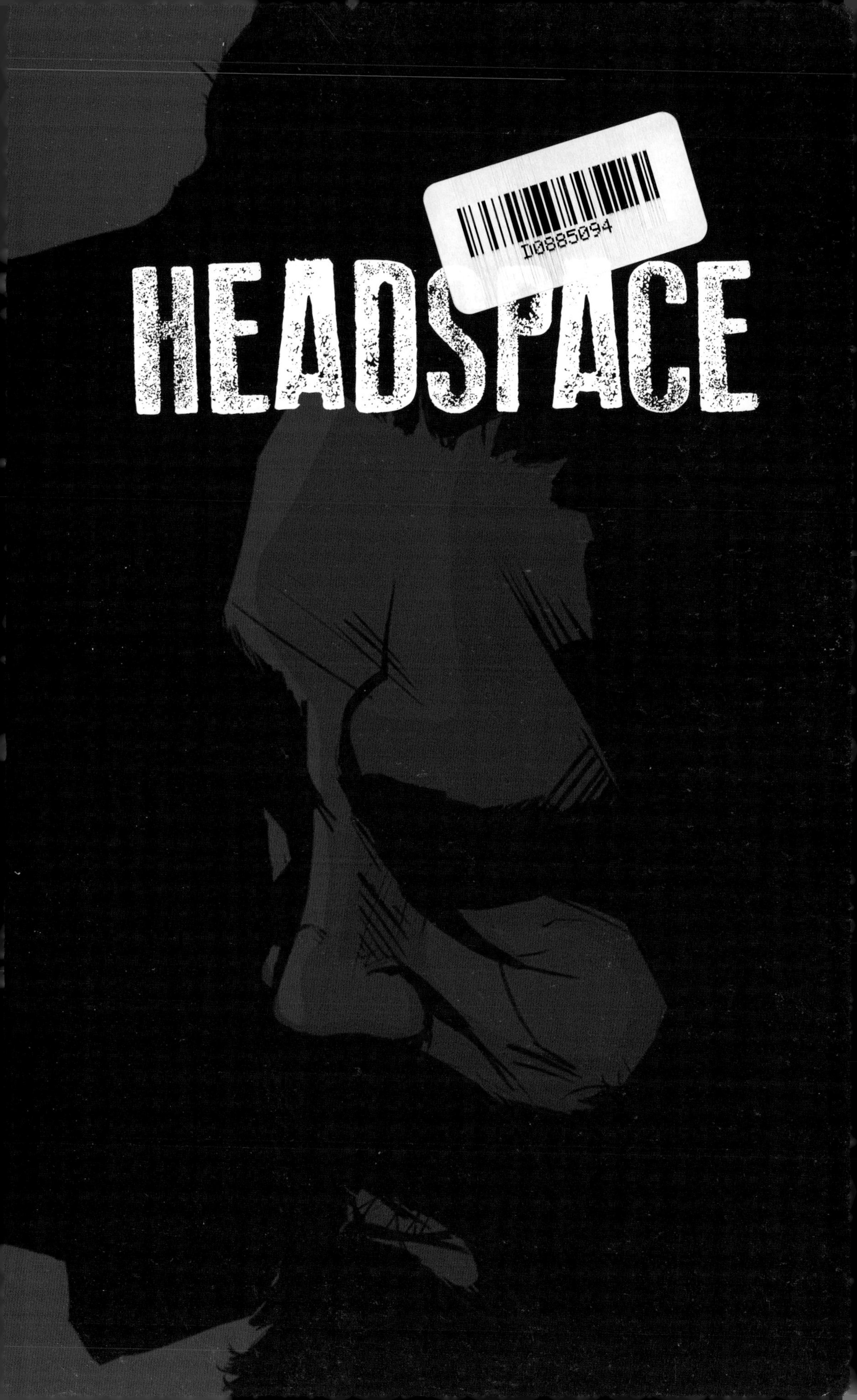
HEADSPACE

Written by **Ryan K. Lindsay**

Illustrated by **Eric Zawadzki & Sebastian Piriz**

Colored by **Eric Zawadzki, Marissa Louise,** and **Dee Cunniffe**

Lettered by **Eric Zawadzki**

Edited by **Dan Hill**

Logo Design by **Ryan Ferrier**

Cover by **Eric Zawadzki**

Collection Edits by **Justin Eisinger** and **Alonzo Simon**

Collection Design by **Clyde Grapa**

Special thanks to Allison Baker and Chris Roberson at Monkeybrain Comics.

ISBN: 978-1-63140-303-3

18 17 16 15   1 2 3 4

IDW®

www.IDWPUBLISHING.com
IDW founded by Ted Adams, Alex Garner, Kris Oprisko, and Robbie Robbins

Ted Adams, CEO & Publisher
Greg Goldstein, President & COO
Robbie Robbins, EVP/Sr. Graphic Artist
Chris Ryall, Chief Creative Officer/Editor-in-Chief
Matthew Ruzicka, CPA, Chief Financial Officer
Alan Payne, VP of Sales
Dirk Wood, VP of Marketing
Lorelei Bunjes, VP of Digital Services
Jeff Webber, VP of Digital Publishing & Business Development

Facebook: facebook.com/idwpublishing
Twitter: @idwpublishing
YouTube: youtube.com/idwpublishing
Instagram: instagram.com/idwpublishing
deviantART: idwpublishing.deviantart.com
Pinterest: pinterest.com/idwpublishing/idw-staff-faves

Foreword

I started reading *HEADSPACE* in the summer months of 2014. It was a very particular summer for me, one that could easily be divided into two halves that made a new whole. Weirdly, it was these two distinct portions of my life that changed the way in which I read *HEADSPACE*.

Before, as a comic reader.

After, as a father.

To say that having a child of my own changed the lens through which I read *HEADSPACE* would not be doing it justice. This is a comic series that affected me equally in the before and the after, for reasons you will find inside.

There's a creeping dread in the weird town of Carpenter Cove, periodically made flesh by the bizarre creatures living in Eric Zawadzki's brain. It infuses itself with a feeling of total helplessness where one floats unhinged in a world with no anchor.

And for those of us who have little ones we call our own, the scariest moments are those shared by a father whose regrets are made from the darkest but most human of thoughts.

When I read the final pages of this book I felt the realest of Ryan Lindsay's fears hit me in my knotted guts. He invited me into Carpenter Cove, threw me into its abyss and led me slowly deeper into hell.

And as haunted as these creators may be, it's those final moments that will play out in my head long after I leave Carpenter Cove.

Kurtis J. Wiebe
(GREEN WAKE, RAT QUEENS)

Chapter 1

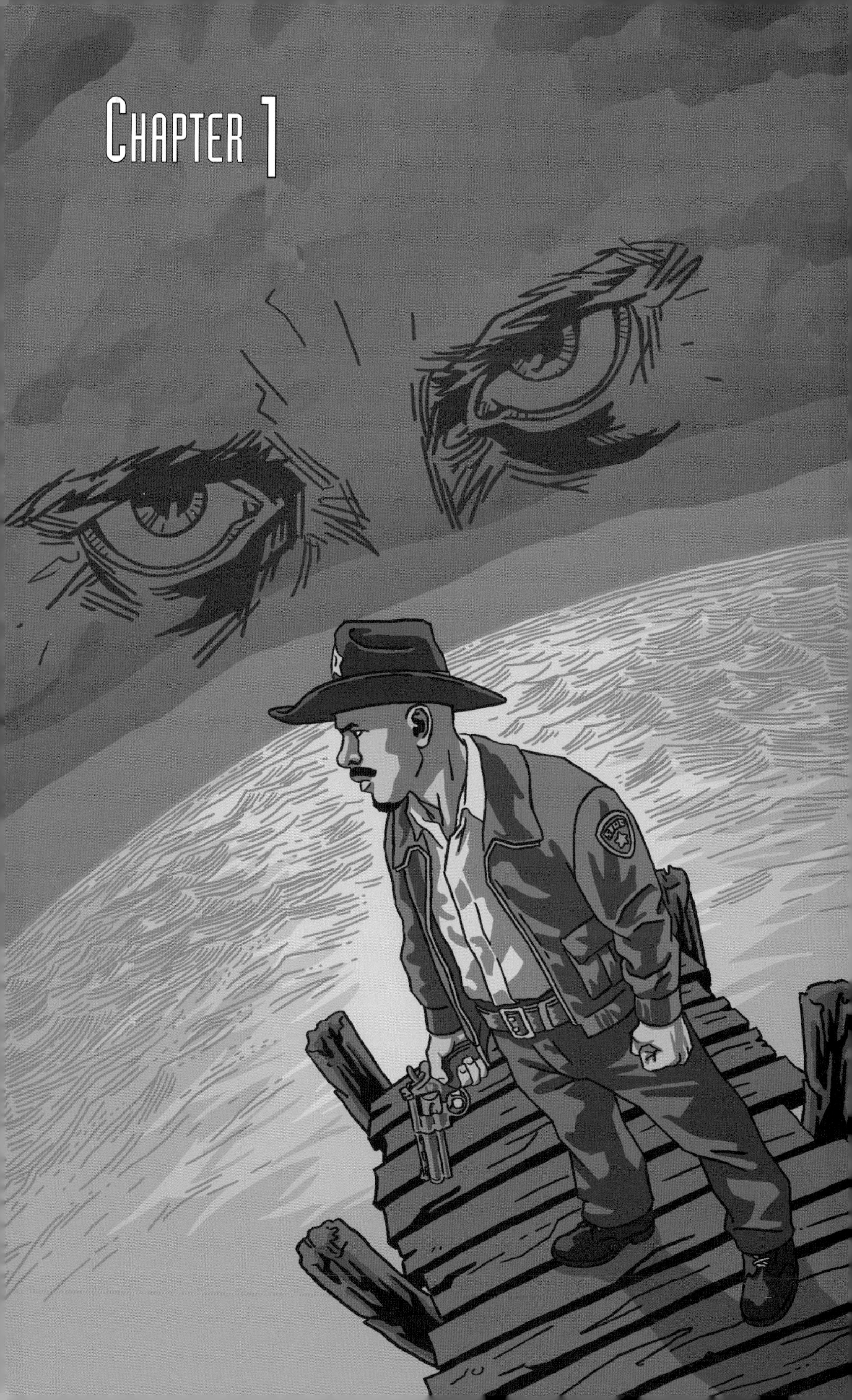

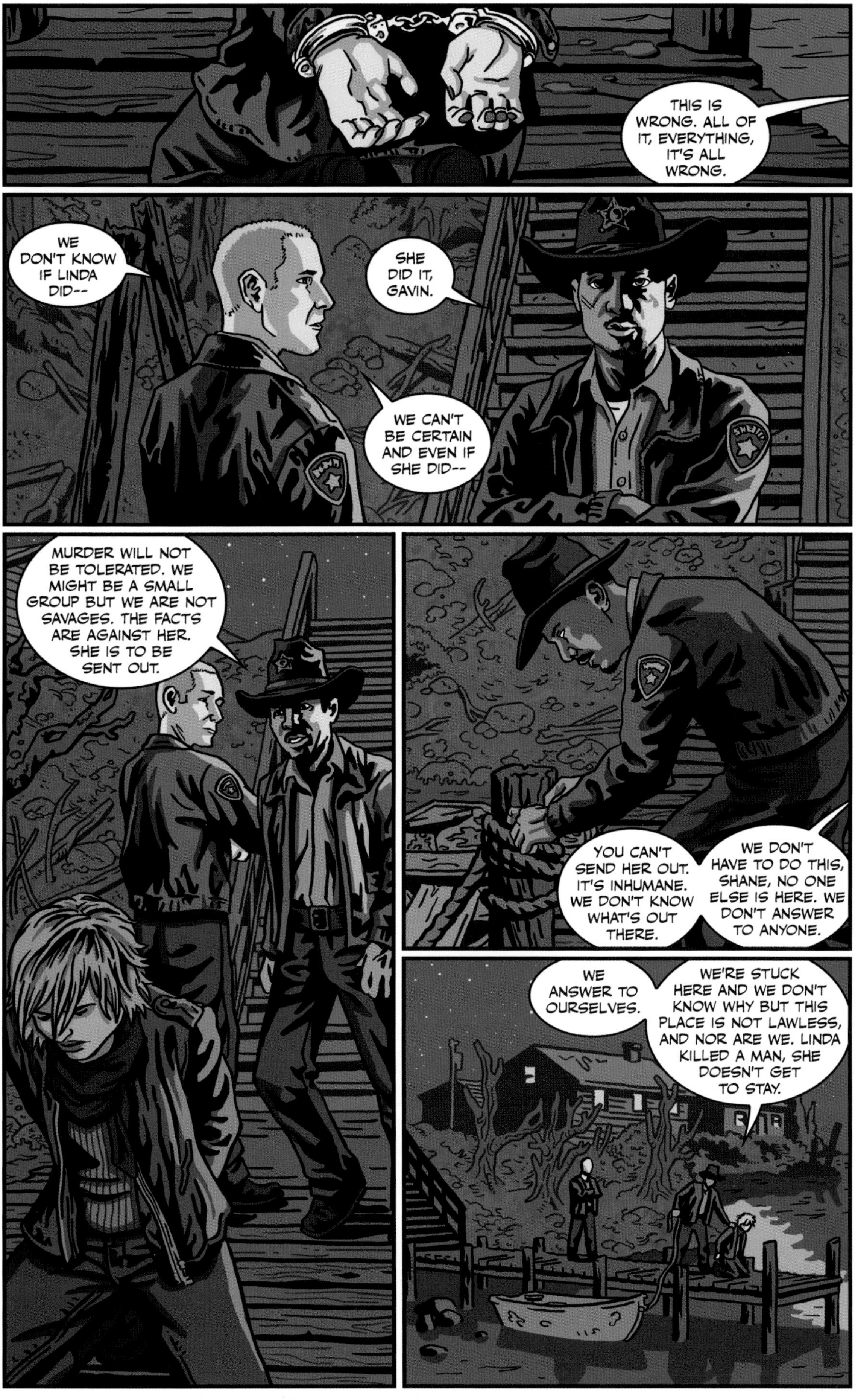
THIS IS WRONG. ALL OF IT, EVERYTHING, IT'S ALL WRONG.
WE DON'T KNOW IF LINDA DID--
SHE DID IT, GAVIN.
WE CAN'T BE CERTAIN AND EVEN IF SHE DID--
MURDER WILL NOT BE TOLERATED. WE MIGHT BE A SMALL GROUP BUT WE ARE NOT SAVAGES. THE FACTS ARE AGAINST HER. SHE IS TO BE SENT OUT.
YOU CAN'T SEND HER OUT. IT'S INHUMANE. WE DON'T KNOW WHAT'S OUT THERE.
WE DON'T HAVE TO DO THIS, SHANE, NO ONE ELSE IS HERE. WE DON'T ANSWER TO ANYONE.
WE ANSWER TO OURSELVES.
WE'RE STUCK HERE AND WE DON'T KNOW WHY BUT THIS PLACE IS NOT LAWLESS, AND NOR ARE WE. LINDA KILLED A MAN, SHE DOESN'T GET TO STAY.

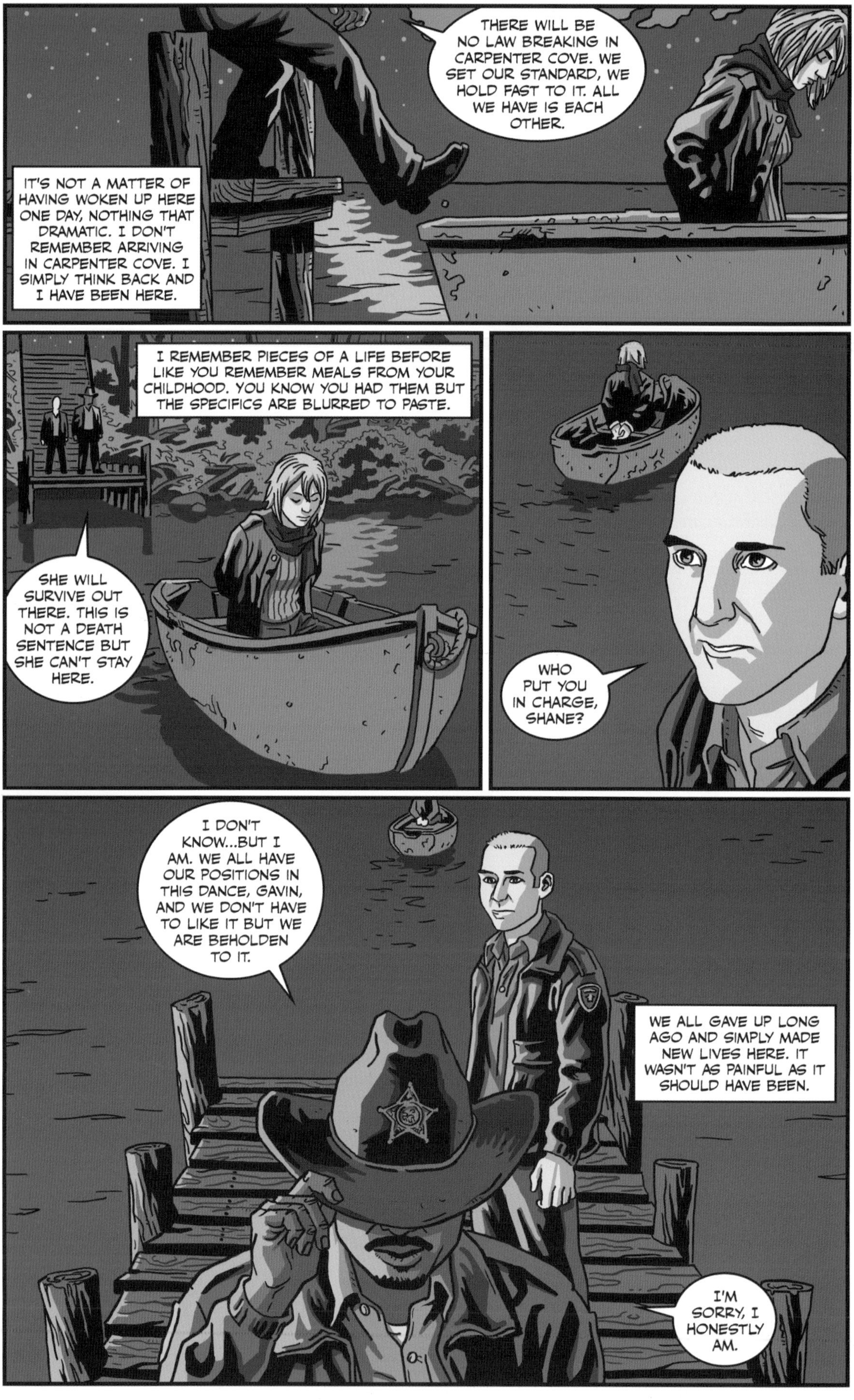
THERE WILL BE NO LAW BREAKING IN CARPENTER COVE. WE SET OUR STANDARD, WE HOLD FAST TO IT. ALL WE HAVE IS EACH OTHER.
IT'S NOT A MATTER OF HAVING WOKEN UP HERE ONE DAY, NOTHING THAT DRAMATIC. I DON'T REMEMBER ARRIVING IN CARPENTER COVE. I SIMPLY THINK BACK AND I HAVE BEEN HERE.
I REMEMBER PIECES OF A LIFE BEFORE LIKE YOU REMEMBER MEALS FROM YOUR CHILDHOOD. YOU KNOW YOU HAD THEM BUT THE SPECIFICS ARE BLURRED TO PASTE.
SHE WILL SURVIVE OUT THERE. THIS IS NOT A DEATH SENTENCE BUT SHE CAN'T STAY HERE.
WHO PUT YOU IN CHARGE, SHANE?
I DON'T KNOW...BUT I AM. WE ALL HAVE OUR POSITIONS IN THIS DANCE, GAVIN, AND WE DON'T HAVE TO LIKE IT BUT WE ARE BEHOLDEN TO IT.
WE ALL GAVE UP LONG AGO AND SIMPLY MADE NEW LIVES HERE. IT WASN'T AS PAINFUL AS IT SHOULD HAVE BEEN.
I'M SORRY, I HONESTLY AM.

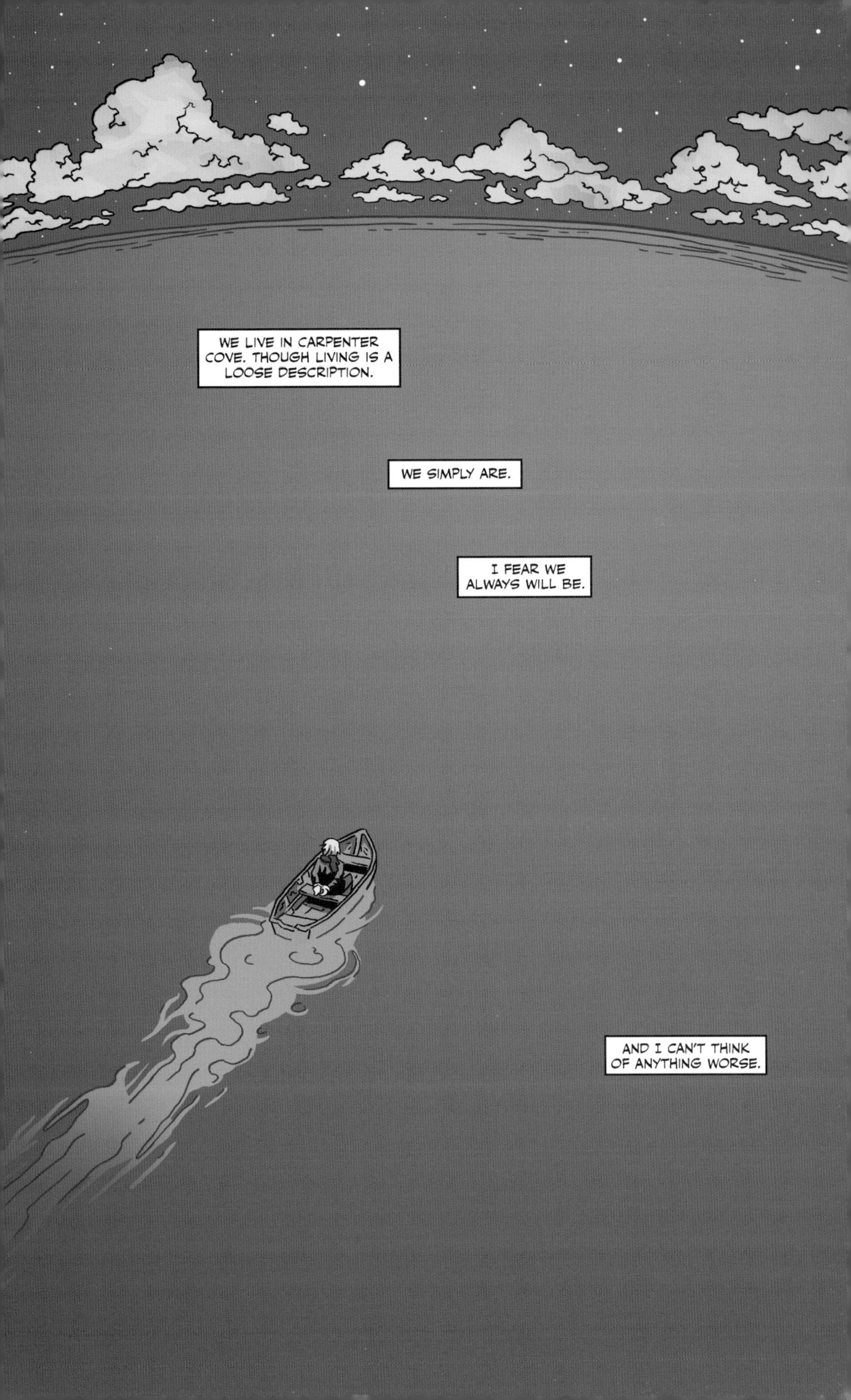
WE LIVE IN CARPENTER COVE. THOUGH LIVING IS A LOOSE DESCRIPTION.
WE SIMPLY ARE.
I FEAR WE ALWAYS WILL BE.
AND I CAN'T THINK OF ANYTHING WORSE.

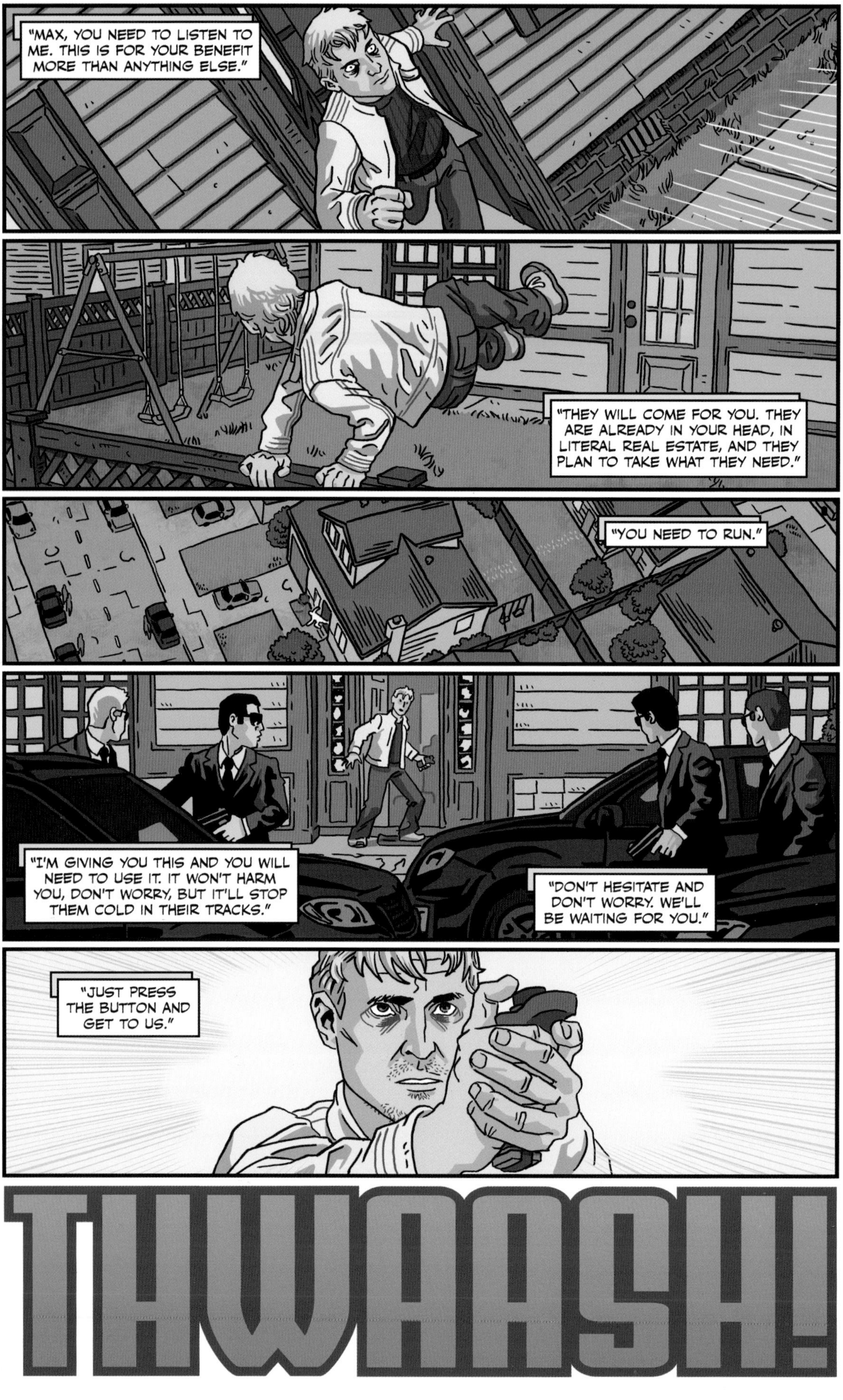
"MAX, YOU NEED TO LISTEN TO ME. THIS IS FOR YOUR BENEFIT MORE THAN ANYTHING ELSE."
"THEY WILL COME FOR YOU. THEY ARE ALREADY IN YOUR HEAD, IN LITERAL REAL ESTATE, AND THEY PLAN TO TAKE WHAT THEY NEED."
"YOU NEED TO RUN."
"I'M GIVING YOU THIS AND YOU WILL NEED TO USE IT. IT WON'T HARM YOU, DON'T WORRY, BUT IT'LL STOP THEM COLD IN THEIR TRACKS."
"DON'T HESITATE AND DON'T WORRY. WE'LL BE WAITING FOR YOU."
"JUST PRESS THE BUTTON AND GET TO US."
THWAASH!

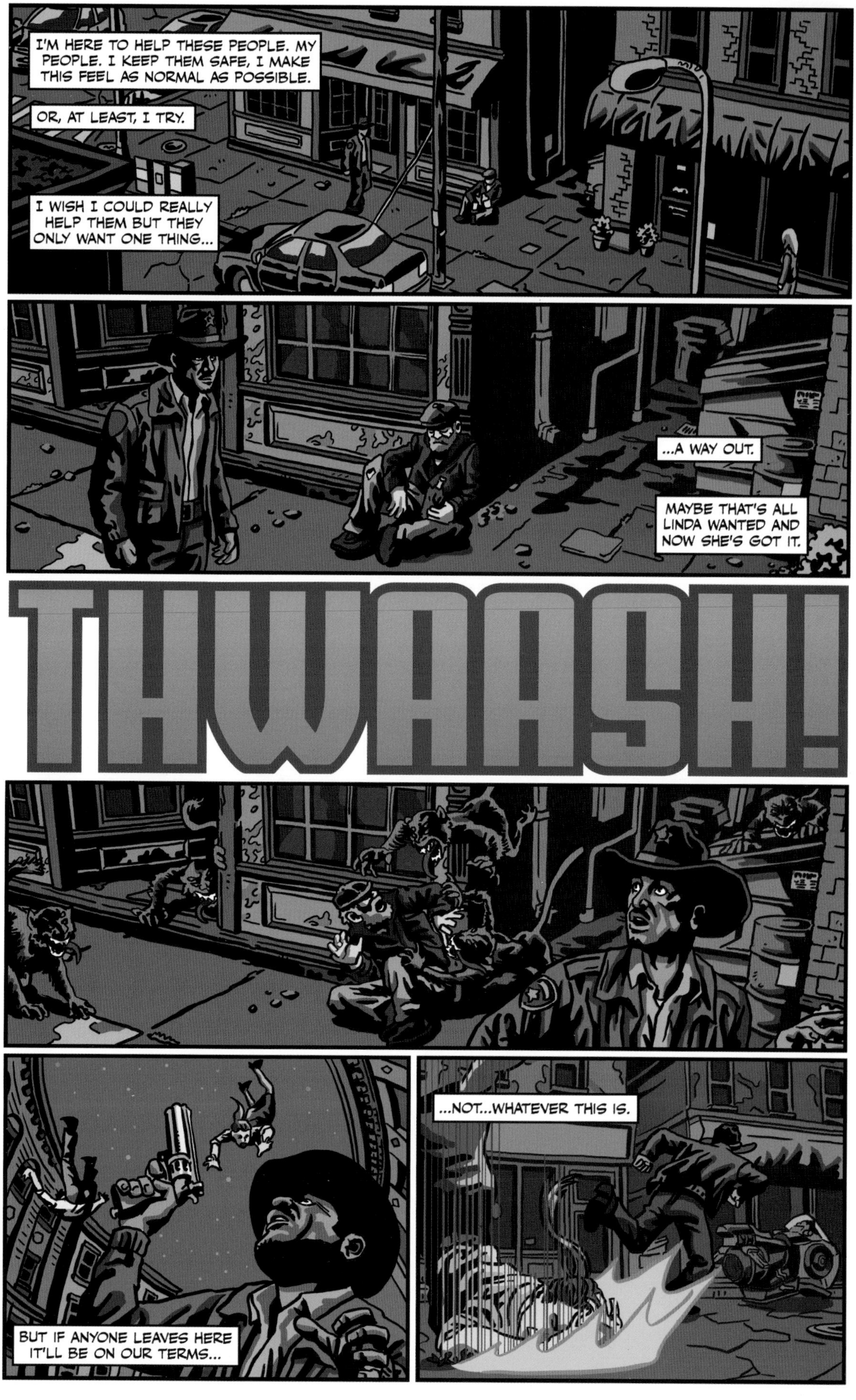
I'M HERE TO HELP THESE PEOPLE. MY PEOPLE. I KEEP THEM SAFE, I MAKE THIS FEEL AS NORMAL AS POSSIBLE.
OR, AT LEAST, I TRY.
I WISH I COULD REALLY HELP THEM BUT THEY ONLY WANT ONE THING...
...A WAY OUT.
MAYBE THAT'S ALL LINDA WANTED AND NOW SHE'S GOT IT.
THWAASH!
BUT IF ANYONE LEAVES HERE IT'LL BE ON OUR TERMS...
...NOT...WHATEVER THIS IS.

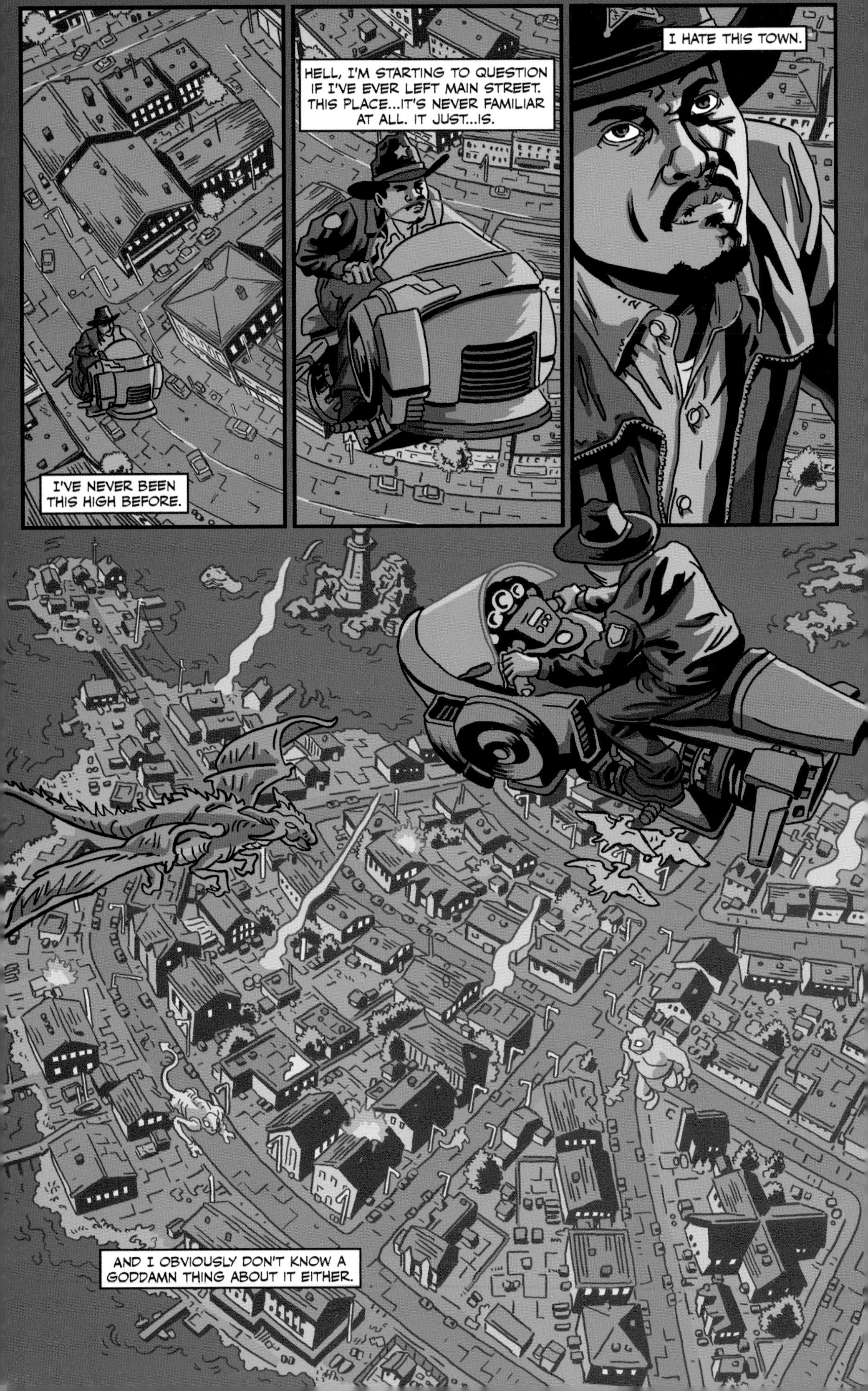
I'VE NEVER BEEN THIS HIGH BEFORE.
HELL, I'M STARTING TO QUESTION IF I'VE EVER LEFT MAIN STREET. THIS PLACE...IT'S NEVER FAMILIAR AT ALL. IT JUST...IS.
I HATE THIS TOWN.
AND I OBVIOUSLY DON'T KNOW A GODDAMN THING ABOUT IT EITHER.

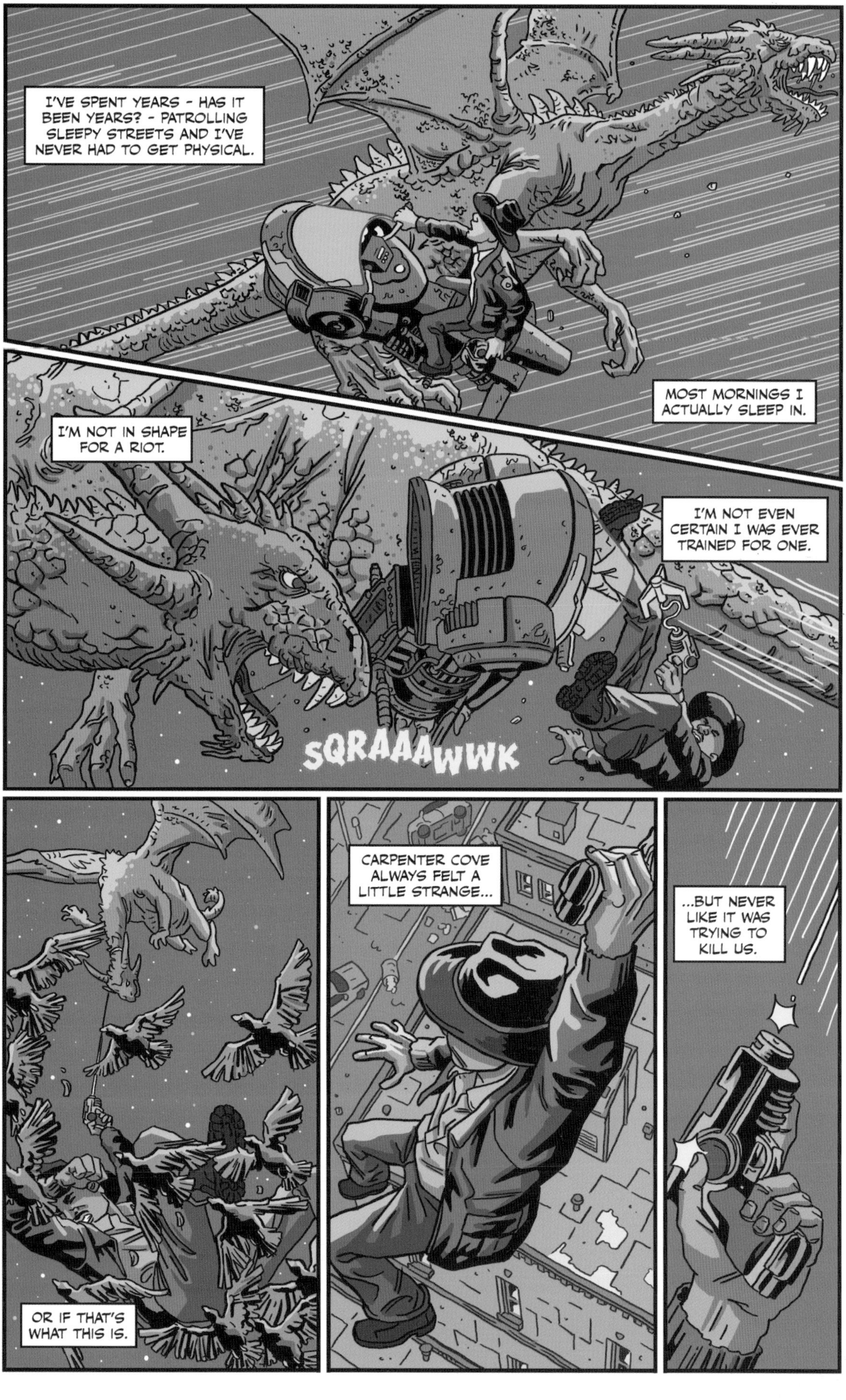
I'VE SPENT YEARS - HAS IT BEEN YEARS? - PATROLLING SLEEPY STREETS AND I'VE NEVER HAD TO GET PHYSICAL.
MOST MORNINGS I ACTUALLY SLEEP IN.
I'M NOT IN SHAPE FOR A RIOT.
I'M NOT EVEN CERTAIN I WAS EVER TRAINED FOR ONE.
SQRAAAWWK
OR IF THAT'S WHAT THIS IS.
CARPENTER COVE ALWAYS FELT A LITTLE STRANGE...
...BUT NEVER LIKE IT WAS TRYING TO KILL US.

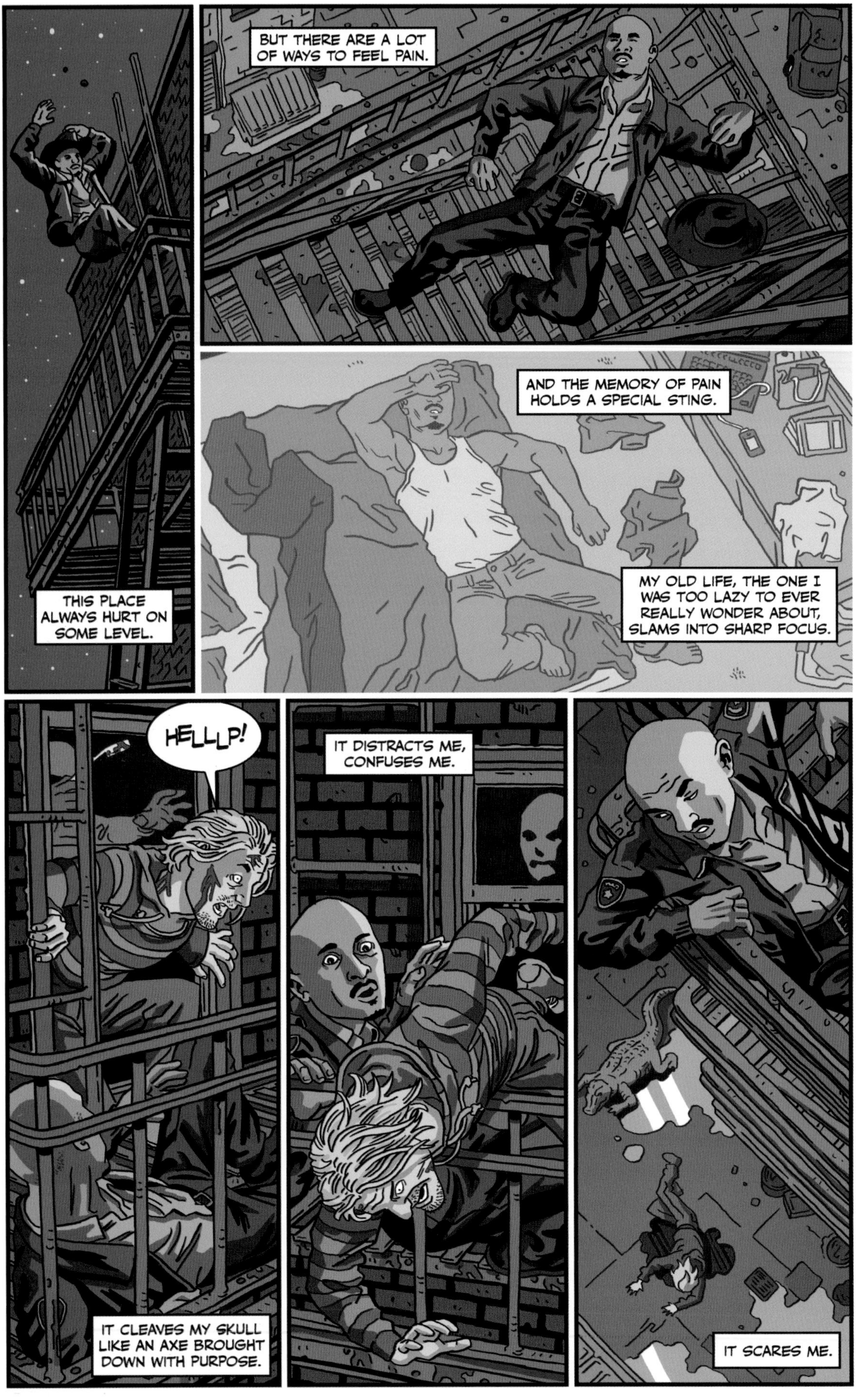
THIS PLACE ALWAYS HURT ON SOME LEVEL.
BUT THERE ARE A LOT OF WAYS TO FEEL PAIN.
AND THE MEMORY OF PAIN HOLDS A SPECIAL STING.
MY OLD LIFE, THE ONE I WAS TOO LAZY TO EVER REALLY WONDER ABOUT, SLAMS INTO SHARP FOCUS.
HELLLP!
IT CLEAVES MY SKULL LIKE AN AXE BROUGHT DOWN WITH PURPOSE.
IT DISTRACTS ME, CONFUSES ME.
IT SCARES ME.

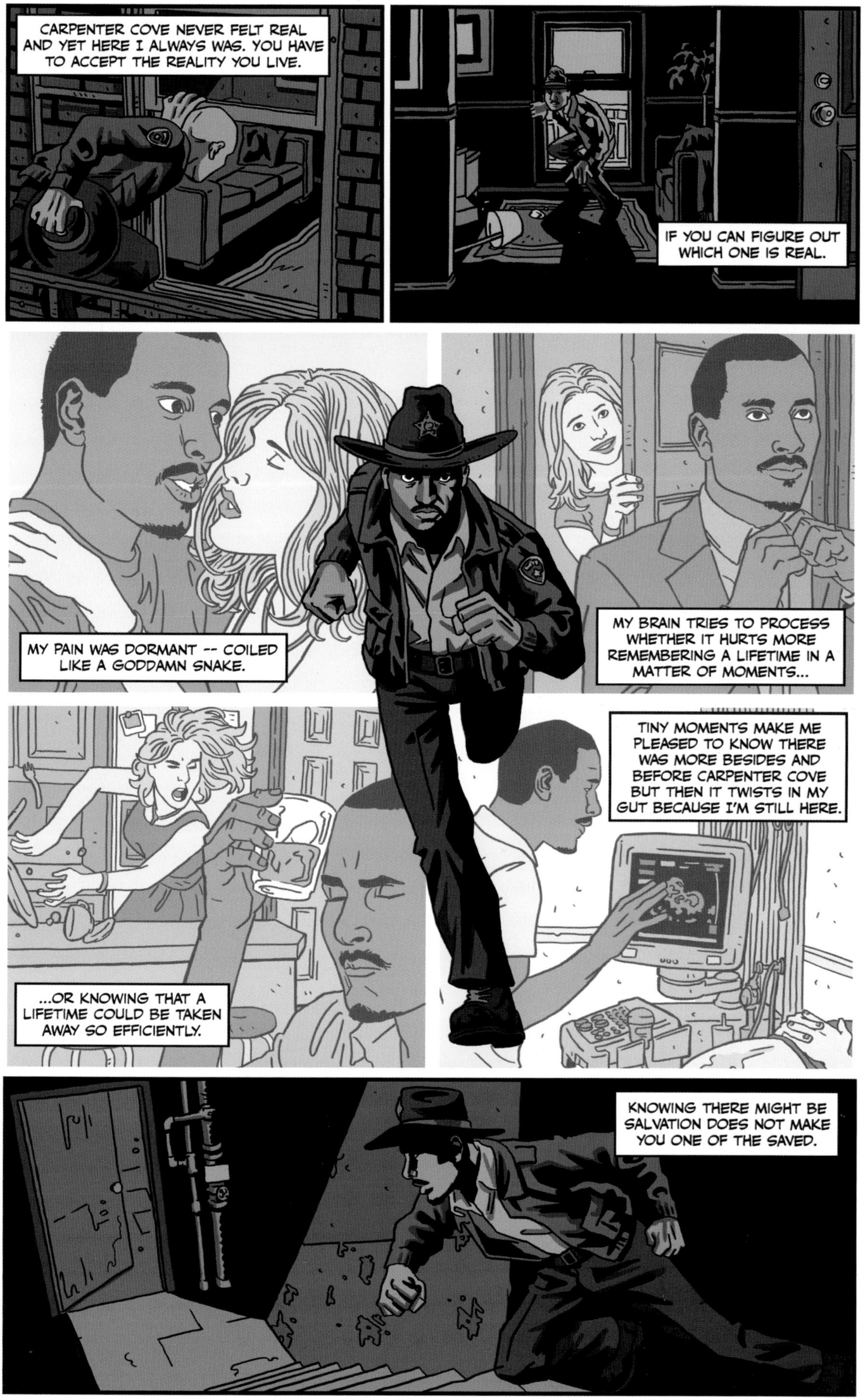
CARPENTER COVE NEVER FELT REAL AND YET HERE I ALWAYS WAS. YOU HAVE TO ACCEPT THE REALITY YOU LIVE.
IF YOU CAN FIGURE OUT WHICH ONE IS REAL.
MY PAIN WAS DORMANT -- COILED LIKE A GODDAMN SNAKE.
MY BRAIN TRIES TO PROCESS WHETHER IT HURTS MORE REMEMBERING A LIFETIME IN A MATTER OF MOMENTS...
TINY MOMENTS MAKE ME PLEASED TO KNOW THERE WAS MORE BESIDES AND BEFORE CARPENTER COVE BUT THEN IT TWISTS IN MY GUT BECAUSE I'M STILL HERE.
...OR KNOWING THAT A LIFETIME COULD BE TAKEN AWAY SO EFFICIENTLY.
KNOWING THERE MIGHT BE SALVATION DOES NOT MAKE YOU ONE OF THE SAVED.

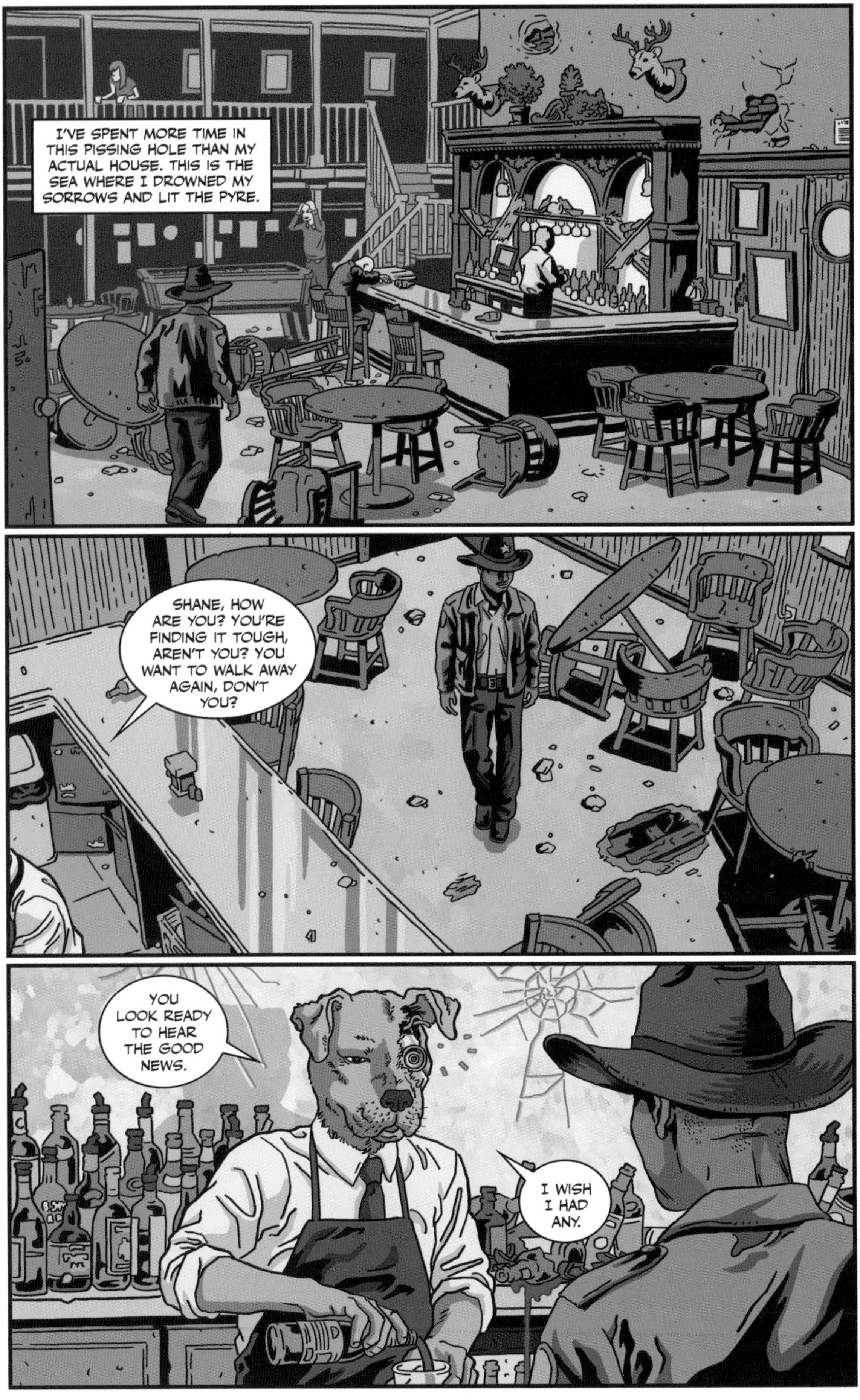
I'VE SPENT MORE TIME IN THIS PISSING HOLE THAN MY ACTUAL HOUSE. THIS IS THE SEA WHERE I DROWNED MY SORROWS AND LIT THE PYRE.
SHANE, HOW ARE YOU? YOU'RE FINDING IT TOUGH, AREN'T YOU? YOU WANT TO WALK AWAY AGAIN, DON'T YOU?
YOU LOOK READY TO HEAR THE GOOD NEWS.
I WISH I HAD ANY.

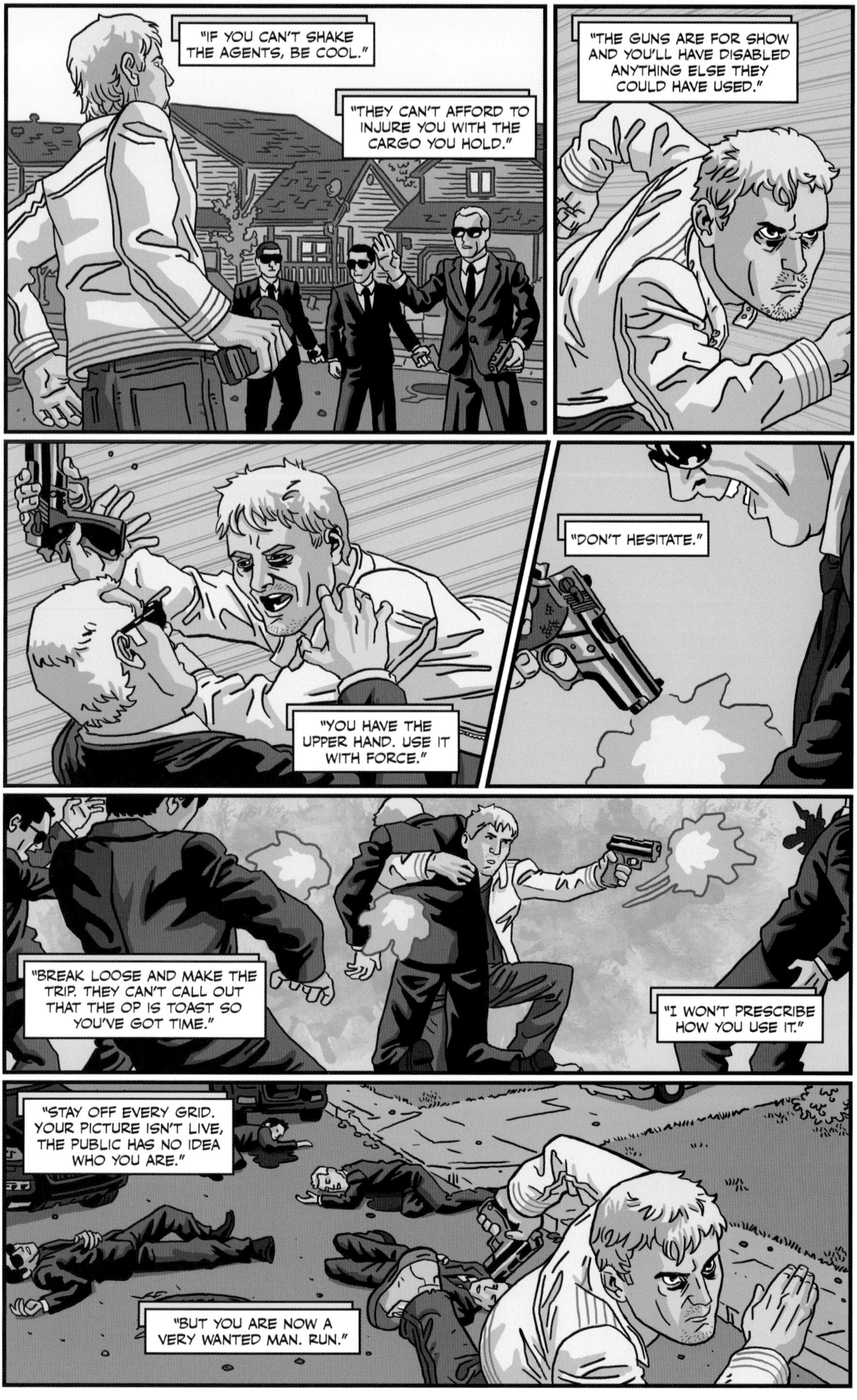
"IF YOU CAN'T SHAKE THE AGENTS, BE COOL."
"THEY CAN'T AFFORD TO INJURE YOU WITH THE CARGO YOU HOLD."
"THE GUNS ARE FOR SHOW AND YOU'LL HAVE DISABLED ANYTHING ELSE THEY COULD HAVE USED."
"YOU HAVE THE UPPER HAND. USE IT WITH FORCE."
"DON'T HESITATE."
"BREAK LOOSE AND MAKE THE TRIP. THEY CAN'T CALL OUT THAT THE OP IS TOAST SO YOU'VE GOT TIME."
"I WON'T PRESCRIBE HOW YOU USE IT."
"STAY OFF EVERY GRID. YOUR PICTURE ISN'T LIVE, THE PUBLIC HAS NO IDEA WHO YOU ARE."
"BUT YOU ARE NOW A VERY WANTED MAN. RUN."

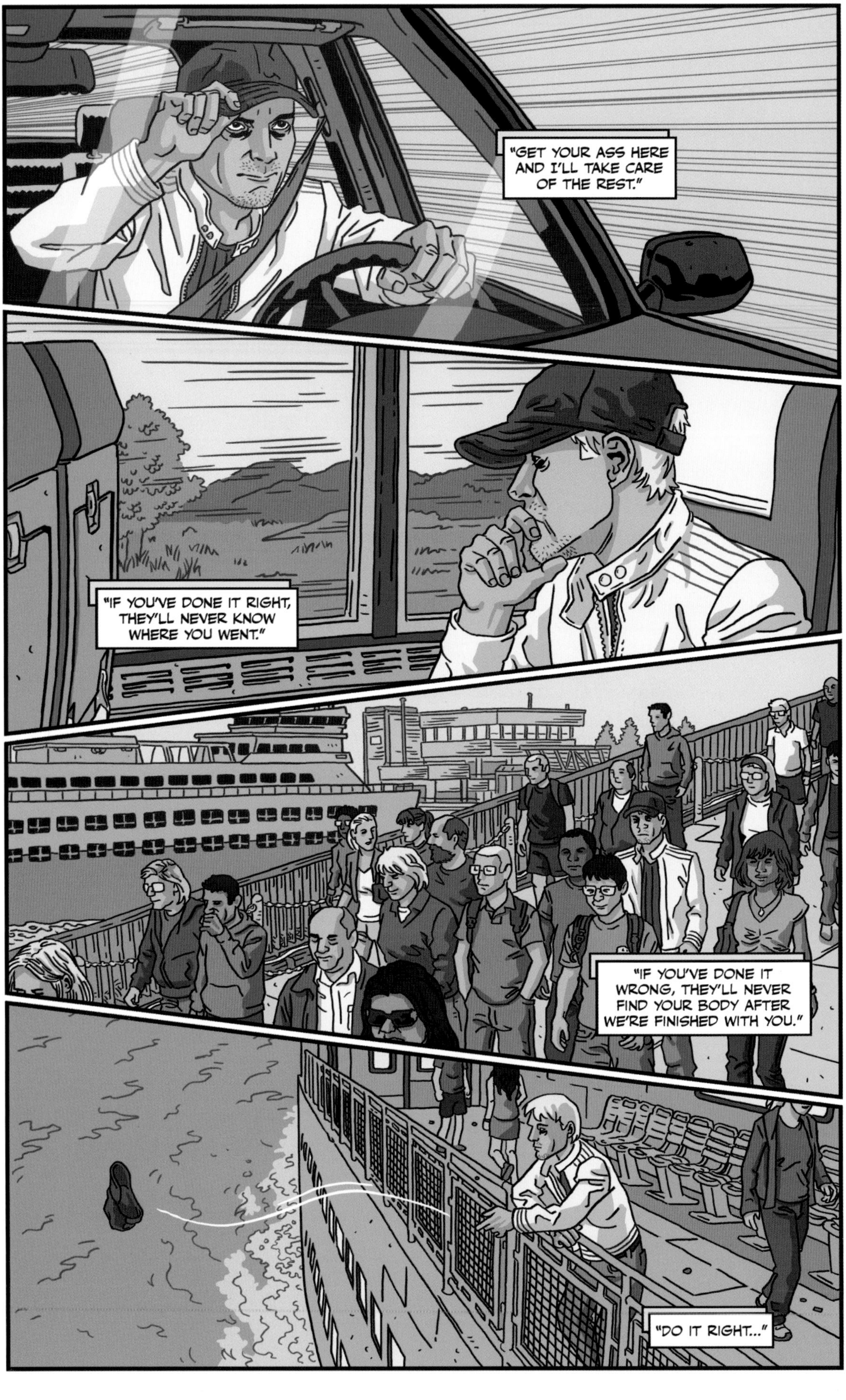
"GET YOUR ASS HERE AND I'LL TAKE CARE OF THE REST."
"IF YOU'VE DONE IT RIGHT, THEY'LL NEVER KNOW WHERE YOU WENT."
"IF YOU'VE DONE IT WRONG, THEY'LL NEVER FIND YOUR BODY AFTER WE'RE FINISHED WITH YOU."
"DO IT RIGHT..."

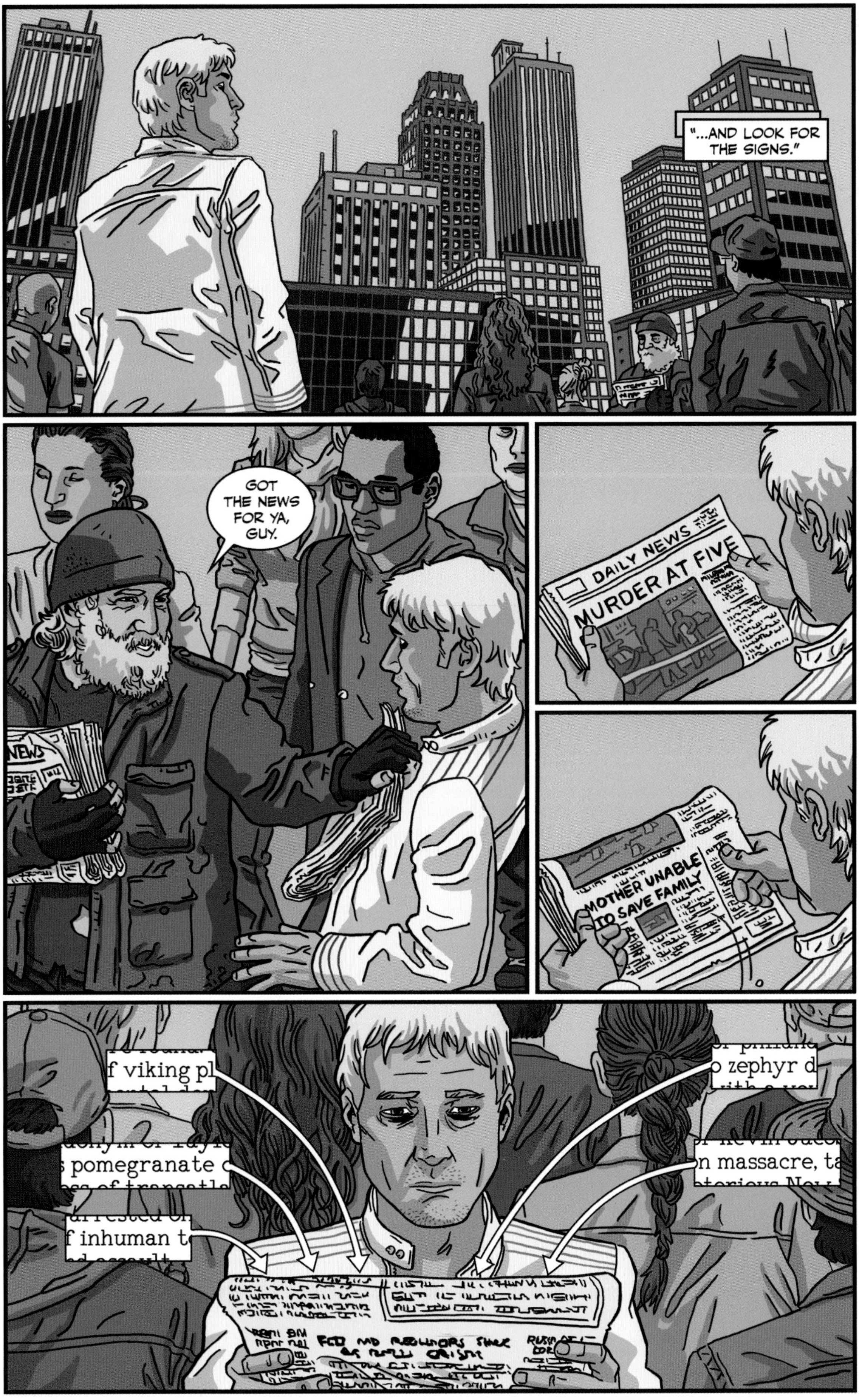
"...AND LOOK FOR THE SIGNS."
GOT THE NEWS FOR YA, GUY.
DAILY NEWS
MURDER AT FIVE
MOTHER UNABLE TO SAVE FAMILY
f viking pl
o zephyr d
s pomegranate c
n massacre, ta
f inhuman t

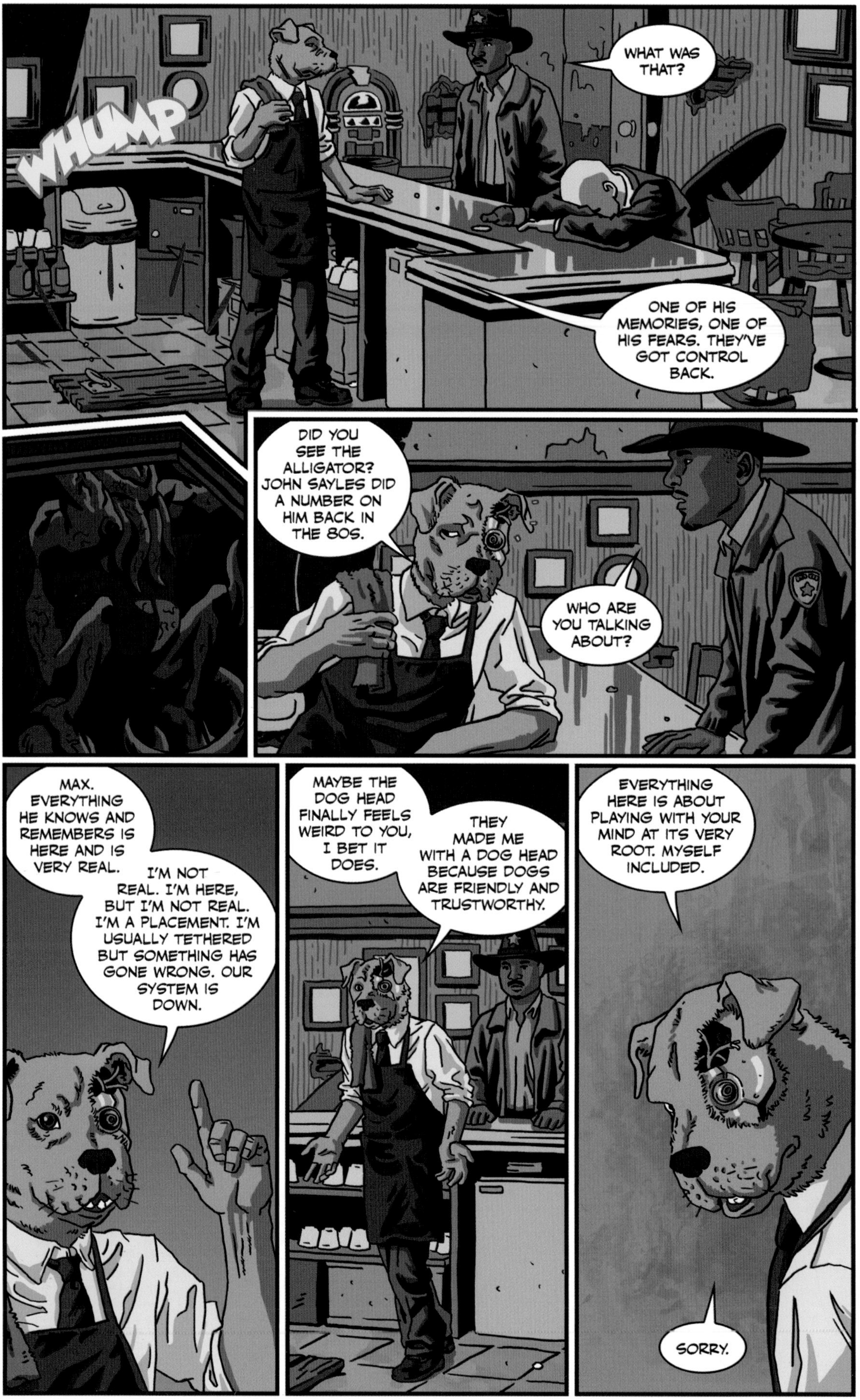
WHUMP
WHAT WAS THAT?
ONE OF HIS MEMORIES, ONE OF HIS FEARS. THEY'VE GOT CONTROL BACK.
DID YOU SEE THE ALLIGATOR? JOHN SAYLES DID A NUMBER ON HIM BACK IN THE 80S.
WHO ARE YOU TALKING ABOUT?
MAX. EVERYTHING HE KNOWS AND REMEMBERS IS HERE AND IS VERY REAL.
I'M NOT REAL. I'M HERE, BUT I'M NOT REAL. I'M A PLACEMENT. I'M USUALLY TETHERED BUT SOMETHING HAS GONE WRONG. OUR SYSTEM IS DOWN.
MAYBE THE DOG HEAD FINALLY FEELS WEIRD TO YOU, I BET IT DOES.
THEY MADE ME WITH A DOG HEAD BECAUSE DOGS ARE FRIENDLY AND TRUSTWORTHY.
EVERYTHING HERE IS ABOUT PLAYING WITH YOUR MIND AT ITS VERY ROOT. MYSELF INCLUDED.
SORRY.

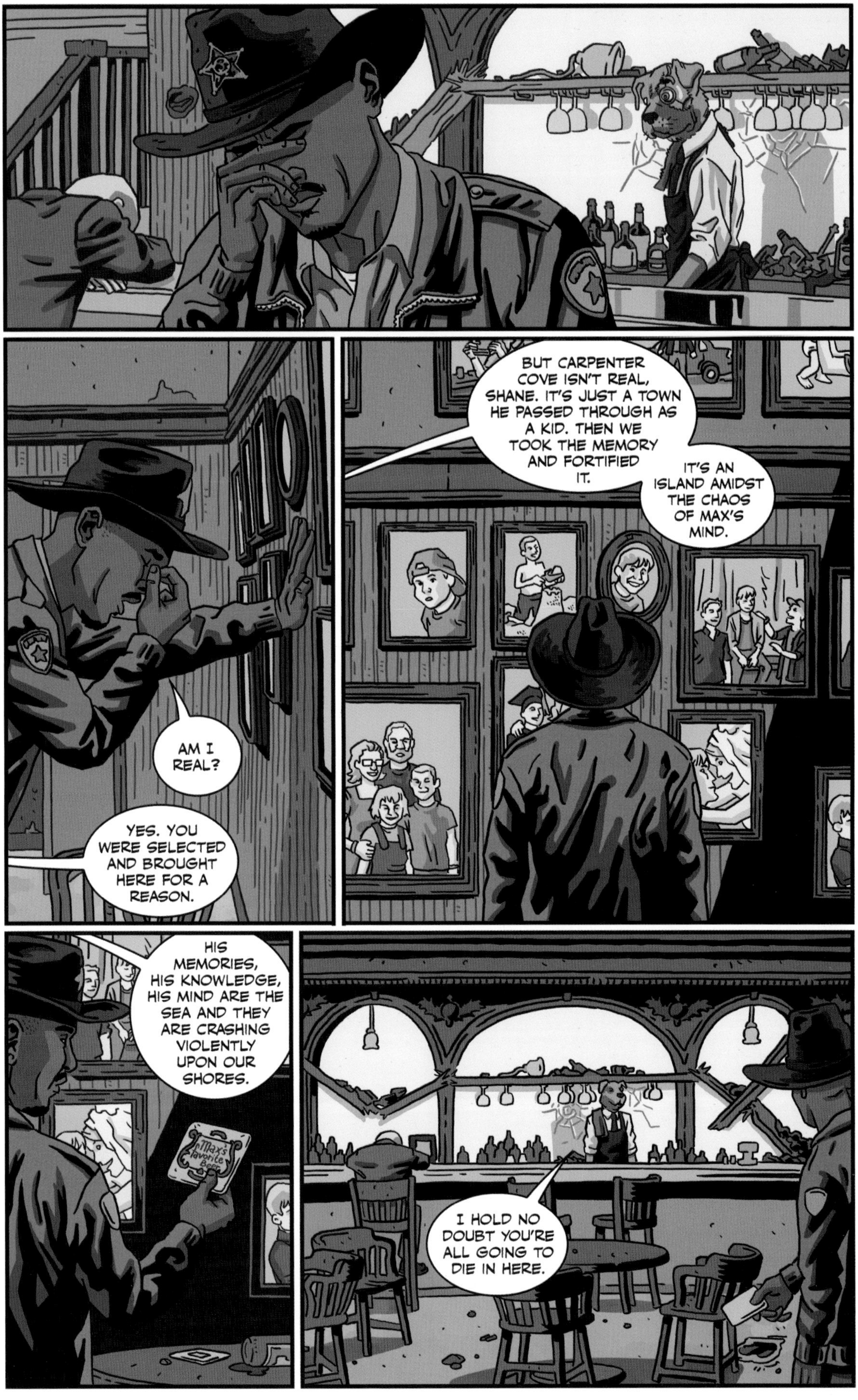
AM I REAL?
YES. YOU WERE SELECTED AND BROUGHT HERE FOR A REASON.
BUT CARPENTER COVE ISN'T REAL, SHANE. IT'S JUST A TOWN HE PASSED THROUGH AS A KID. THEN WE TOOK THE MEMORY AND FORTIFIED IT.
IT'S AN ISLAND AMIDST THE CHAOS OF MAX'S MIND.
HIS MEMORIES, HIS KNOWLEDGE, HIS MIND ARE THE SEA AND THEY ARE CRASHING VIOLENTLY UPON OUR SHORES.
Max's Favorite Beer
I HOLD NO DOUBT YOU'RE ALL GOING TO DIE IN HERE.

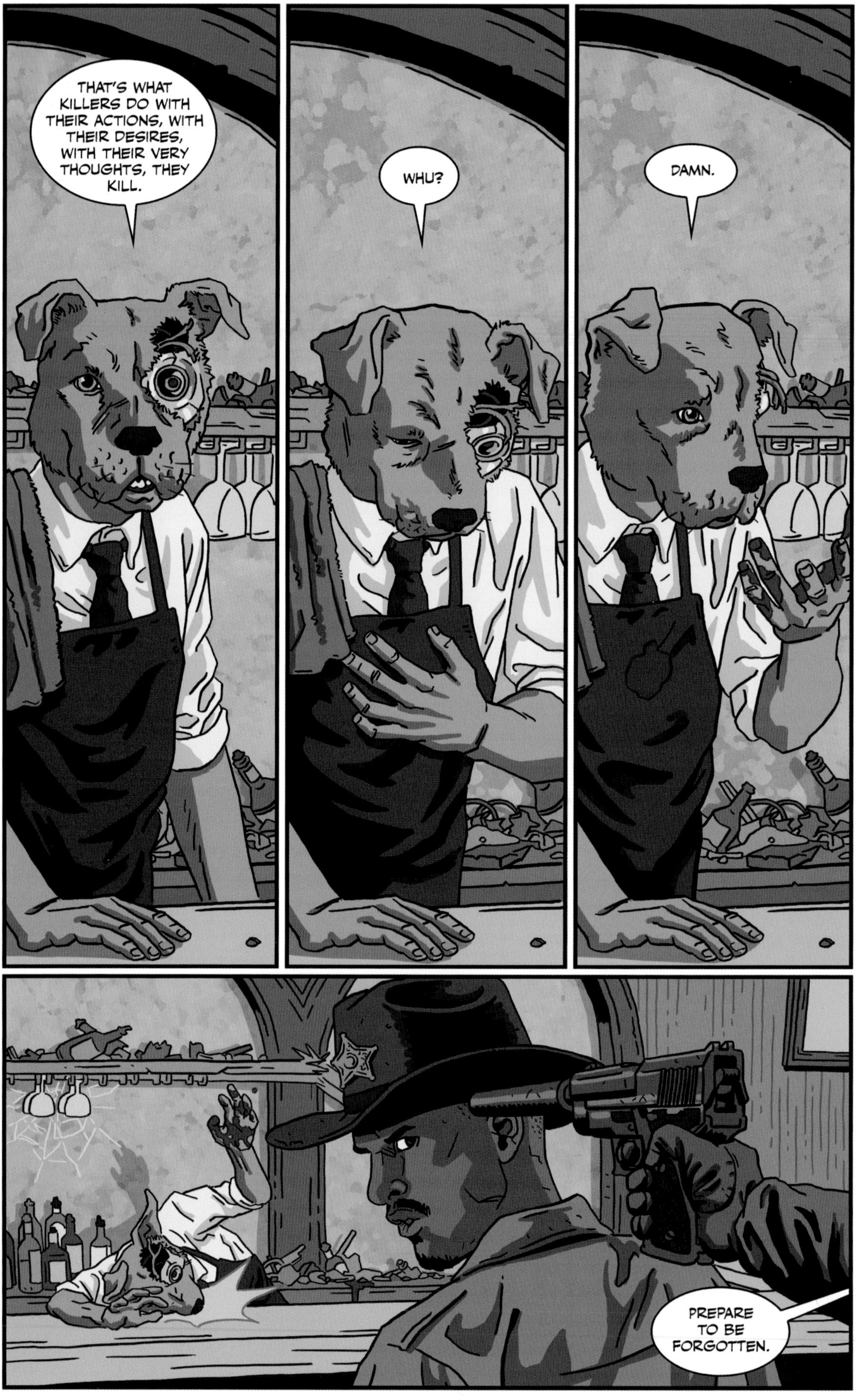
THAT'S WHAT KILLERS DO WITH THEIR ACTIONS, WITH THEIR DESIRES, WITH THEIR VERY THOUGHTS, THEY KILL.
WHU?
DAMN.
PREPARE TO BE FORGOTTEN.

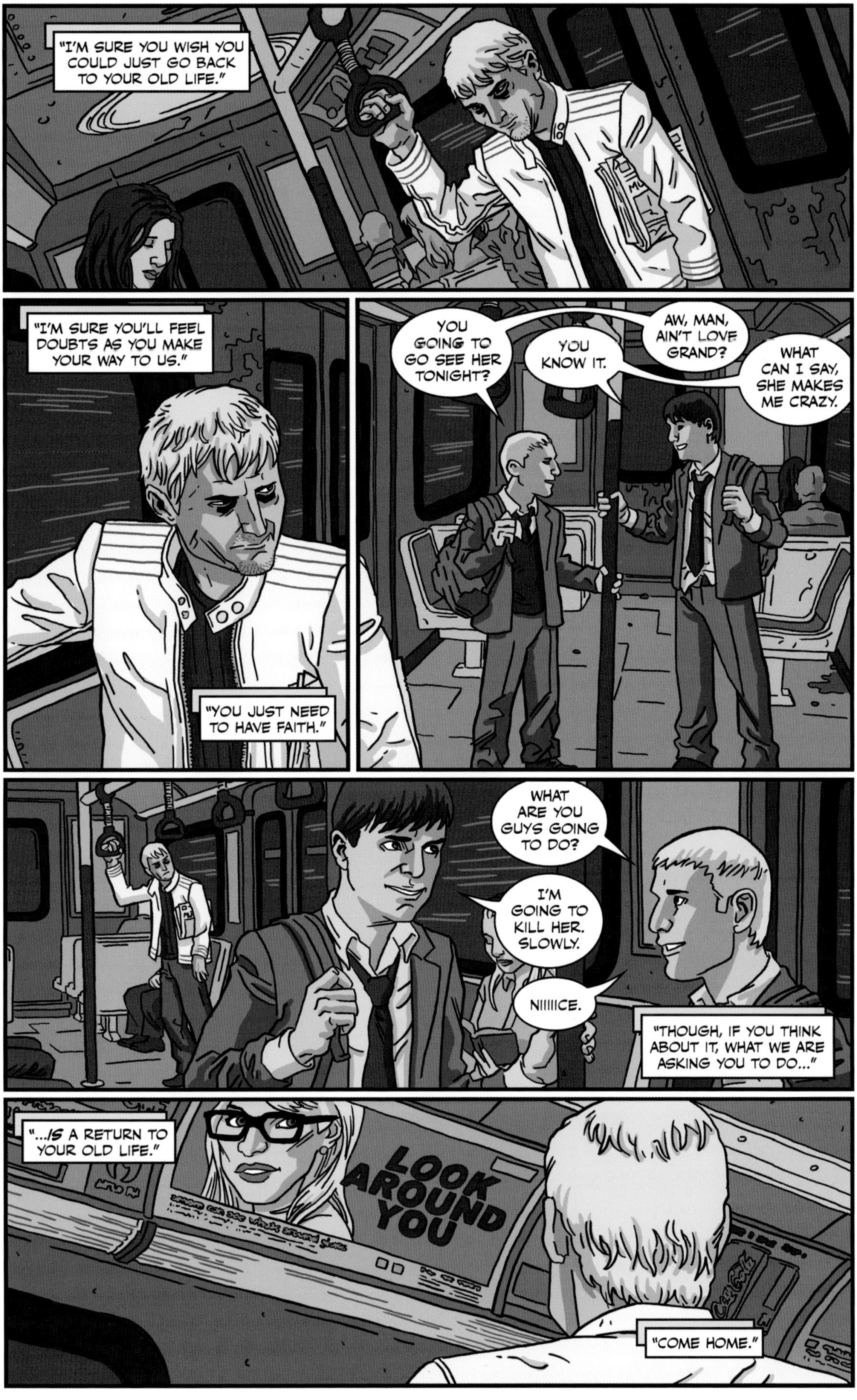
"I'M SURE YOU WISH YOU COULD JUST GO BACK TO YOUR OLD LIFE."
"I'M SURE YOU'LL FEEL DOUBTS AS YOU MAKE YOUR WAY TO US."
"YOU JUST NEED TO HAVE FAITH."
YOU GOING TO GO SEE HER TONIGHT?
YOU KNOW IT.
AW, MAN, AIN'T LOVE GRAND?
WHAT CAN I SAY, SHE MAKES ME CRAZY.
WHAT ARE YOU GUYS GOING TO DO?
I'M GOING TO KILL HER. SLOWLY.
NIIIIICE.
"THOUGH, IF YOU THINK ABOUT IT, WHAT WE ARE ASKING YOU TO DO..."
"...*IS* A RETURN TO YOUR OLD LIFE."
LOOK AROUND YOU
"COME HOME."

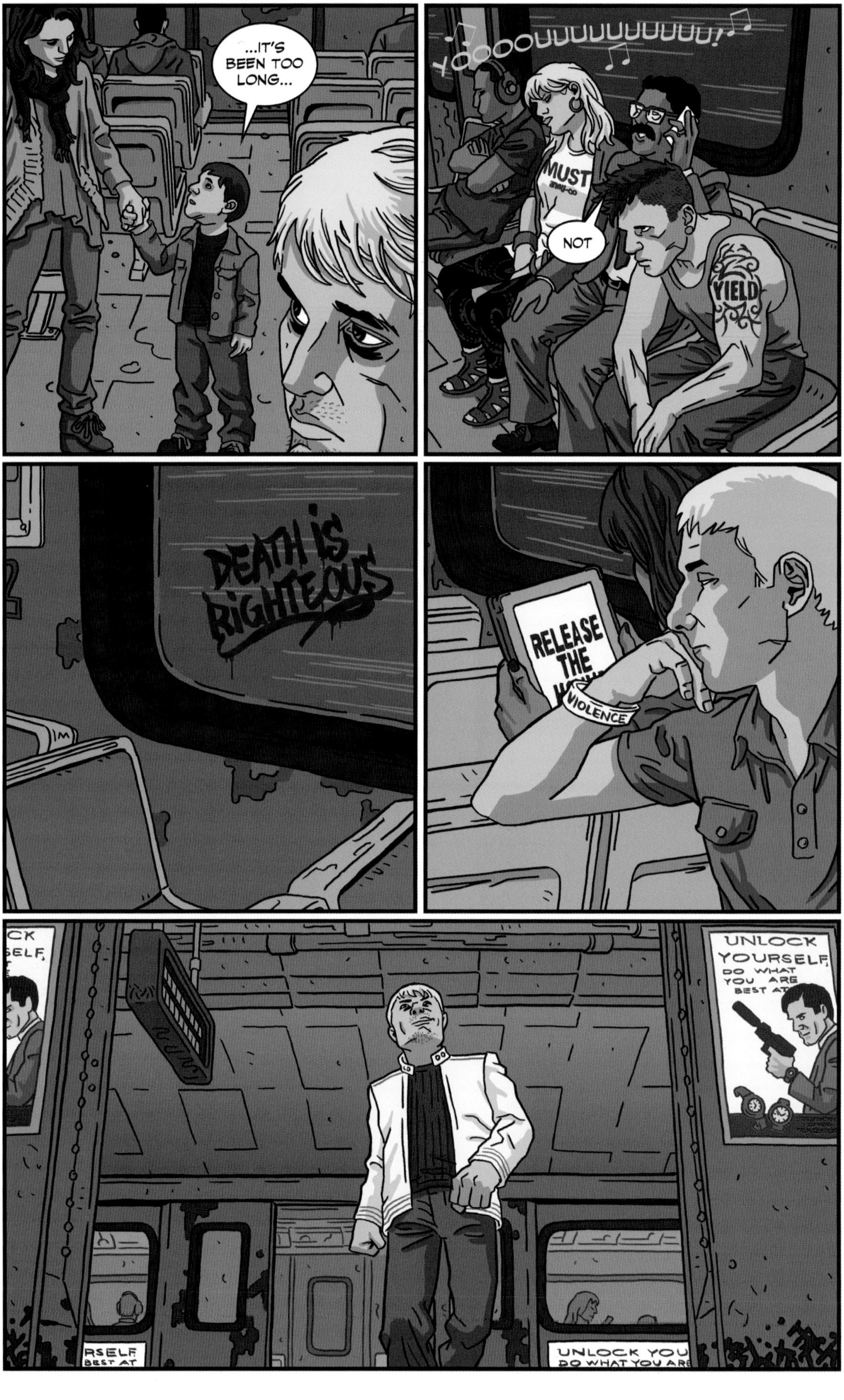
...IT'S BEEN TOO LONG...
YOOOOOUUUUUUUUUU!
MUST
NOT
YIELD
DEATH IS RIGHTEOUS
RELEASE THE
VIOLENCE
UNLOCK YOURSELF, DO WHAT YOU ARE BEST AT
UNLOCK YOU DO WHAT YOU ARE
RSELF BEST AT

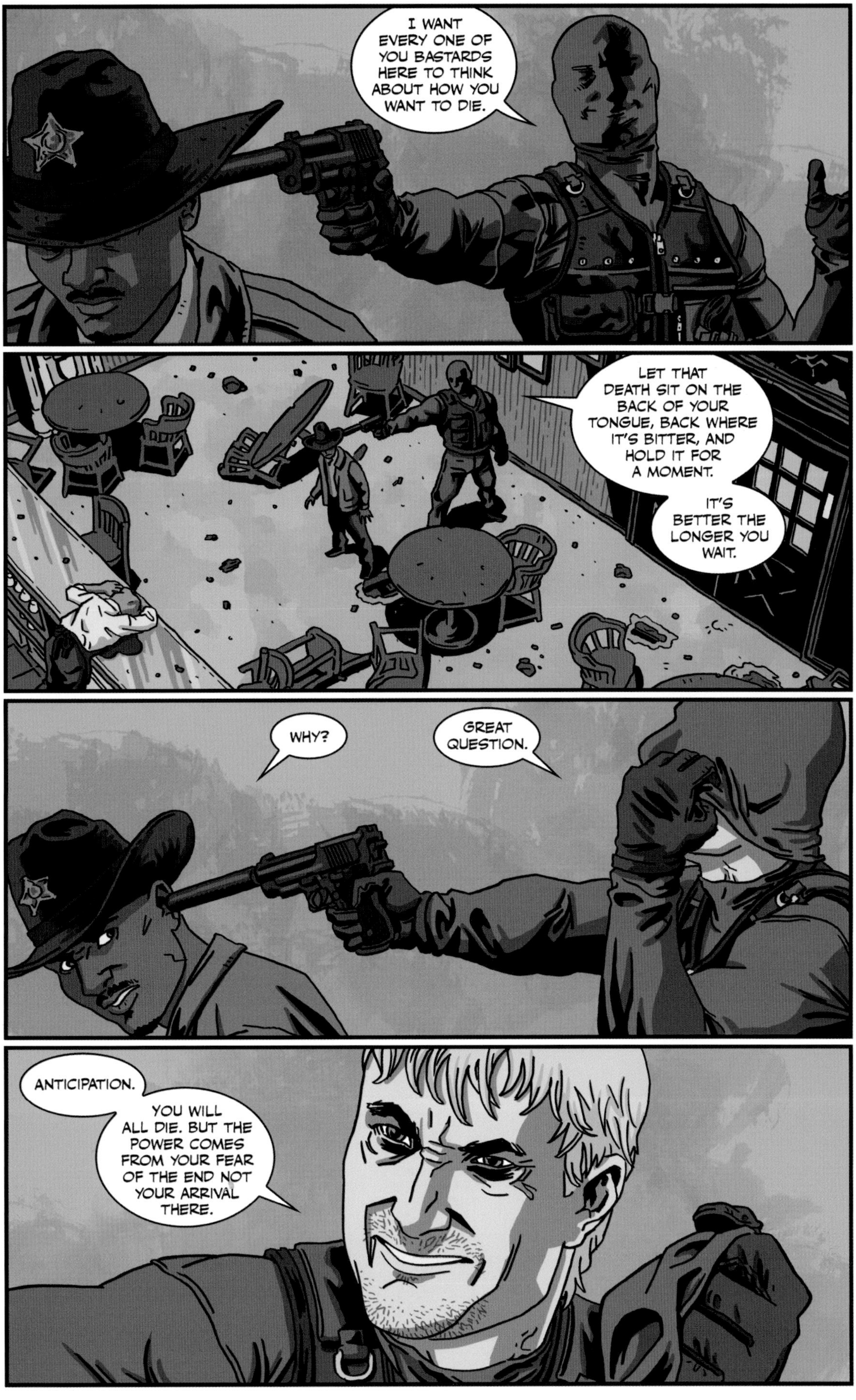
I WANT EVERY ONE OF YOU BASTARDS HERE TO THINK ABOUT HOW YOU WANT TO DIE.
LET THAT DEATH SIT ON THE BACK OF YOUR TONGUE, BACK WHERE IT'S BITTER, AND HOLD IT FOR A MOMENT.
IT'S BETTER THE LONGER YOU WAIT.
WHY?
GREAT QUESTION.
ANTICIPATION.
YOU WILL ALL DIE. BUT THE POWER COMES FROM YOUR FEAR OF THE END NOT YOUR ARRIVAL THERE.

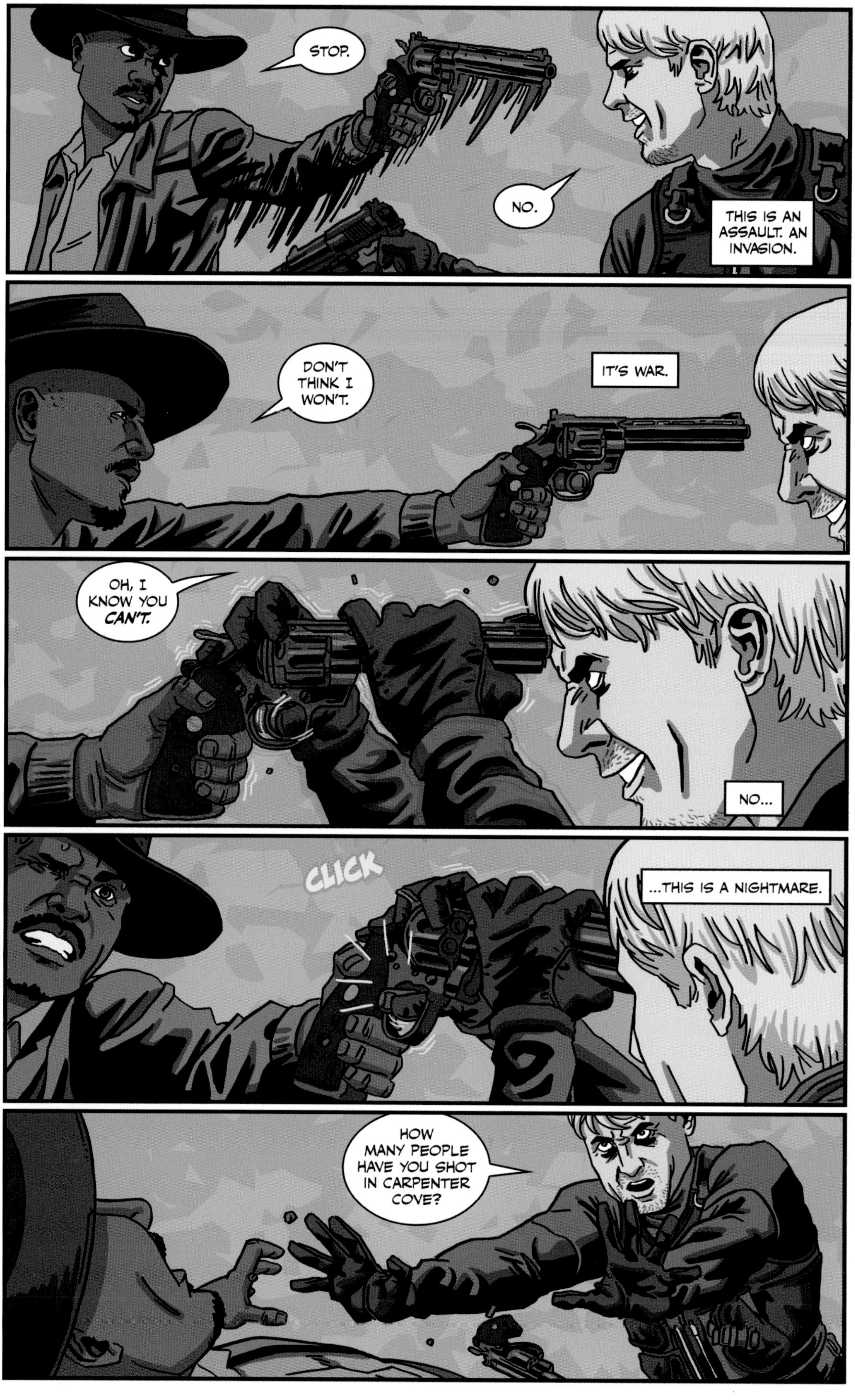
STOP.
NO.
THIS IS AN ASSAULT. AN INVASION.
DON'T THINK I WON'T.
IT'S WAR.
OH, I KNOW YOU *CAN'T.*
NO...
CLICK
...THIS IS A NIGHTMARE.
HOW MANY PEOPLE HAVE YOU SHOT IN CARPENTER COVE?

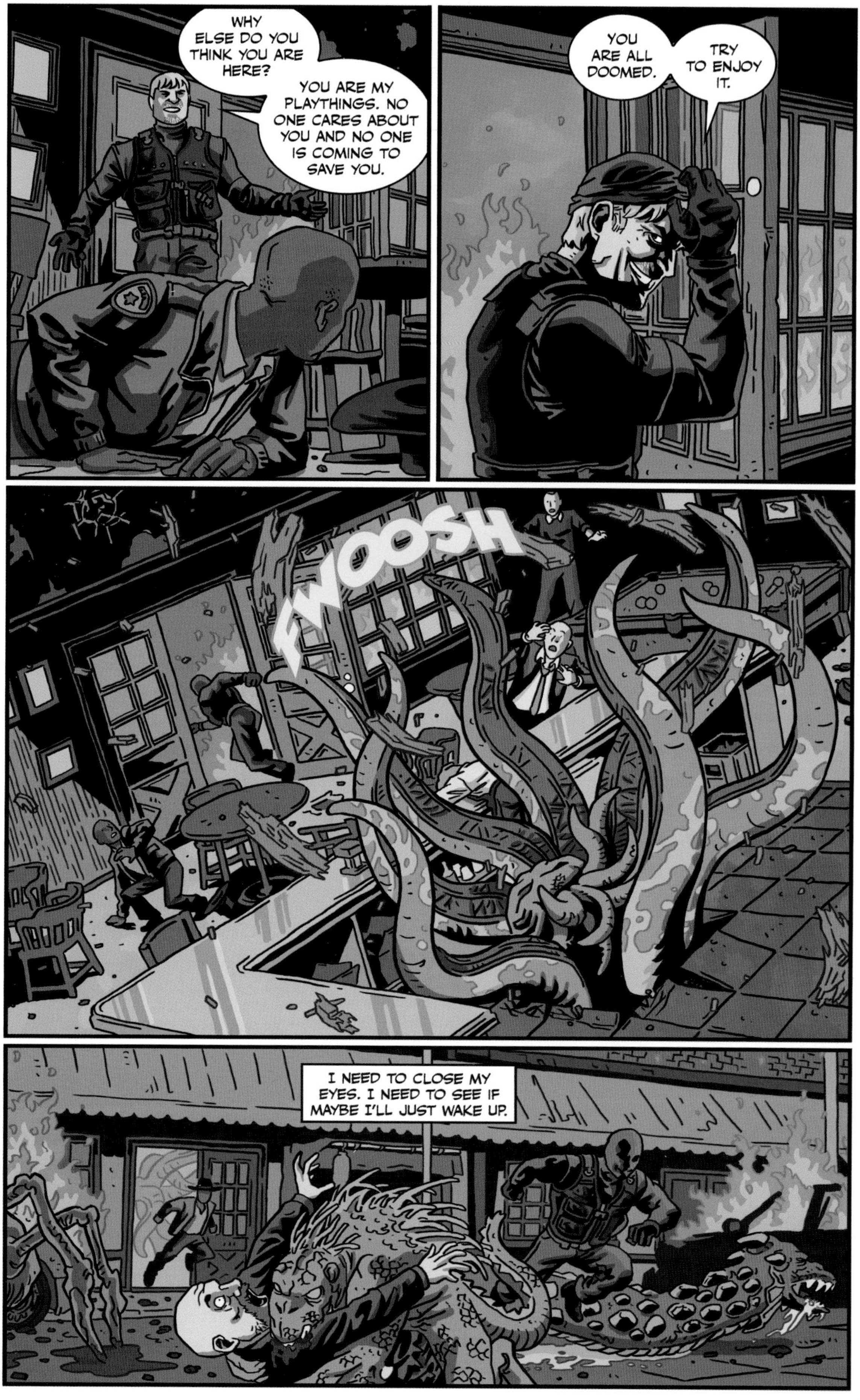
WHY ELSE DO YOU THINK YOU ARE HERE?
YOU ARE MY PLAYTHINGS. NO ONE CARES ABOUT YOU AND NO ONE IS COMING TO SAVE YOU.
YOU ARE ALL DOOMED.
TRY TO ENJOY IT.
FWOOSH
I NEED TO CLOSE MY EYES. I NEED TO SEE IF MAYBE I'LL JUST WAKE UP.

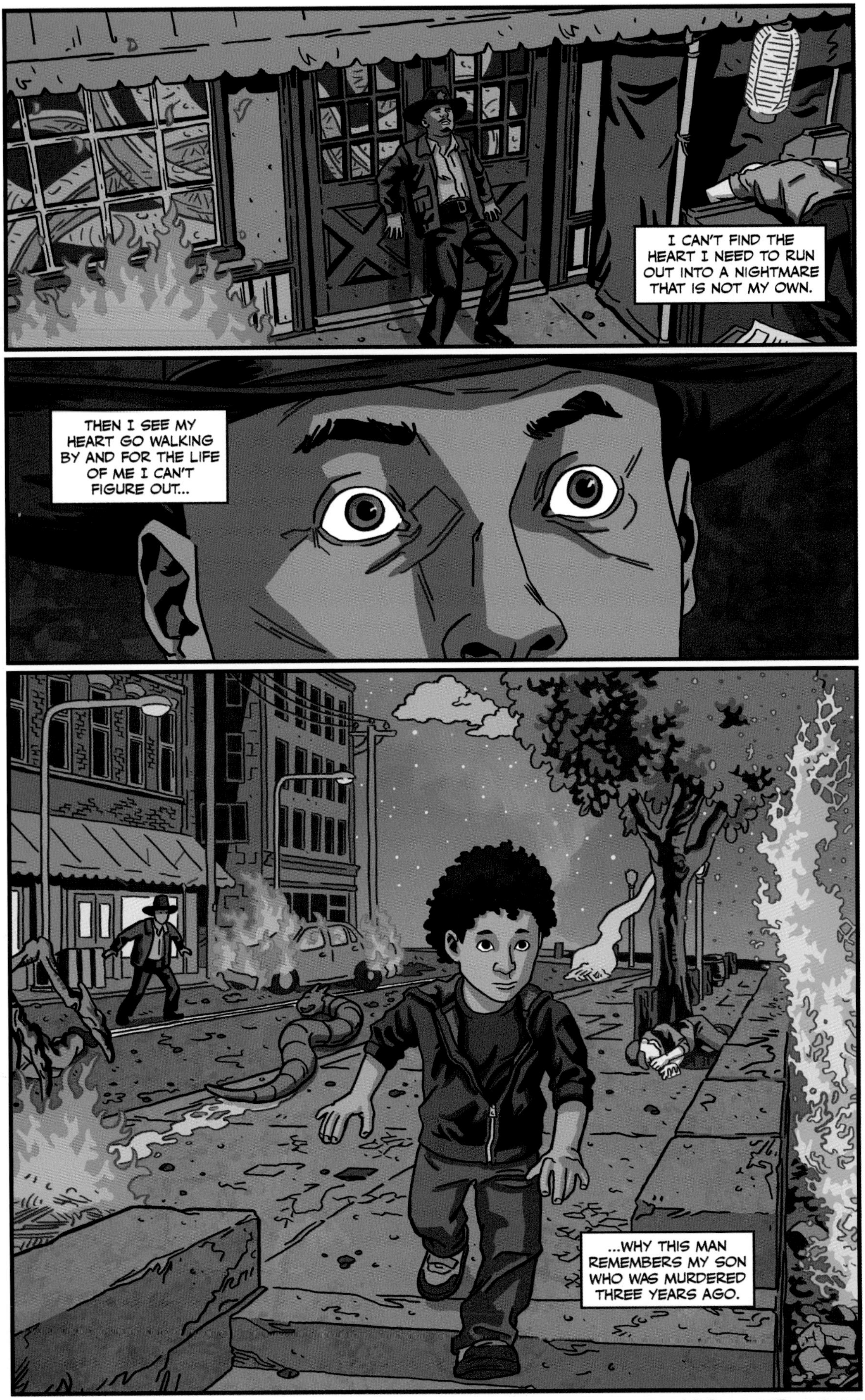
I CAN'T FIND THE HEART I NEED TO RUN OUT INTO A NIGHTMARE THAT IS NOT MY OWN.
THEN I SEE MY HEART GO WALKING BY AND FOR THE LIFE OF ME I CAN'T FIGURE OUT...
...WHY THIS MAN REMEMBERS MY SON WHO WAS MURDERED THREE YEARS AGO.

NEXT: THE DEAD MEN OF CARPENTER COVE

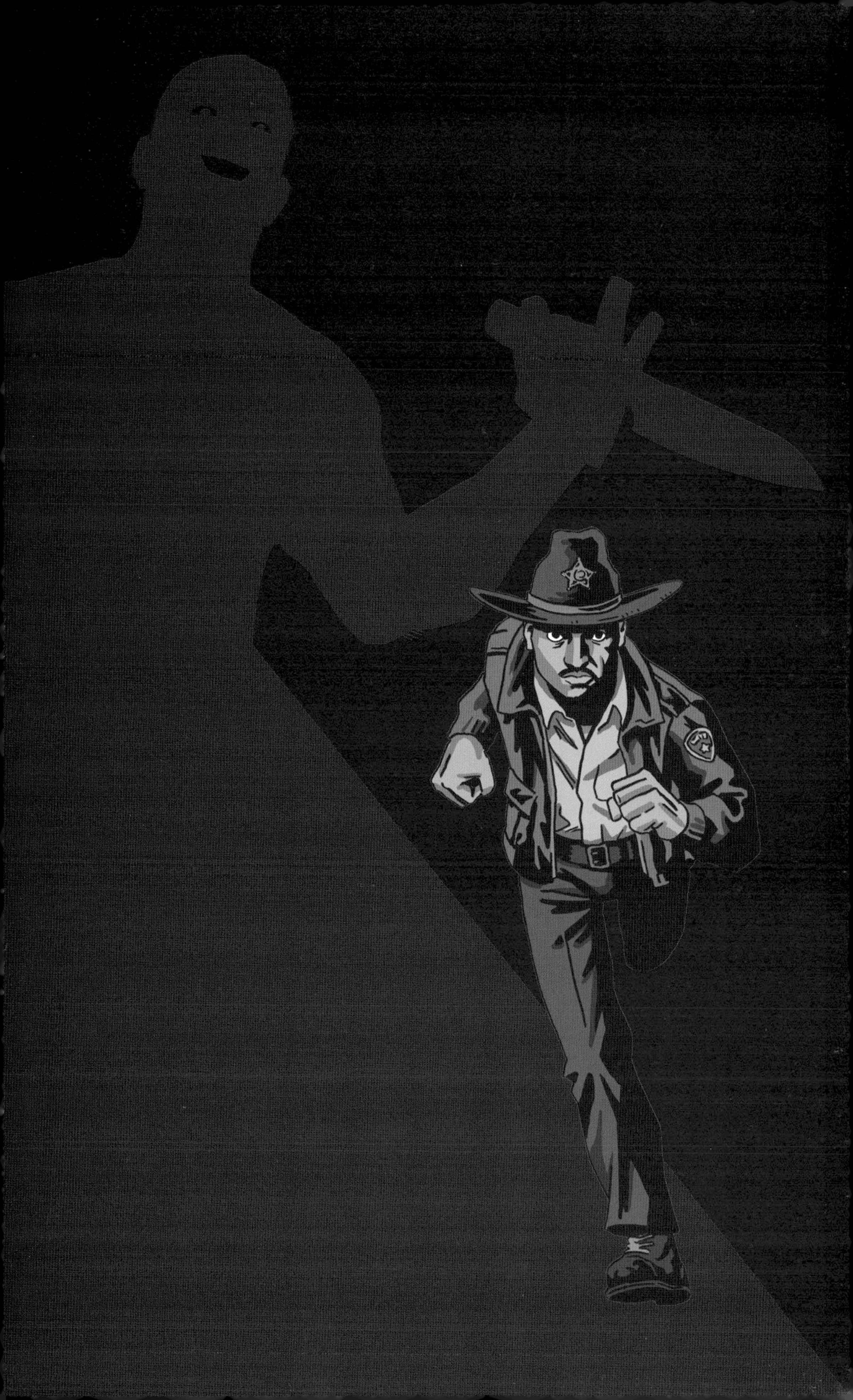

CHAPTER 2

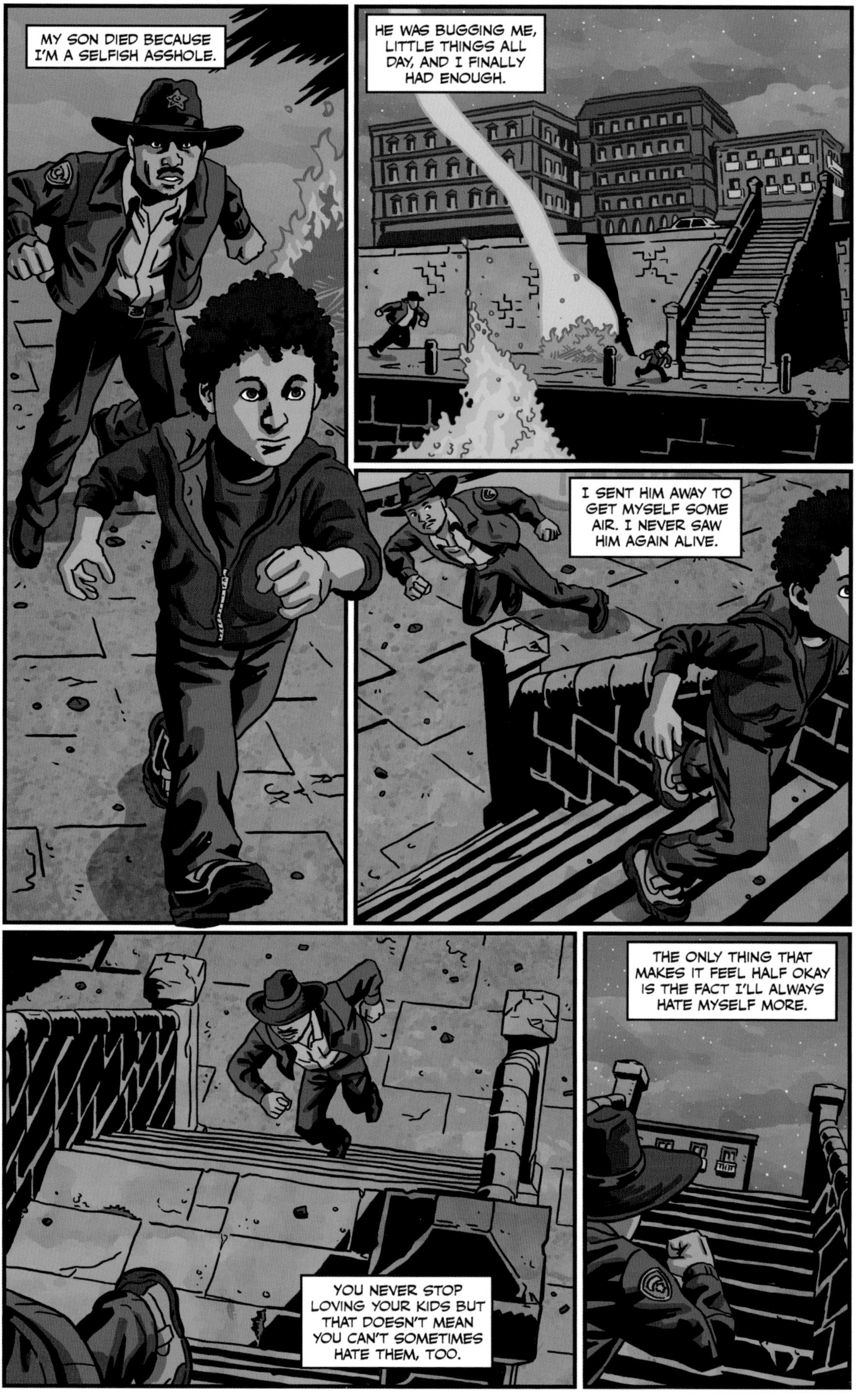
MY SON DIED BECAUSE I'M A SELFISH ASSHOLE.
HE WAS BUGGING ME, LITTLE THINGS ALL DAY, AND I FINALLY HAD ENOUGH.
I SENT HIM AWAY TO GET MYSELF SOME AIR. I NEVER SAW HIM AGAIN ALIVE.
YOU NEVER STOP LOVING YOUR KIDS BUT THAT DOESN'T MEAN YOU CAN'T SOMETIMES HATE THEM, TOO.
THE ONLY THING THAT MAKES IT FEEL HALF OKAY IS THE FACT I'LL ALWAYS HATE MYSELF MORE.

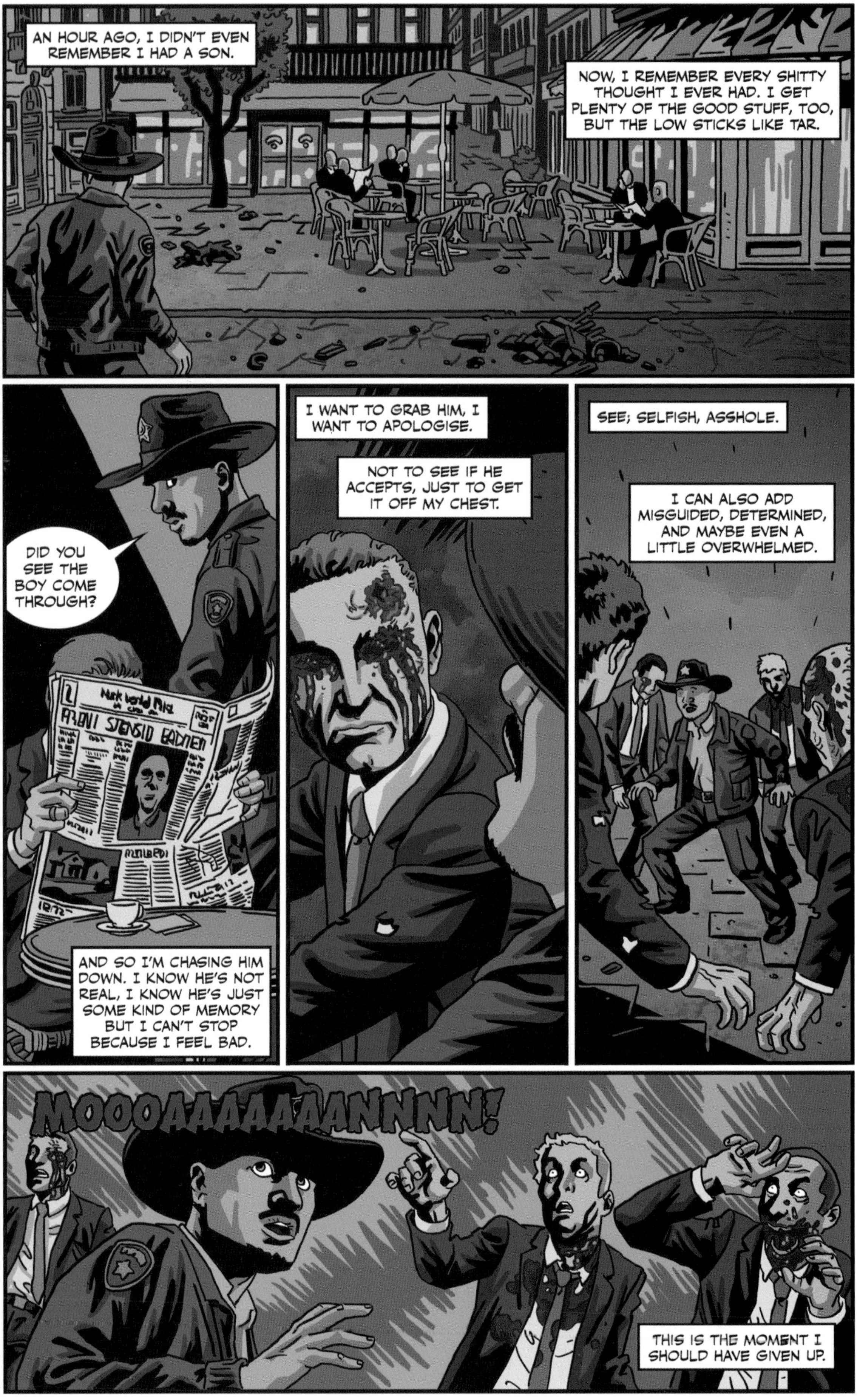
AN HOUR AGO, I DIDN'T EVEN REMEMBER I HAD A SON.
NOW, I REMEMBER EVERY SHITTY THOUGHT I EVER HAD. I GET PLENTY OF THE GOOD STUFF, TOO, BUT THE LOW STICKS LIKE TAR.
DID YOU SEE THE BOY COME THROUGH?
AND SO I'M CHASING HIM DOWN. I KNOW HE'S NOT REAL, I KNOW HE'S JUST SOME KIND OF MEMORY BUT I CAN'T STOP BECAUSE I FEEL BAD.
I WANT TO GRAB HIM, I WANT TO APOLOGISE.
NOT TO SEE IF HE ACCEPTS, JUST TO GET IT OFF MY CHEST.
SEE; SELFISH, ASSHOLE.
I CAN ALSO ADD MISGUIDED, DETERMINED, AND MAYBE EVEN A LITTLE OVERWHELMED.
MOOOAAAAAAAANNNNN!
THIS IS THE MOMENT I SHOULD HAVE GIVEN UP.

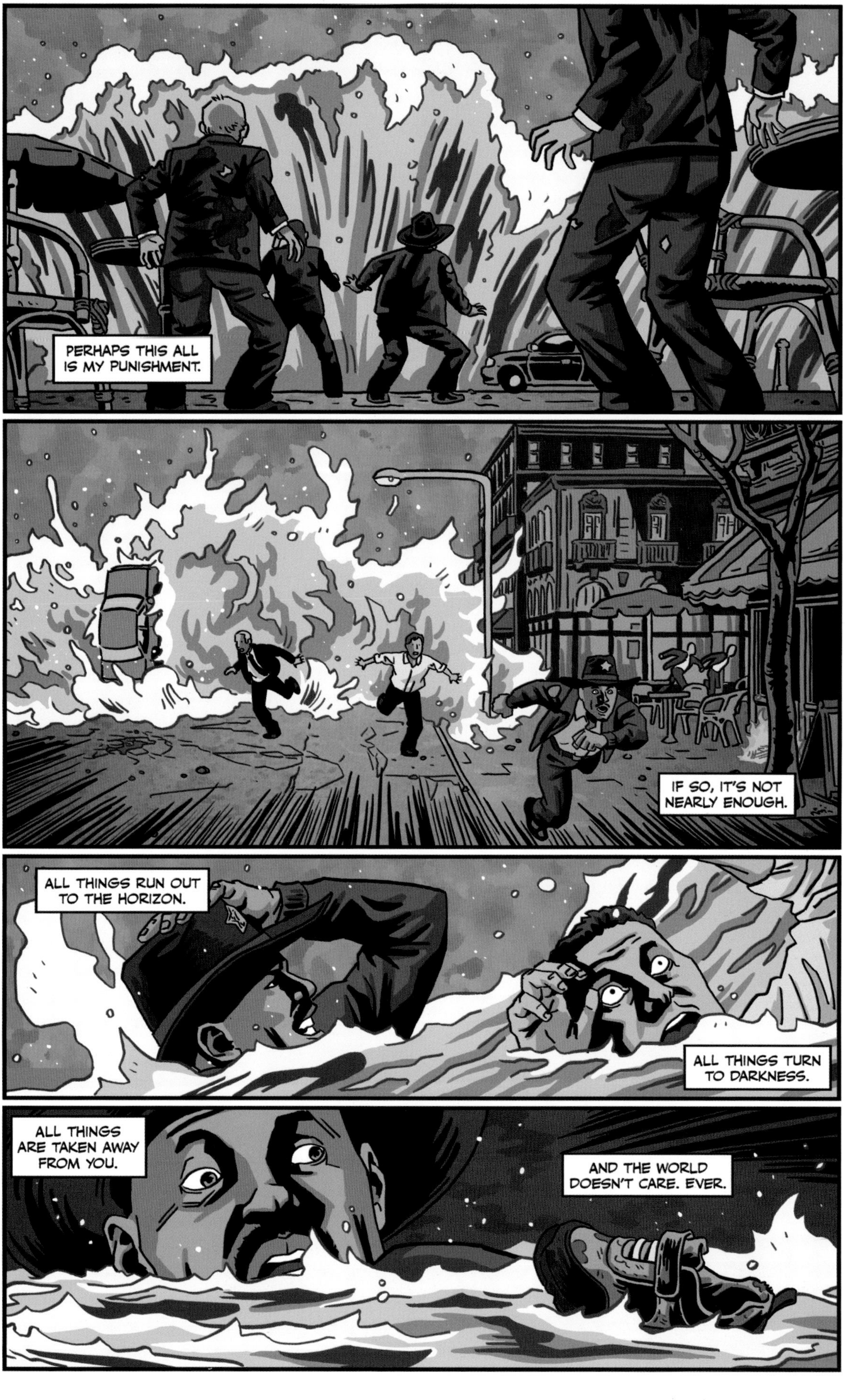
PERHAPS THIS ALL IS MY PUNISHMENT.
IF SO, IT'S NOT NEARLY ENOUGH.
ALL THINGS RUN OUT TO THE HORIZON.
ALL THINGS TURN TO DARKNESS.
ALL THINGS ARE TAKEN AWAY FROM YOU.
AND THE WORLD DOESN'T CARE. EVER.

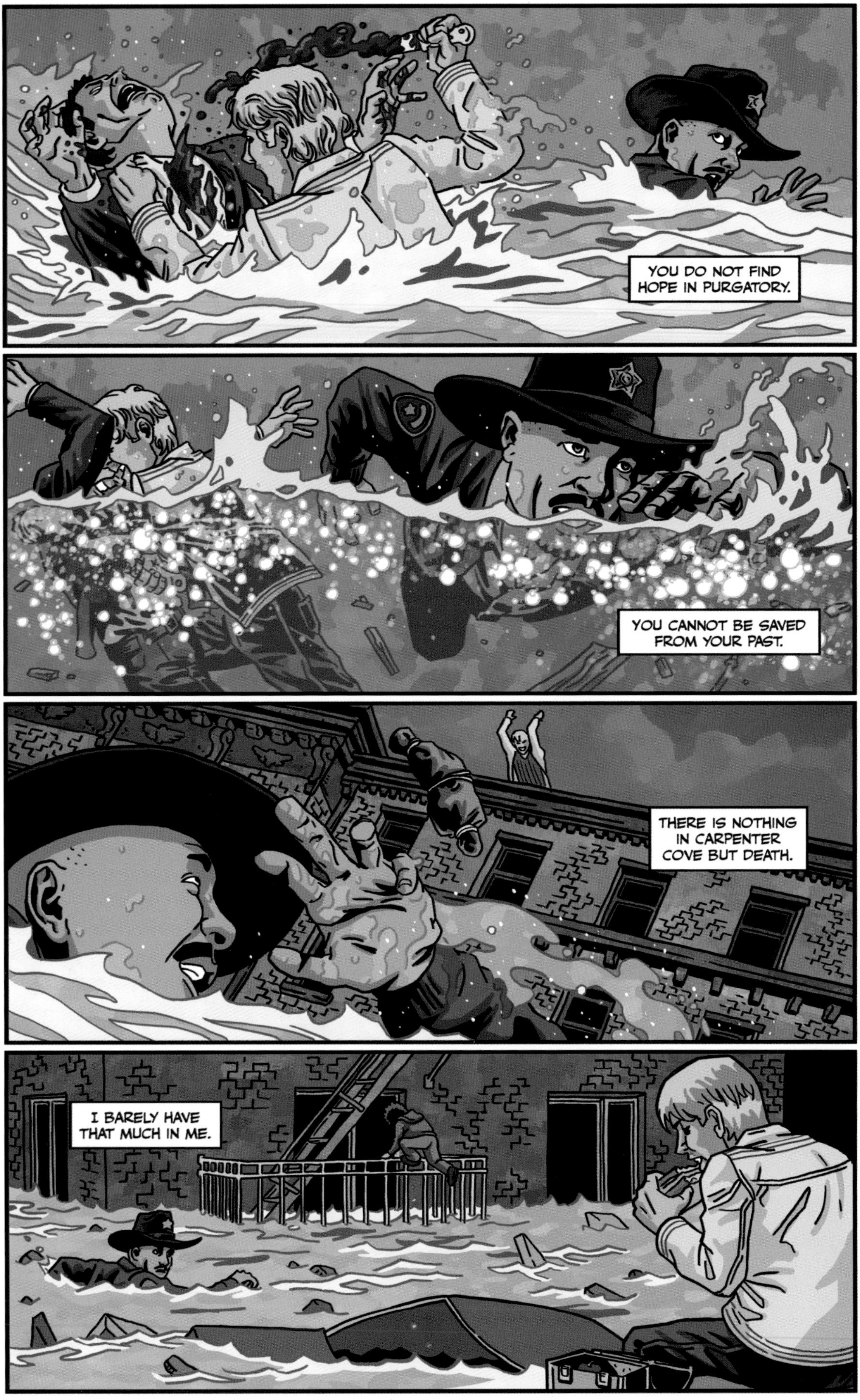
YOU DO NOT FIND HOPE IN PURGATORY.
YOU CANNOT BE SAVED FROM YOUR PAST.
THERE IS NOTHING IN CARPENTER COVE BUT DEATH.
I BARELY HAVE THAT MUCH IN ME.

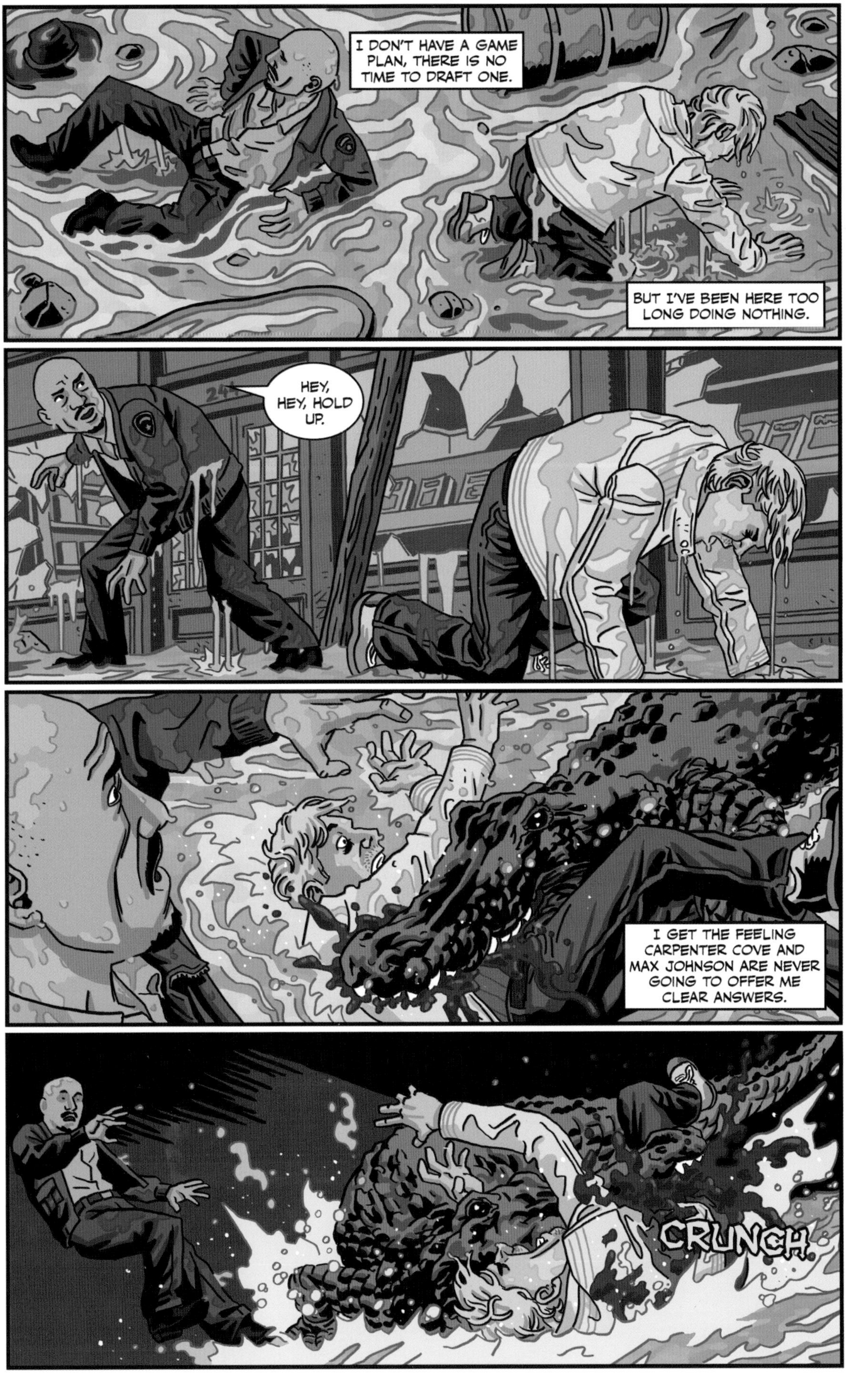
I DON'T HAVE A GAME PLAN, THERE IS NO TIME TO DRAFT ONE.
BUT I'VE BEEN HERE TOO LONG DOING NOTHING.
HEY, HEY, HOLD UP.
I GET THE FEELING CARPENTER COVE AND MAX JOHNSON ARE NEVER GOING TO OFFER ME CLEAR ANSWERS.
CRUNCH.

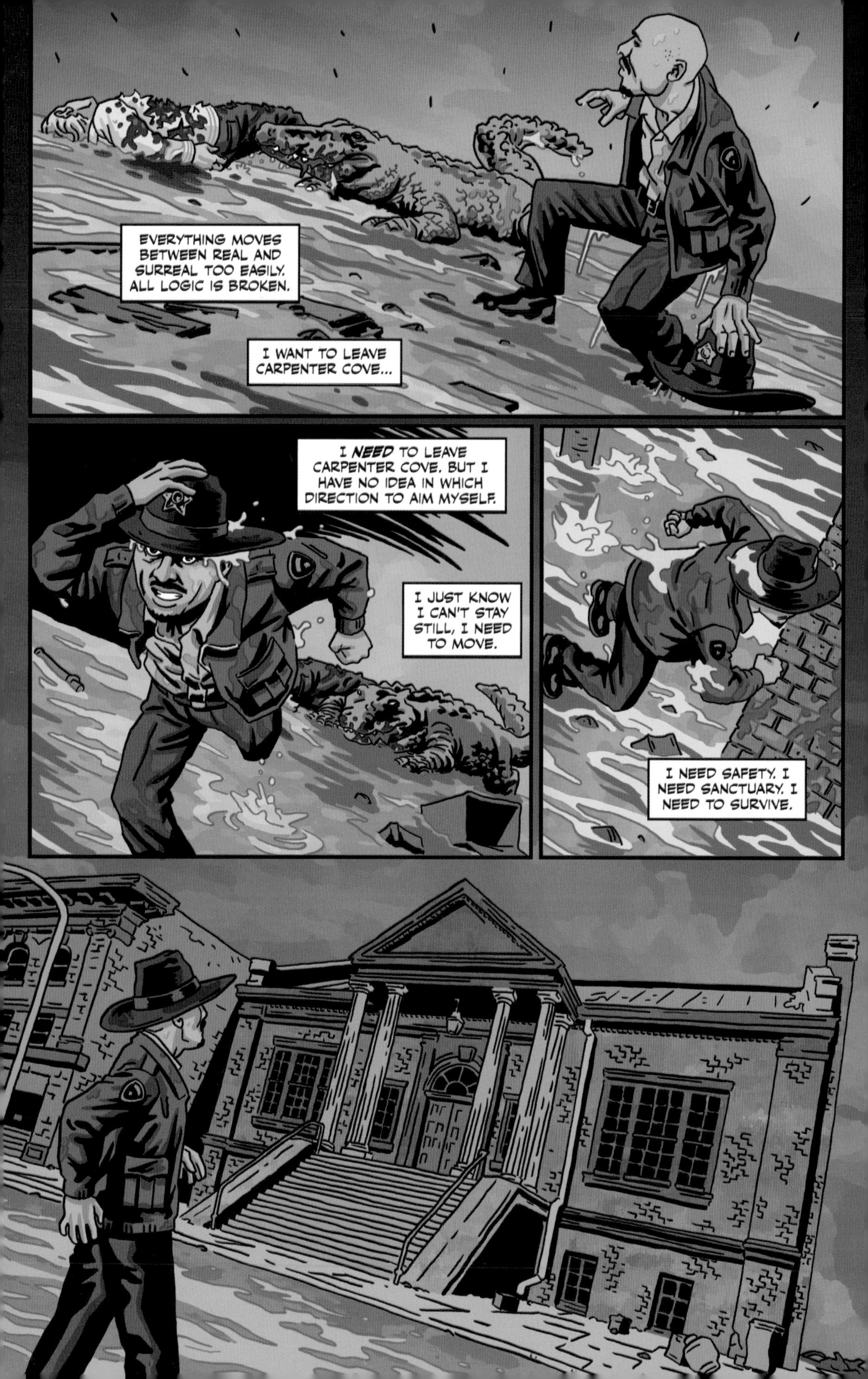
EVERYTHING MOVES BETWEEN REAL AND SURREAL TOO EASILY. ALL LOGIC IS BROKEN.
I WANT TO LEAVE CARPENTER COVE...
I NEED TO LEAVE CARPENTER COVE. BUT I HAVE NO IDEA IN WHICH DIRECTION TO AIM MYSELF.
I JUST KNOW I CAN'T STAY STILL, I NEED TO MOVE.
I NEED SAFETY. I NEED SANCTUARY. I NEED TO SURVIVE.

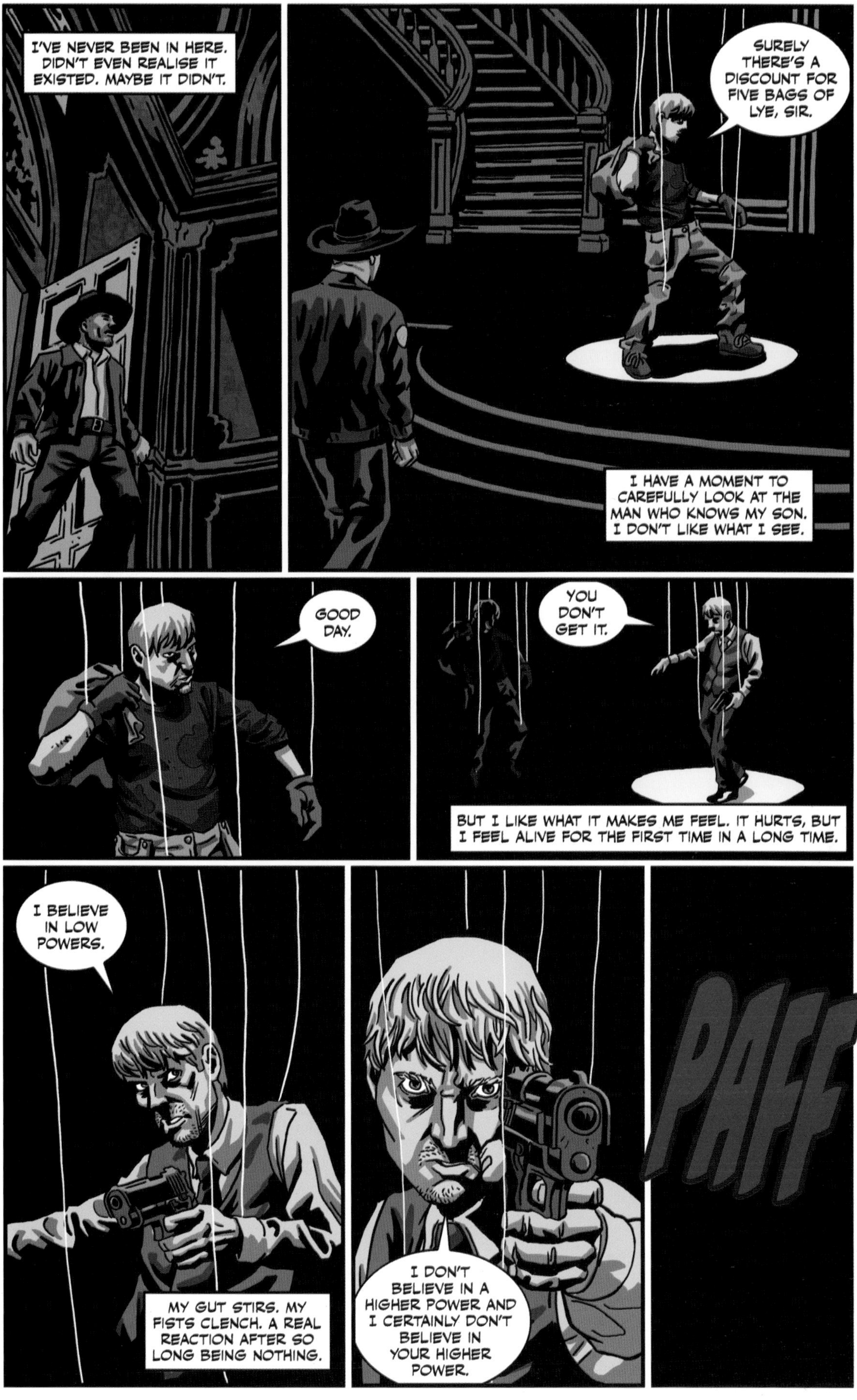
I'VE NEVER BEEN IN HERE. DIDN'T EVEN REALISE IT EXISTED. MAYBE IT DIDN'T.
SURELY THERE'S A DISCOUNT FOR FIVE BAGS OF LYE, SIR.
I HAVE A MOMENT TO CAREFULLY LOOK AT THE MAN WHO KNOWS MY SON. I DON'T LIKE WHAT I SEE.
GOOD DAY.
YOU DON'T GET IT.
BUT I LIKE WHAT IT MAKES ME FEEL. IT HURTS, BUT I FEEL ALIVE FOR THE FIRST TIME IN A LONG TIME.
I BELIEVE IN LOW POWERS.
MY GUT STIRS. MY FISTS CLENCH. A REAL REACTION AFTER SO LONG BEING NOTHING.
I DON'T BELIEVE IN A HIGHER POWER AND I CERTAINLY DON'T BELIEVE IN YOUR HIGHER POWER.
PAFF

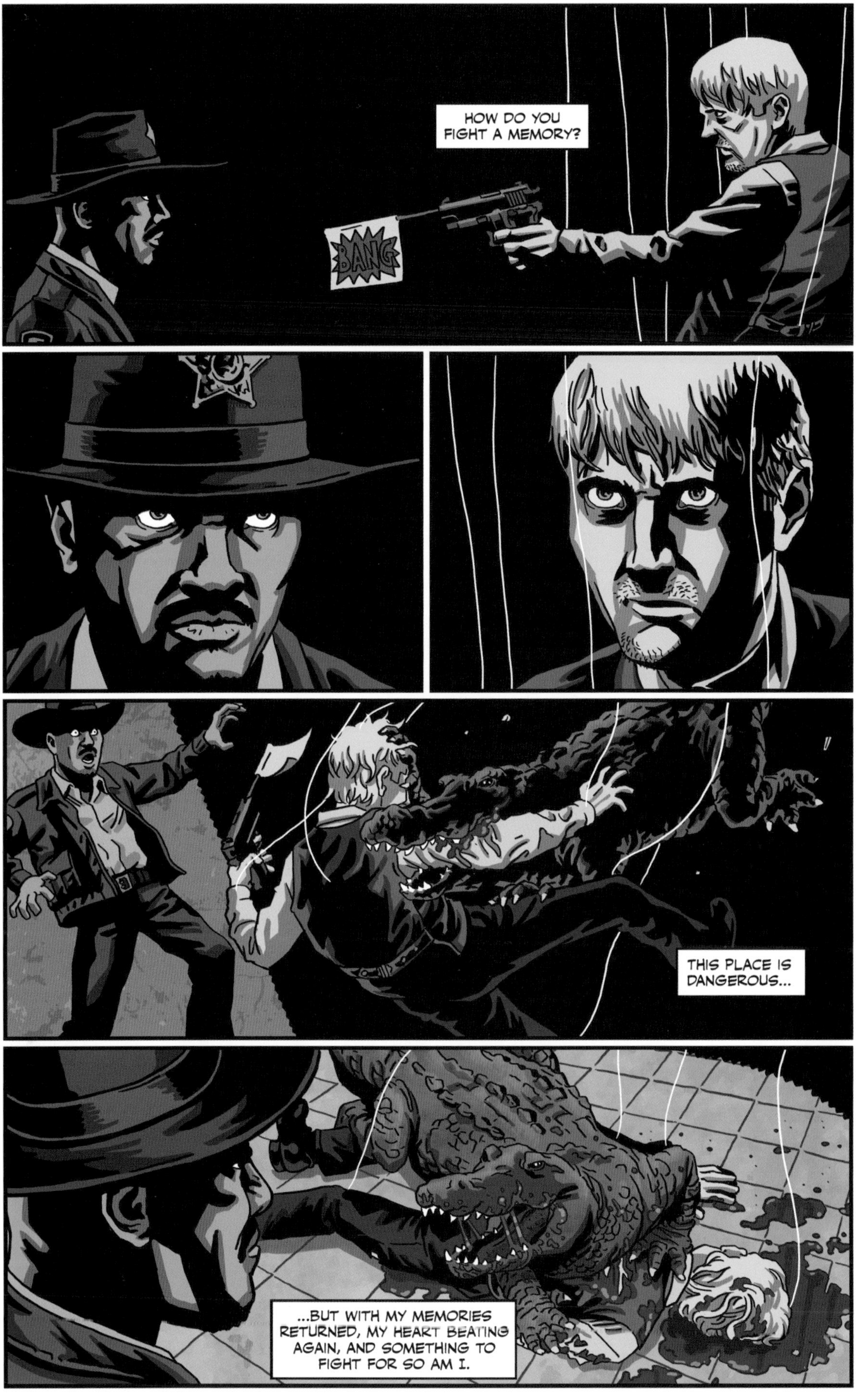
HOW DO YOU
FIGHT A MEMORY?
BANG
THIS PLACE IS
DANGEROUS...
...BUT WITH MY MEMORIES
RETURNED, MY HEART BEATING
AGAIN, AND SOMETHING TO
FIGHT FOR SO AM I.

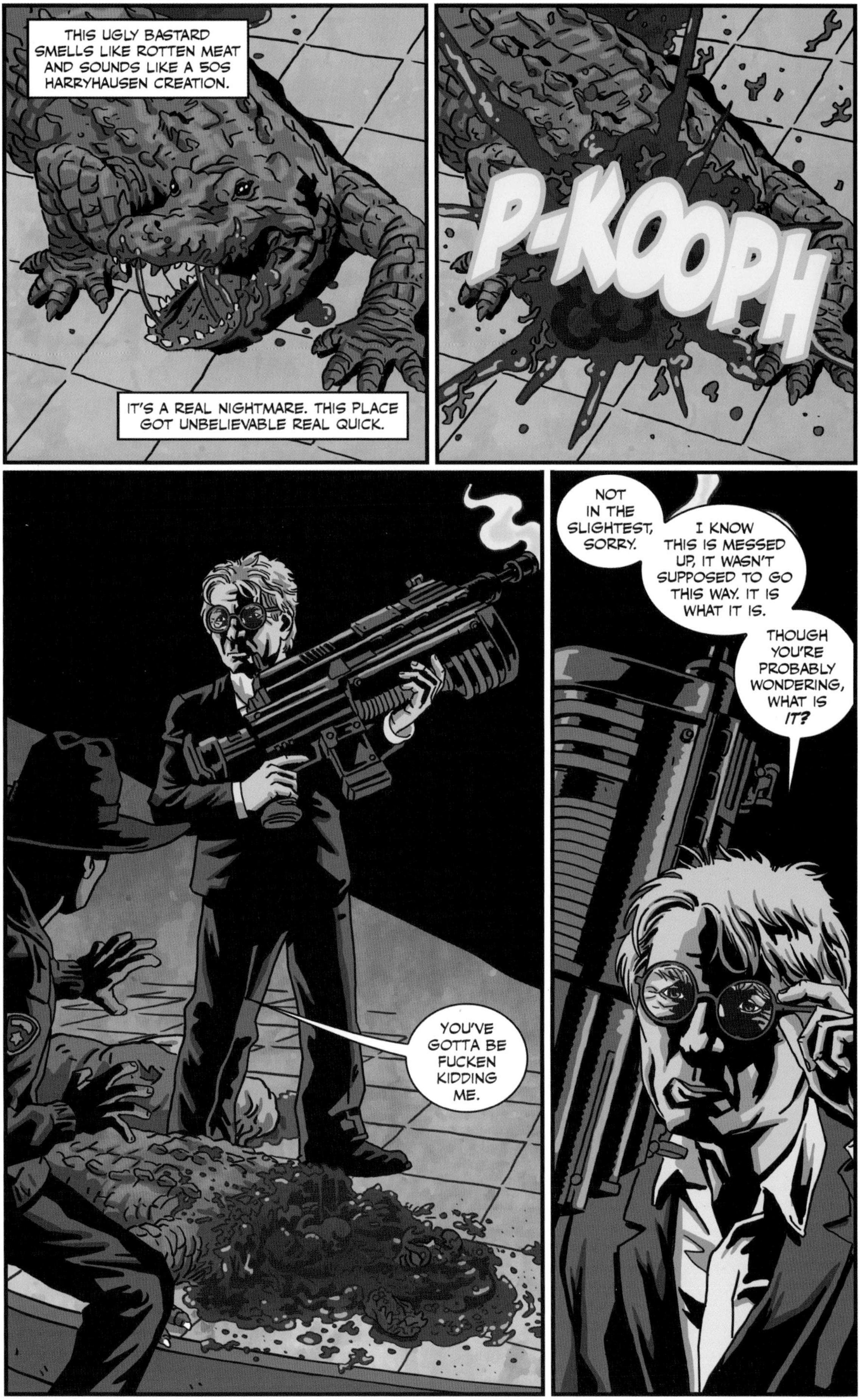
THIS UGLY BASTARD SMELLS LIKE ROTTEN MEAT AND SOUNDS LIKE A 50S HARRYHAUSEN CREATION.
IT'S A REAL NIGHTMARE. THIS PLACE GOT UNBELIEVABLE REAL QUICK.
P-KOOPH
YOU'VE GOTTA BE FUCKEN KIDDING ME.
NOT IN THE SLIGHTEST, SORRY.
I KNOW THIS IS MESSED UP, IT WASN'T SUPPOSED TO GO THIS WAY. IT IS WHAT IT IS.
THOUGH YOU'RE PROBABLY WONDERING, WHAT IS *IT?*

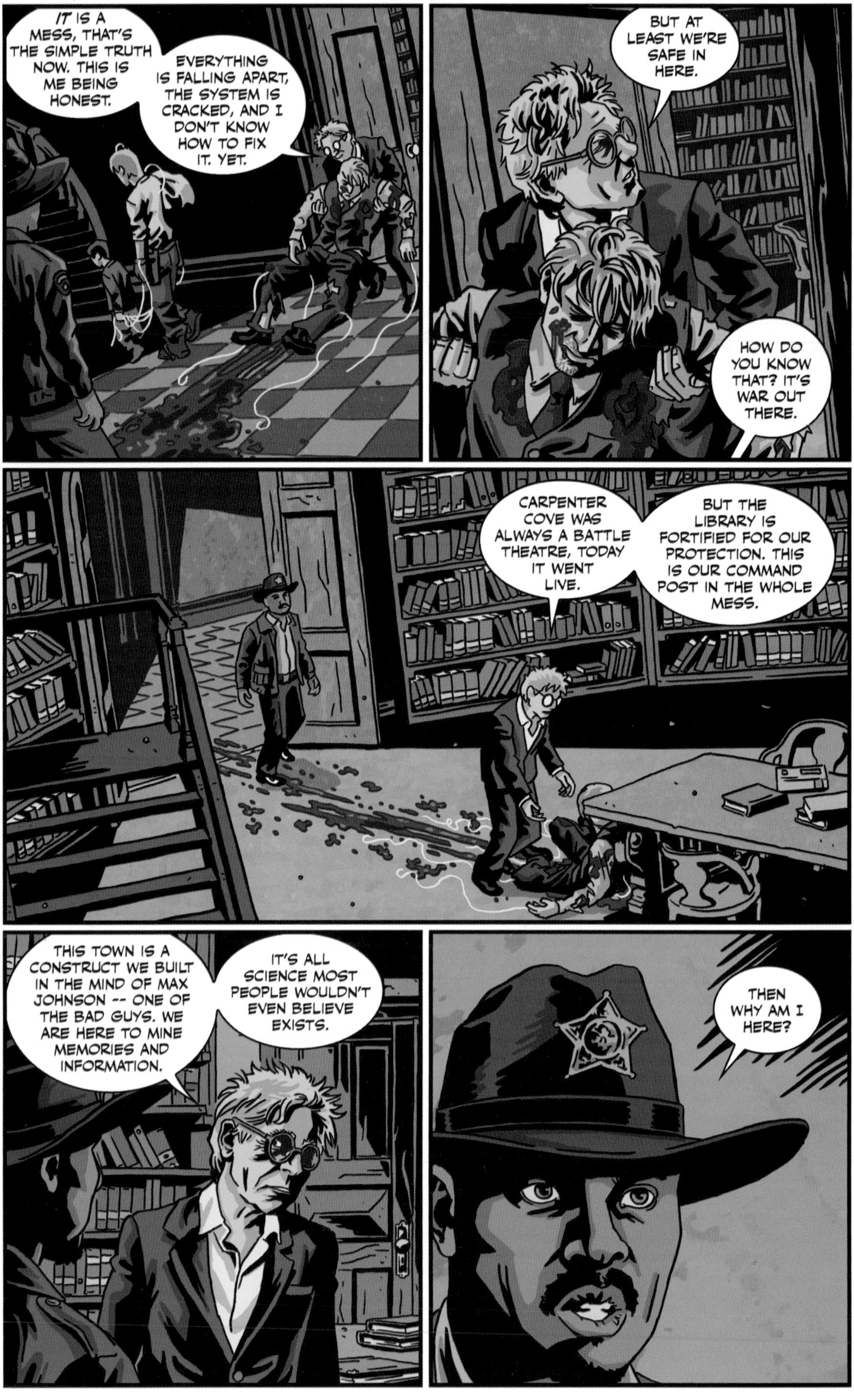
IT IS A MESS, THAT'S THE SIMPLE TRUTH NOW. THIS IS ME BEING HONEST.
EVERYTHING IS FALLING APART, THE SYSTEM IS CRACKED, AND I DON'T KNOW HOW TO FIX IT. YET.
BUT AT LEAST WE'RE SAFE IN HERE.
HOW DO YOU KNOW THAT? IT'S WAR OUT THERE.
CARPENTER COVE WAS ALWAYS A BATTLE THEATRE, TODAY IT WENT LIVE.
BUT THE LIBRARY IS FORTIFIED FOR OUR PROTECTION. THIS IS OUR COMMAND POST IN THE WHOLE MESS.
THIS TOWN IS A CONSTRUCT WE BUILT IN THE MIND OF MAX JOHNSON -- ONE OF THE BAD GUYS. WE ARE HERE TO MINE MEMORIES AND INFORMATION.
IT'S ALL SCIENCE MOST PEOPLE WOULDN'T EVEN BELIEVE EXISTS.
THEN WHY AM I HERE?

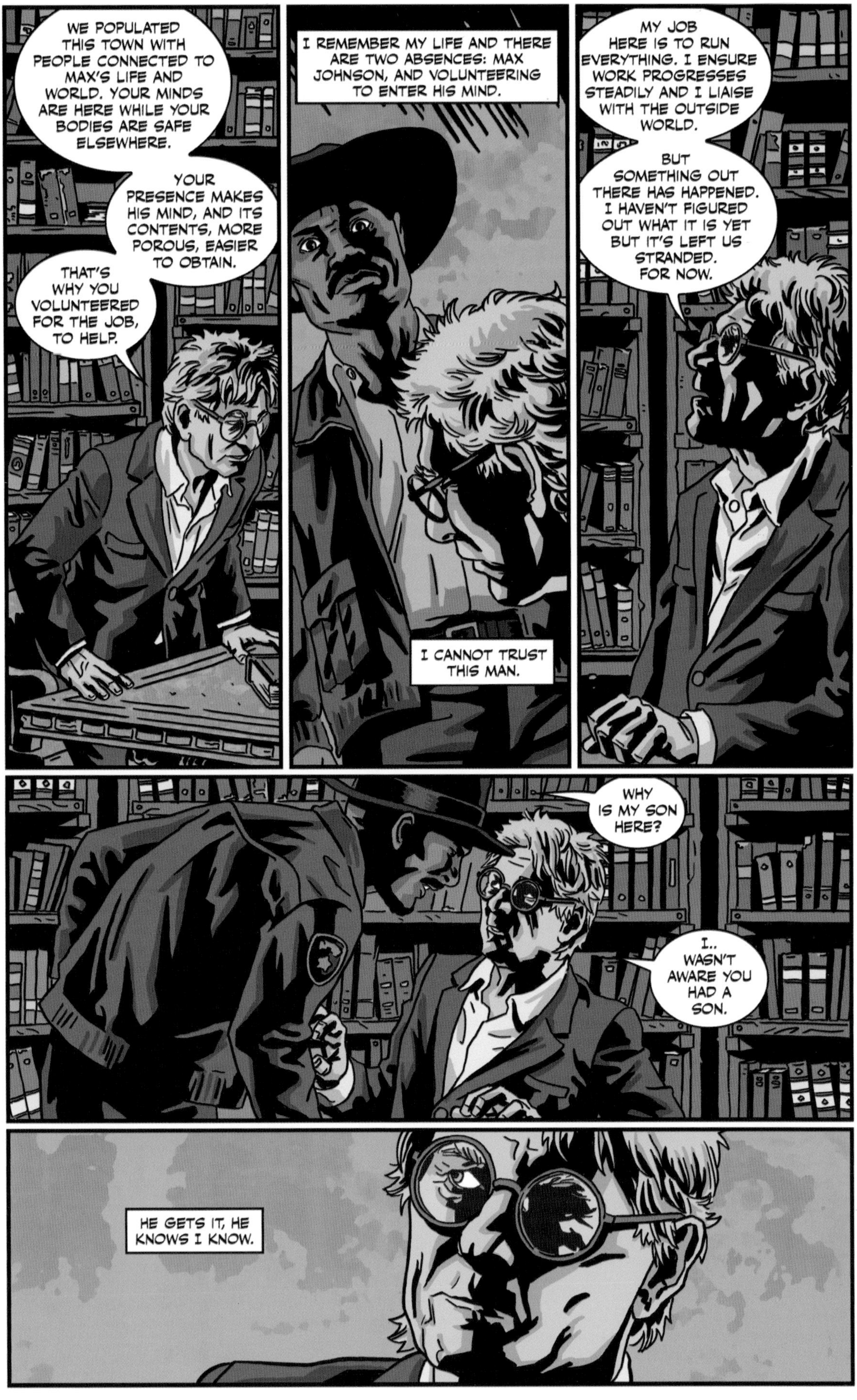
WE POPULATED THIS TOWN WITH PEOPLE CONNECTED TO MAX'S LIFE AND WORLD. YOUR MINDS ARE HERE WHILE YOUR BODIES ARE SAFE ELSEWHERE.
YOUR PRESENCE MAKES HIS MIND, AND ITS CONTENTS, MORE POROUS, EASIER TO OBTAIN.
THAT'S WHY YOU VOLUNTEERED FOR THE JOB, TO HELP.
I REMEMBER MY LIFE AND THERE ARE TWO ABSENCES: MAX JOHNSON, AND VOLUNTEERING TO ENTER HIS MIND.
I CANNOT TRUST THIS MAN.
MY JOB HERE IS TO RUN EVERYTHING. I ENSURE WORK PROGRESSES STEADILY AND I LIAISE WITH THE OUTSIDE WORLD.
BUT SOMETHING OUT THERE HAS HAPPENED. I HAVEN'T FIGURED OUT WHAT IT IS YET BUT IT'S LEFT US STRANDED. FOR NOW.
WHY IS MY SON HERE?
I.. WASN'T AWARE YOU HAD A SON.
HE GETS IT, HE KNOWS I KNOW.

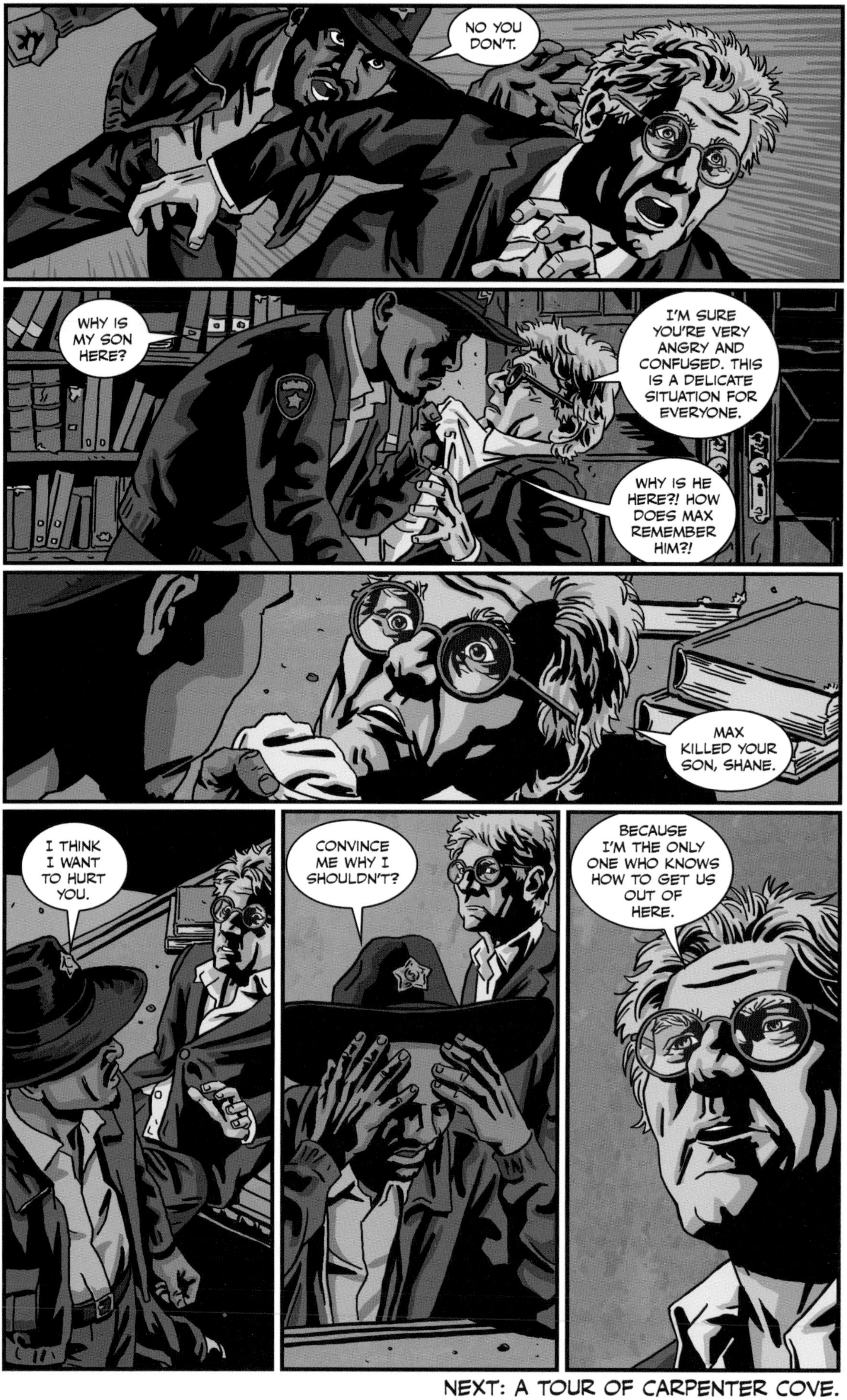
NO YOU DON'T.
WHY IS MY SON HERE?
I'M SURE YOU'RE VERY ANGRY AND CONFUSED. THIS IS A DELICATE SITUATION FOR EVERYONE.
WHY IS HE HERE?! HOW DOES MAX REMEMBER HIM?!
MAX KILLED YOUR SON, SHANE.
I THINK I WANT TO HURT YOU.
CONVINCE ME WHY I SHOULDN'T?
BECAUSE I'M THE ONLY ONE WHO KNOWS HOW TO GET US OUT OF HERE.

NEXT: A TOUR OF CARPENTER COVE.

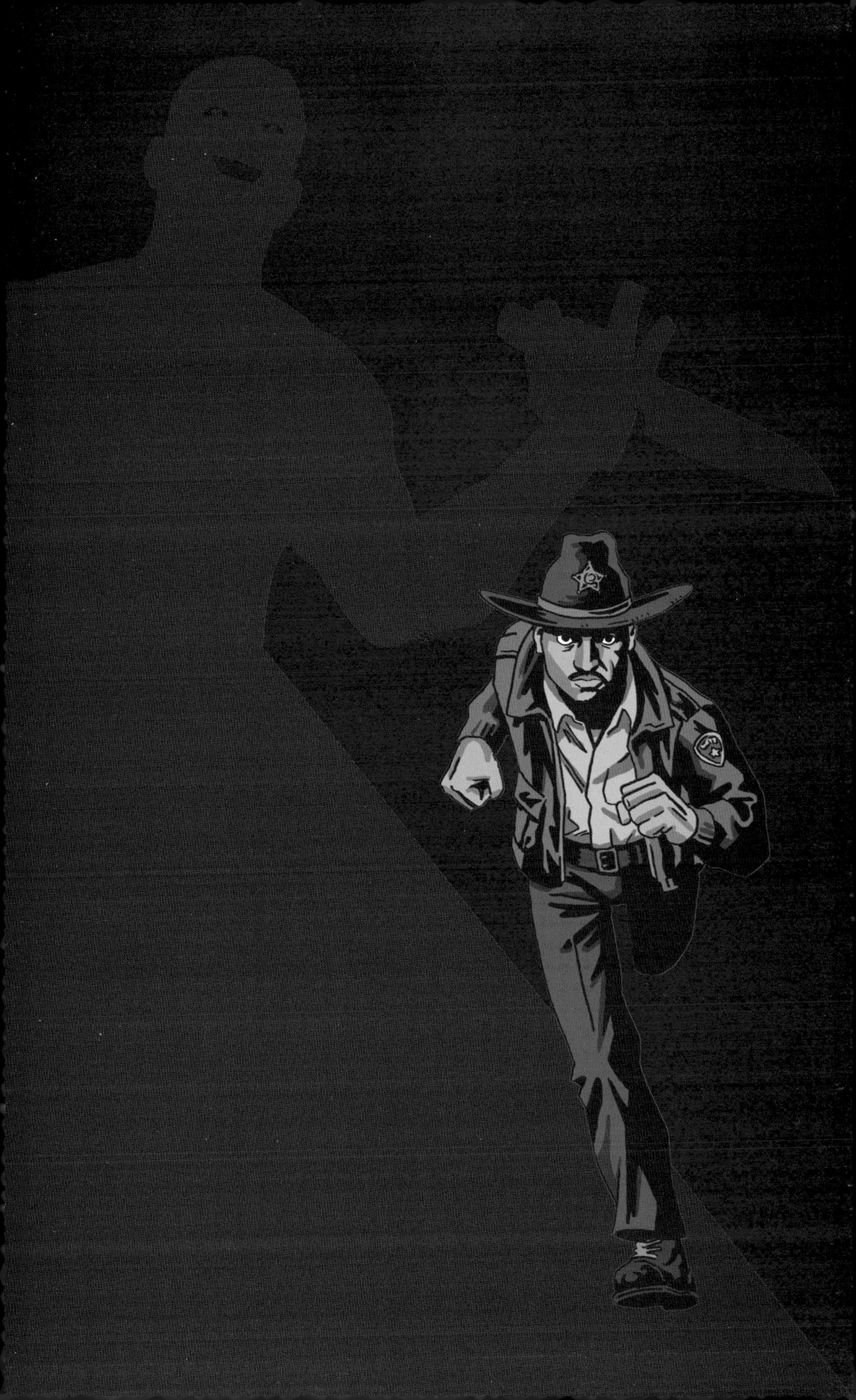

Chapter 3

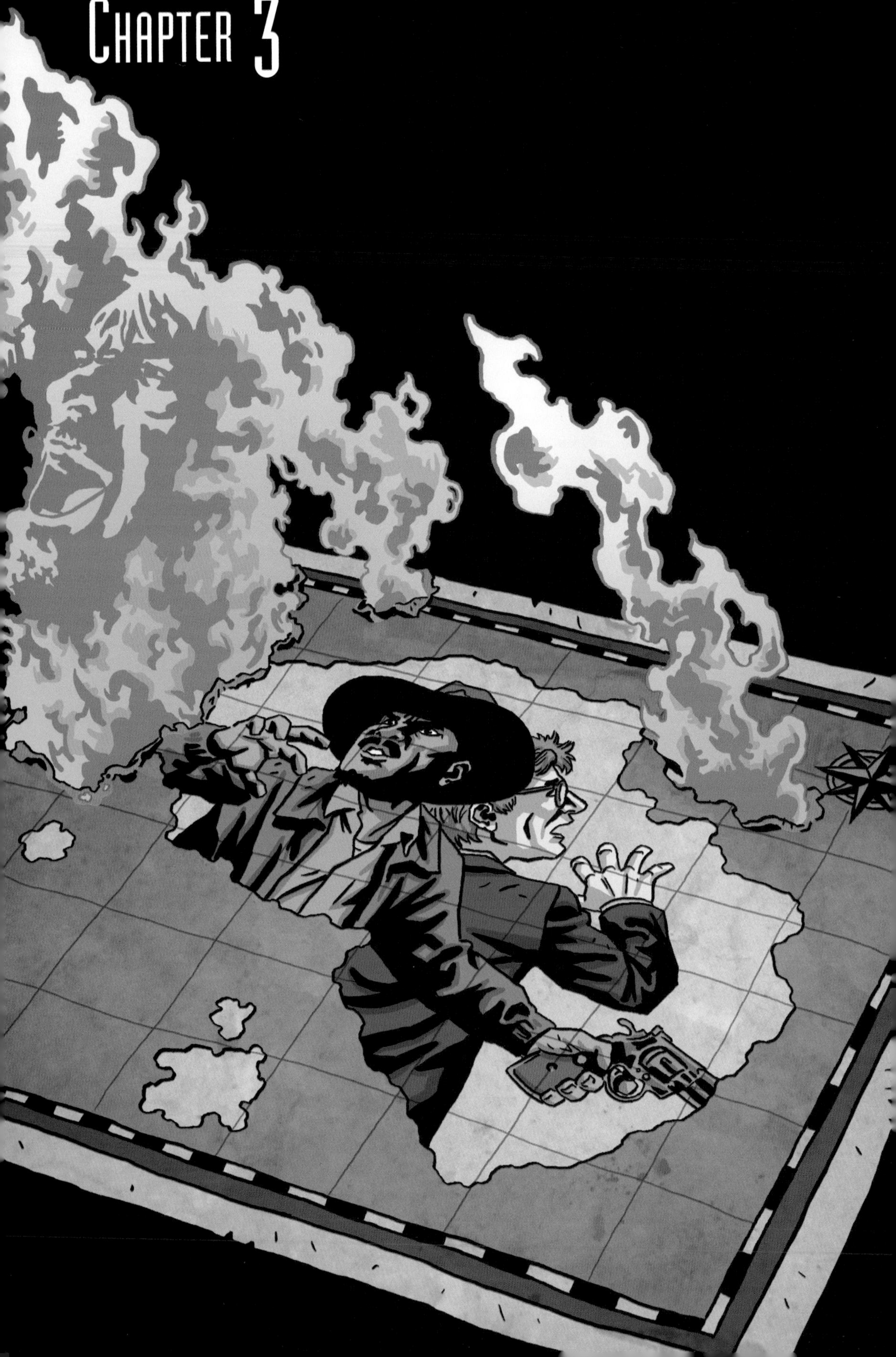

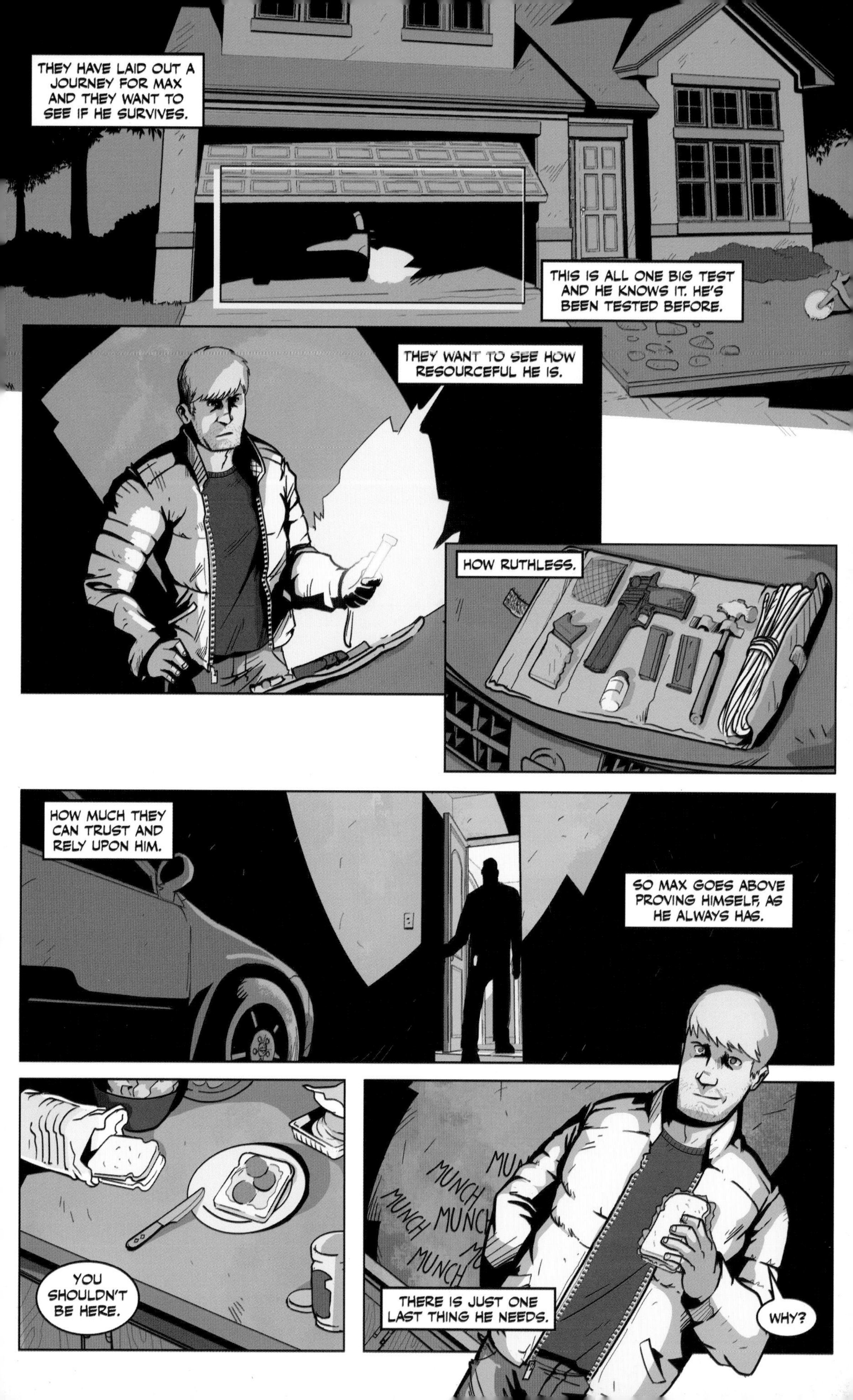
THEY HAVE LAID OUT A JOURNEY FOR MAX AND THEY WANT TO SEE IF HE SURVIVES.
THIS IS ALL ONE BIG TEST AND HE KNOWS IT. HE'S BEEN TESTED BEFORE.
THEY WANT TO SEE HOW RESOURCEFUL HE IS.
HOW RUTHLESS.
HOW MUCH THEY CAN TRUST AND RELY UPON HIM.
SO MAX GOES ABOVE PROVING HIMSELF, AS HE ALWAYS HAS.
YOU SHOULDN'T BE HERE.
MUNCH
MUNCH
MUNCH
MUNCH
THERE IS JUST ONE LAST THING HE NEEDS.
WHY?

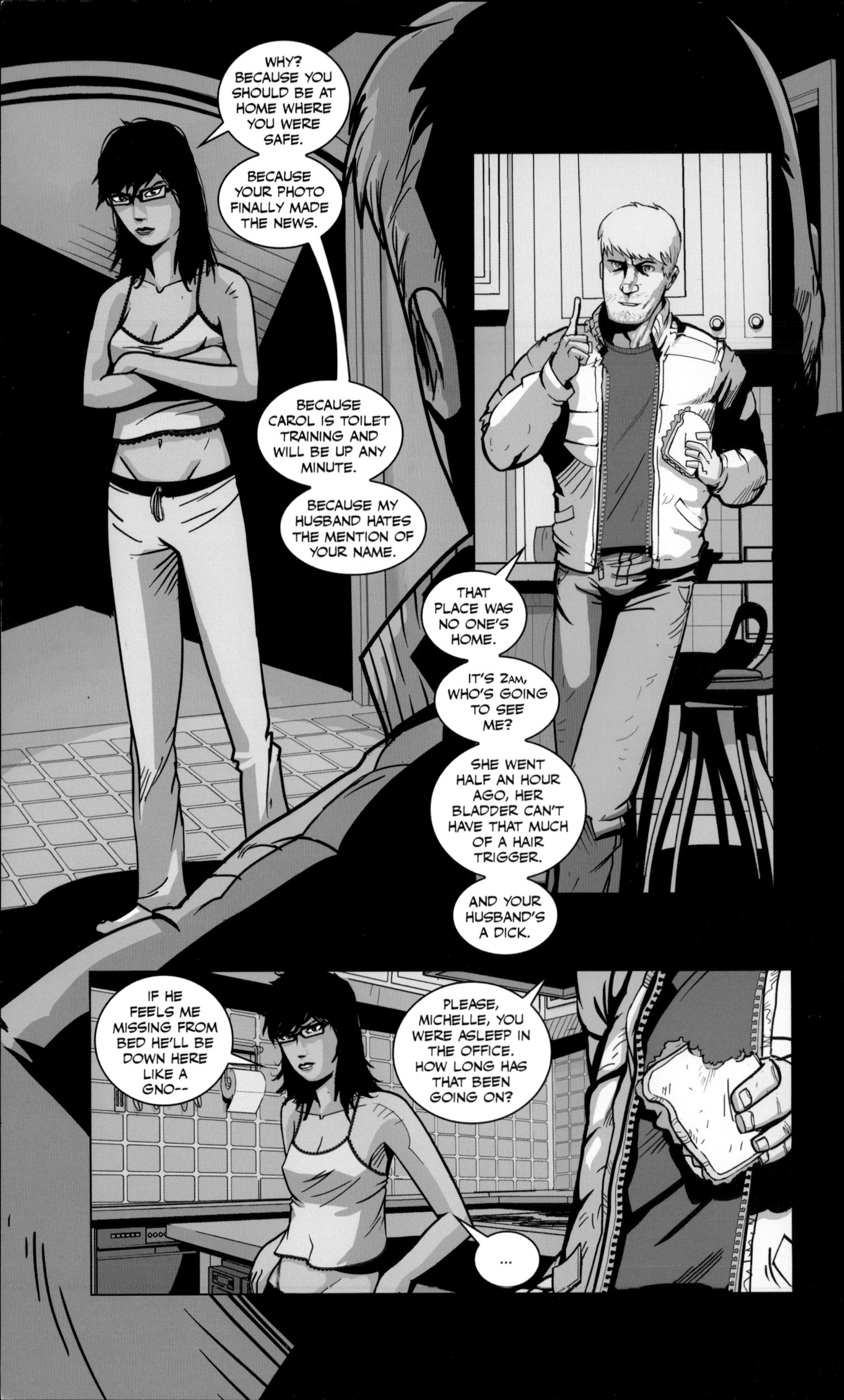
WHY? BECAUSE YOU SHOULD BE AT HOME WHERE YOU WERE SAFE.
BECAUSE YOUR PHOTO FINALLY MADE THE NEWS.
BECAUSE CAROL IS TOILET TRAINING AND WILL BE UP ANY MINUTE.
BECAUSE MY HUSBAND HATES THE MENTION OF YOUR NAME.
THAT PLACE WAS NO ONE'S HOME.
IT'S ZAM, WHO'S GOING TO SEE ME?
SHE WENT HALF AN HOUR AGO, HER BLADDER CAN'T HAVE THAT MUCH OF A HAIR TRIGGER.
AND YOUR HUSBAND'S A DICK.
IF HE FEELS ME MISSING FROM BED HE'LL BE DOWN HERE LIKE A GNO--
PLEASE, MICHELLE, YOU WERE ASLEEP IN THE OFFICE. HOW LONG HAS THAT BEEN GOING ON?
...

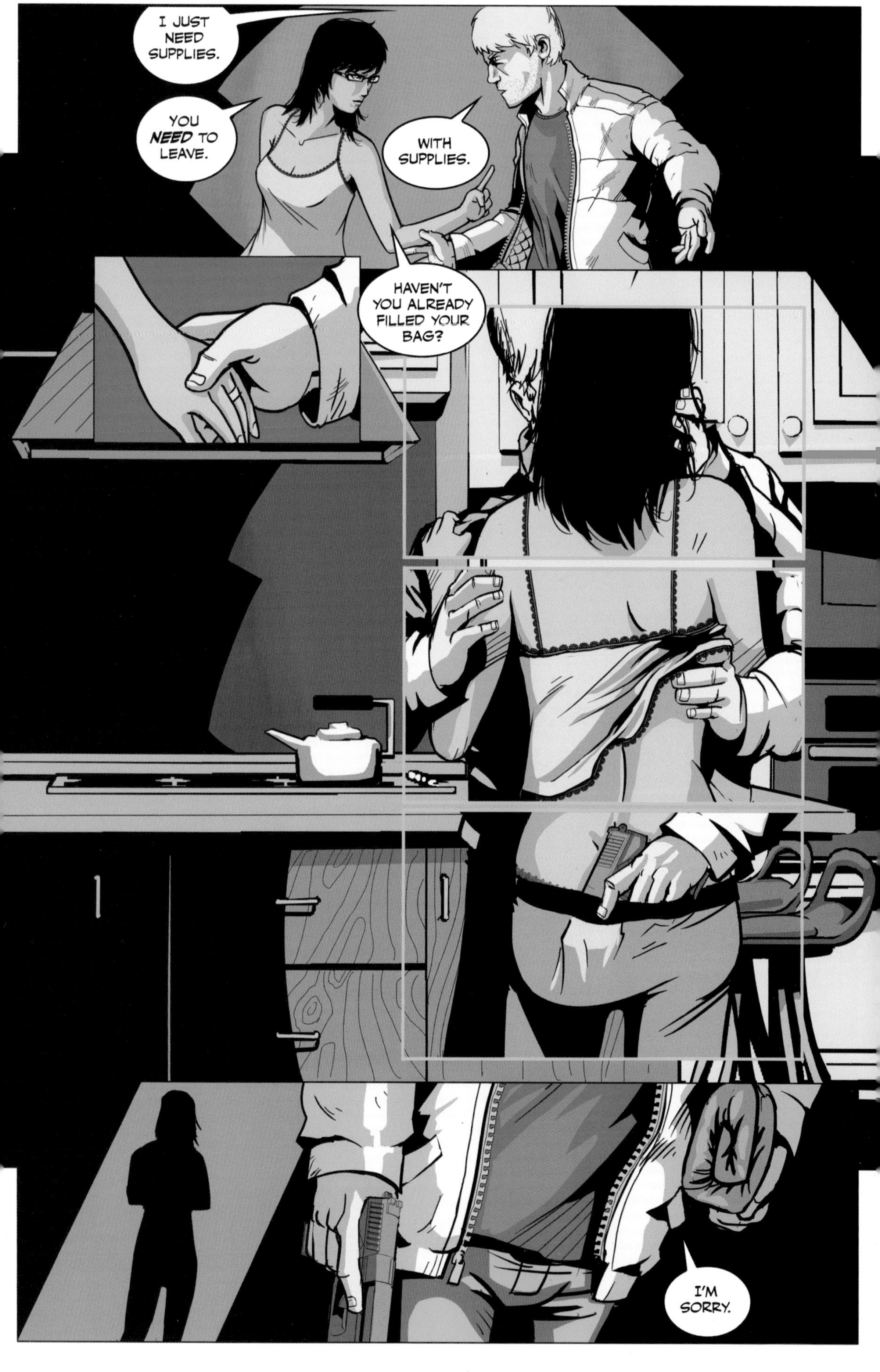
I JUST NEED SUPPLIES.
YOU NEED TO LEAVE.
WITH SUPPLIES.
HAVEN'T YOU ALREADY FILLED YOUR BAG?
I'M SORRY.

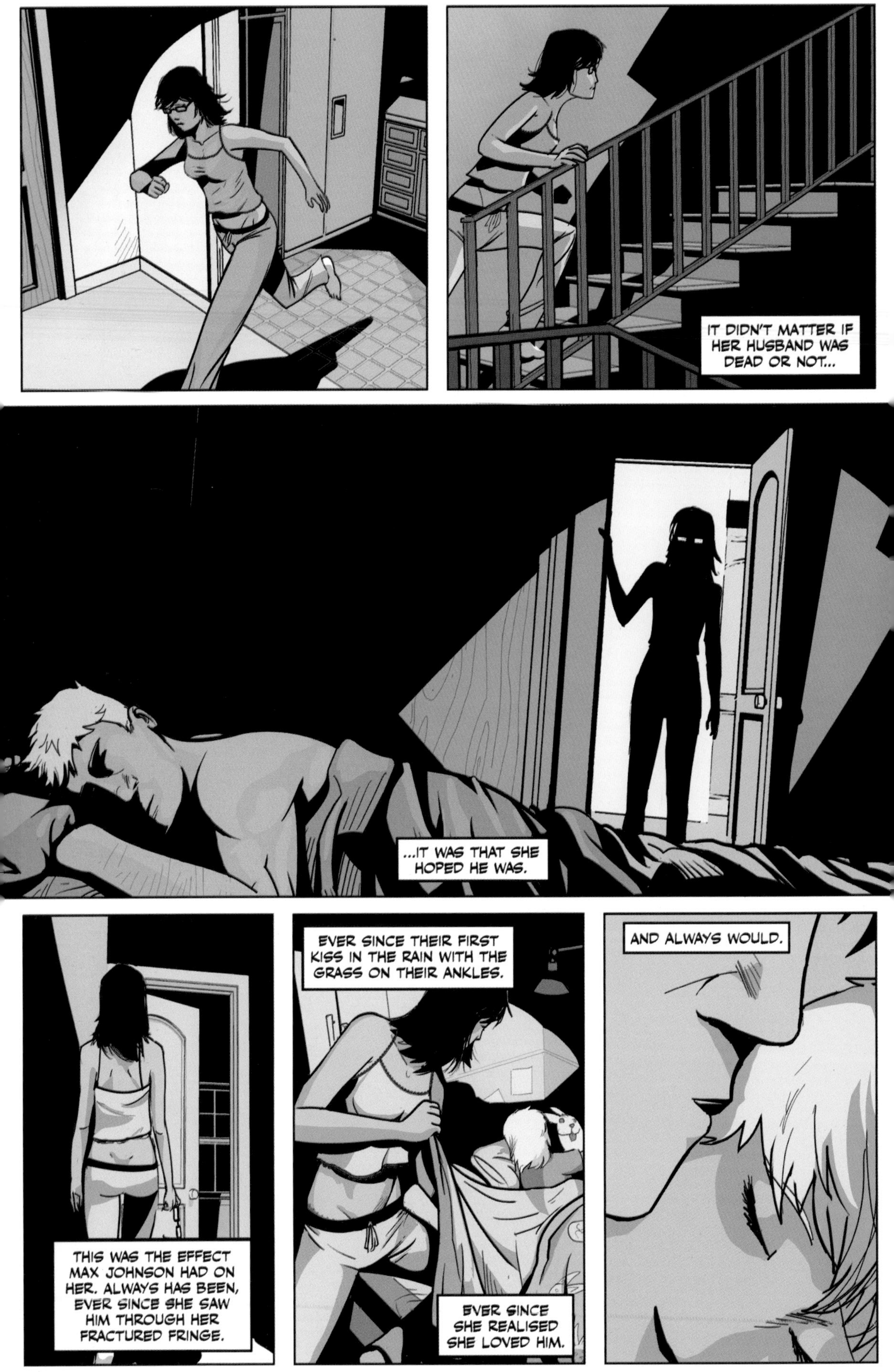
IT DIDN'T MATTER IF HER HUSBAND WAS DEAD OR NOT...
...IT WAS THAT SHE HOPED HE WAS.
THIS WAS THE EFFECT MAX JOHNSON HAD ON HER. ALWAYS HAS BEEN, EVER SINCE SHE SAW HIM THROUGH HER FRACTURED FRINGE.
EVER SINCE THEIR FIRST KISS IN THE RAIN WITH THE GRASS ON THEIR ANKLES.
EVER SINCE SHE REALISED SHE LOVED HIM.
AND ALWAYS WOULD.

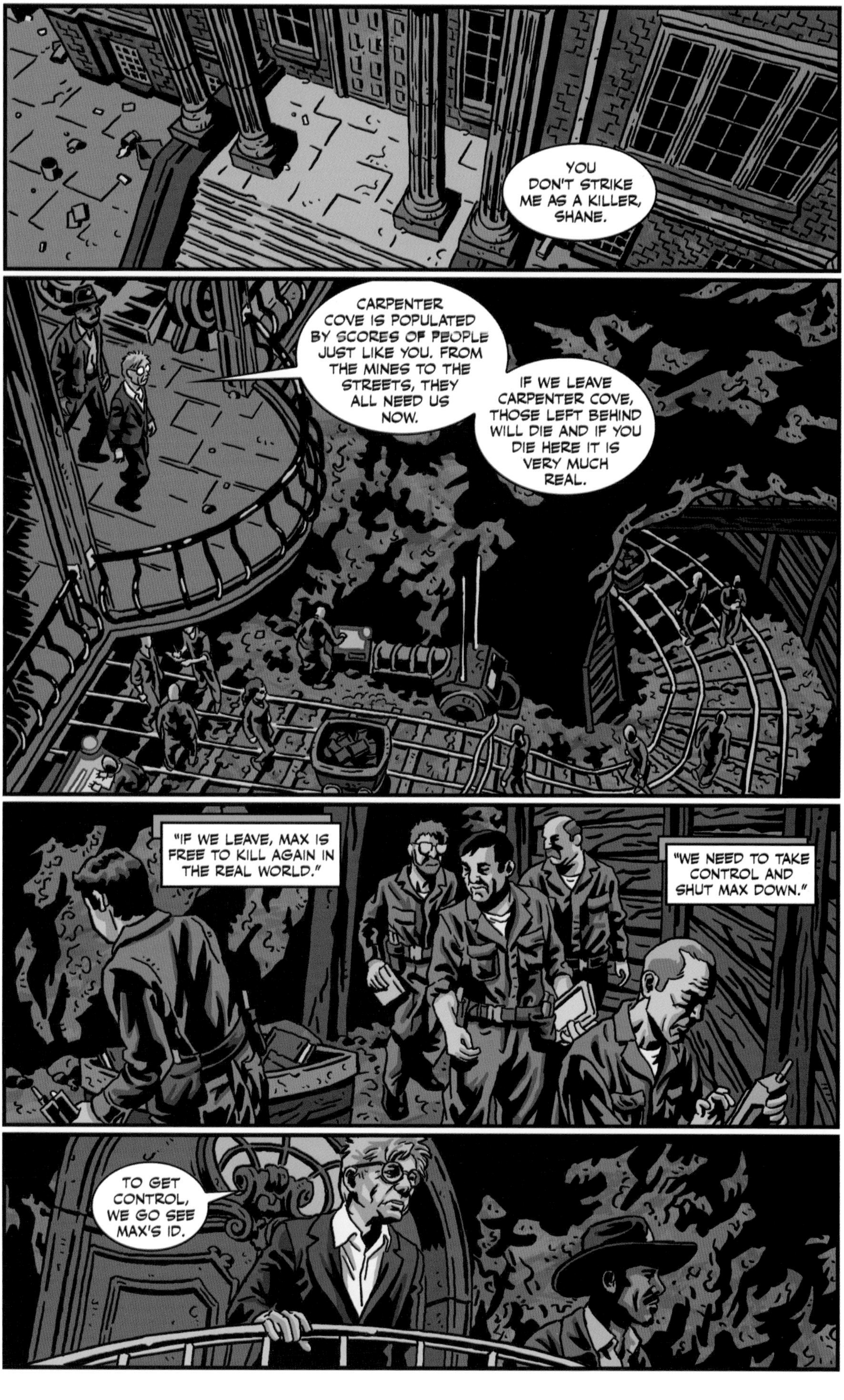
YOU DON'T STRIKE ME AS A KILLER, SHANE.
CARPENTER COVE IS POPULATED BY SCORES OF PEOPLE JUST LIKE YOU. FROM THE MINES TO THE STREETS, THEY ALL NEED US NOW.
IF WE LEAVE CARPENTER COVE, THOSE LEFT BEHIND WILL DIE AND IF YOU DIE HERE IT IS VERY MUCH REAL.
"IF WE LEAVE, MAX IS FREE TO KILL AGAIN IN THE REAL WORLD."
"WE NEED TO TAKE CONTROL AND SHUT MAX DOWN."
TO GET CONTROL, WE GO SEE MAX'S ID.

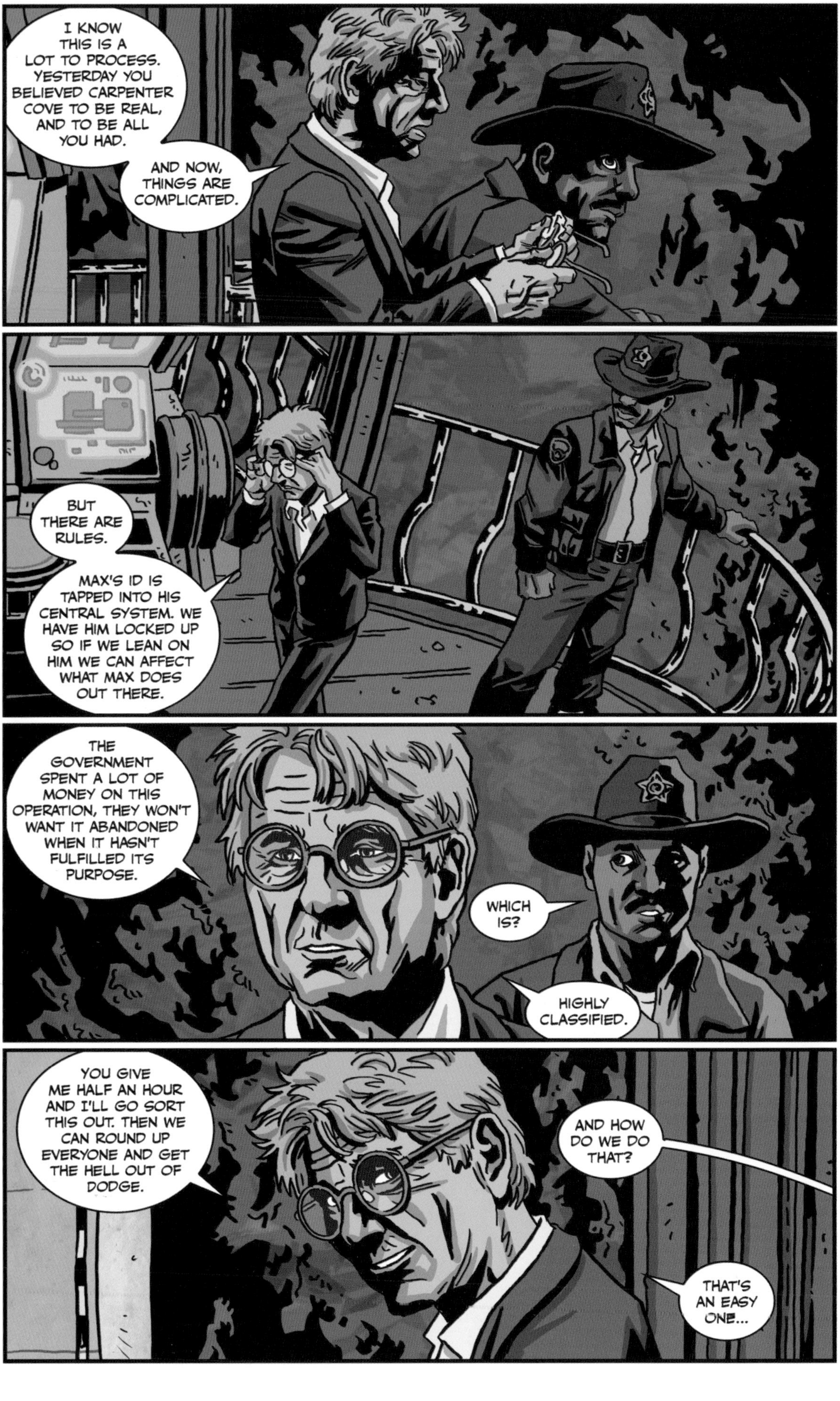
I KNOW THIS IS A LOT TO PROCESS. YESTERDAY YOU BELIEVED CARPENTER COVE TO BE REAL, AND TO BE ALL YOU HAD.
AND NOW, THINGS ARE COMPLICATED.
BUT THERE ARE RULES.
MAX'S ID IS TAPPED INTO HIS CENTRAL SYSTEM. WE HAVE HIM LOCKED UP SO IF WE LEAN ON HIM WE CAN AFFECT WHAT MAX DOES OUT THERE.
THE GOVERNMENT SPENT A LOT OF MONEY ON THIS OPERATION, THEY WON'T WANT IT ABANDONED WHEN IT HASN'T FULFILLED ITS PURPOSE.
WHICH IS?
HIGHLY CLASSIFIED.
YOU GIVE ME HALF AN HOUR AND I'LL GO SORT THIS OUT. THEN WE CAN ROUND UP EVERYONE AND GET THE HELL OUT OF DODGE.
AND HOW DO WE DO THAT?
THAT'S AN EASY ONE...

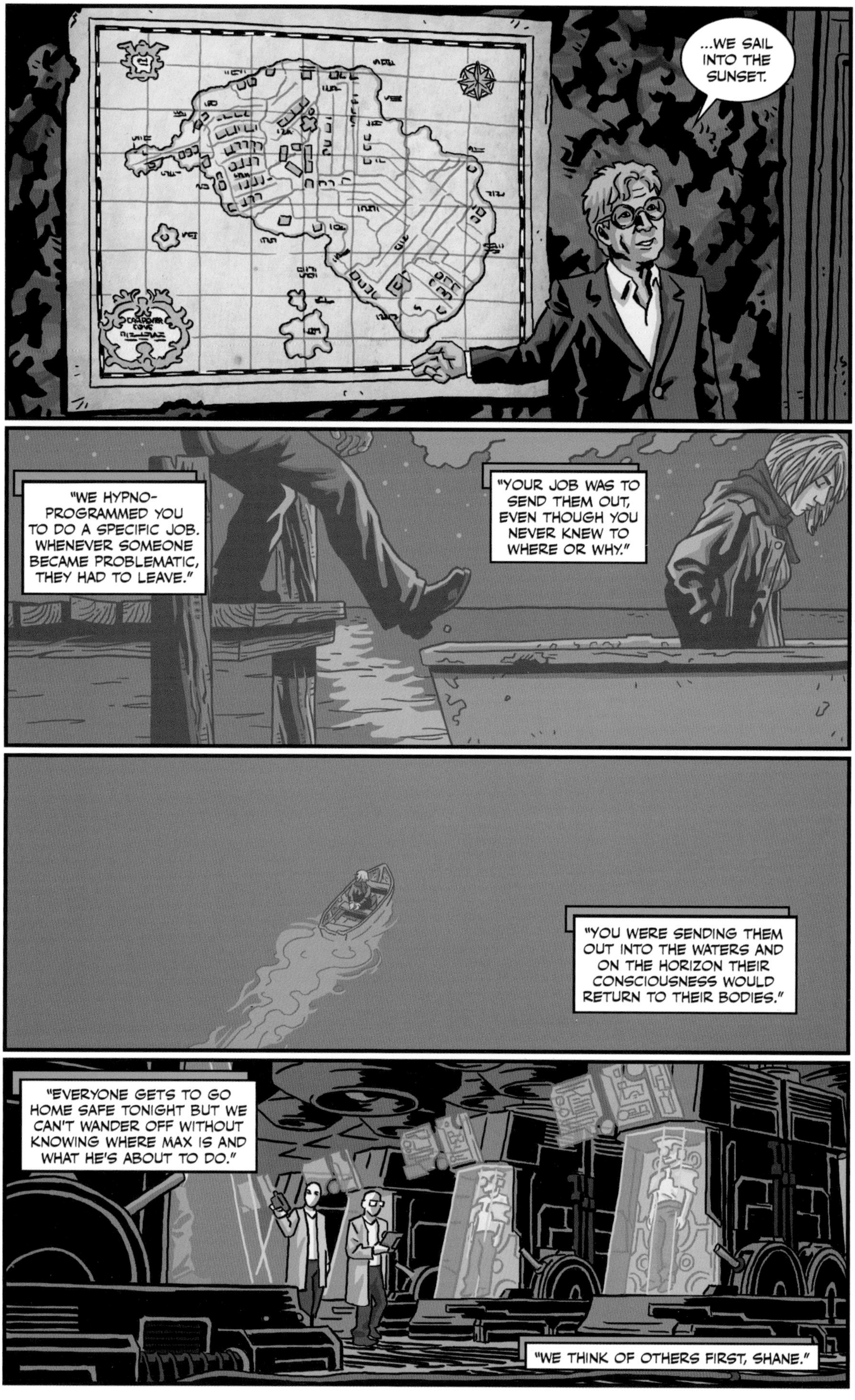
...WE SAIL INTO THE SUNSET.
"WE HYPNO-PROGRAMMED YOU TO DO A SPECIFIC JOB. WHENEVER SOMEONE BECAME PROBLEMATIC, THEY HAD TO LEAVE."
"YOUR JOB WAS TO SEND THEM OUT, EVEN THOUGH YOU NEVER KNEW TO WHERE OR WHY."
"YOU WERE SENDING THEM OUT INTO THE WATERS AND ON THE HORIZON THEIR CONSCIOUSNESS WOULD RETURN TO THEIR BODIES."
"EVERYONE GETS TO GO HOME SAFE TONIGHT BUT WE CAN'T WANDER OFF WITHOUT KNOWING WHERE MAX IS AND WHAT HE'S ABOUT TO DO."
"WE THINK OF OTHERS FIRST, SHANE."

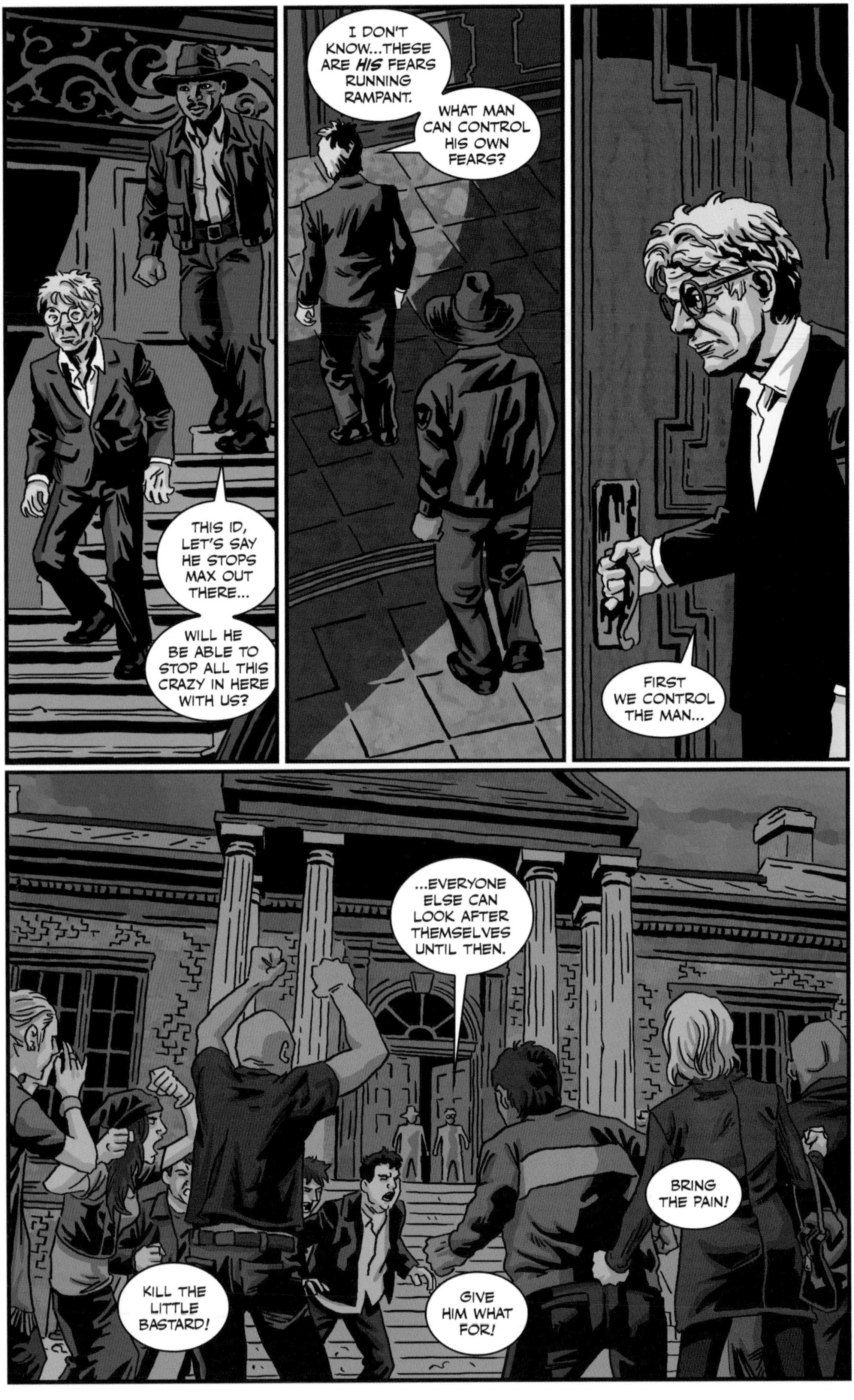
THIS ID, LET'S SAY HE STOPS MAX OUT THERE...
WILL HE BE ABLE TO STOP ALL THIS CRAZY IN HERE WITH US?
I DON'T KNOW...THESE ARE *HIS* FEARS RUNNING RAMPANT.
WHAT MAN CAN CONTROL HIS OWN FEARS?
FIRST WE CONTROL THE MAN...
...EVERYONE ELSE CAN LOOK AFTER THEMSELVES UNTIL THEN.
KILL THE LITTLE BASTARD!
GIVE HIM WHAT FOR!
BRING THE PAIN!

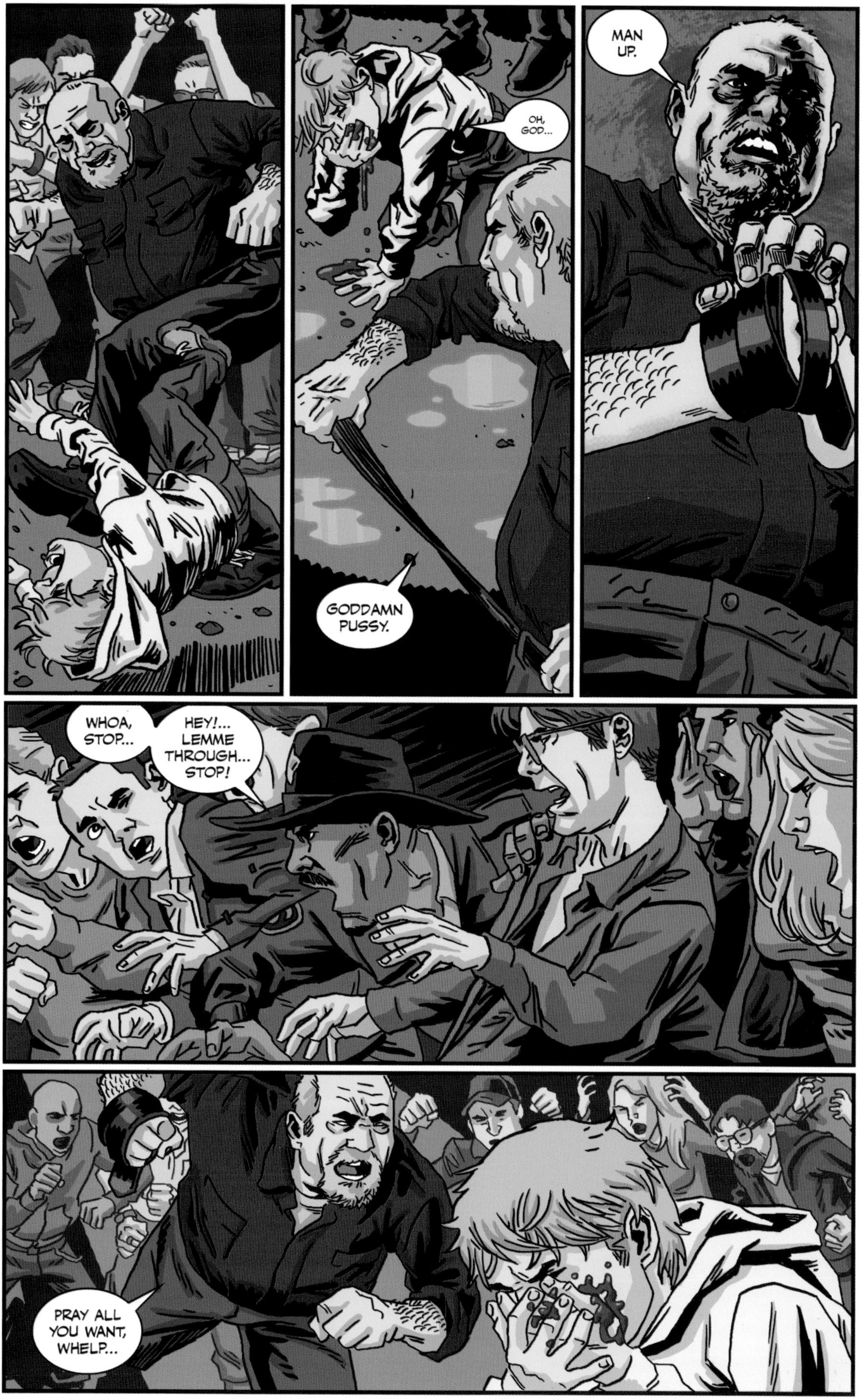
OH, GOD...
GODDAMN PUSSY.
MAN UP.
WHOA, STOP...
HEY!... LEMME THROUGH... STOP!
PRAY ALL YOU WANT, WHELP...

I'LL BE THE ONLY ANSWER YOU EVER GET.

STOP!

OR WHAT?

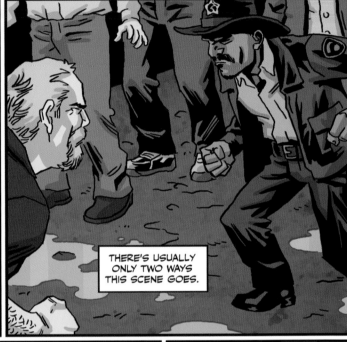

THERE'S USUALLY ONLY TWO WAYS THIS SCENE GOES.

OKAY, MAKE THAT THREE.

CAN'T SAY I KNOW MANY NAMES OF THOSE UNDER MY PROTECTION...

HIS NAME, WHO HE IS, WHAT HE'S DONE, NONE OF IT MATTERS. HE NEEDS MY HELP.

PRESSURE SITUATIONS LIKE THIS BRING OUT THE WORST IN PEOPLE.

A SHAME IT BECAME CONTAGIOUS.

GET THEM INTO THE LIBRARY, BE SAFE, FIND YOUR MINDS...

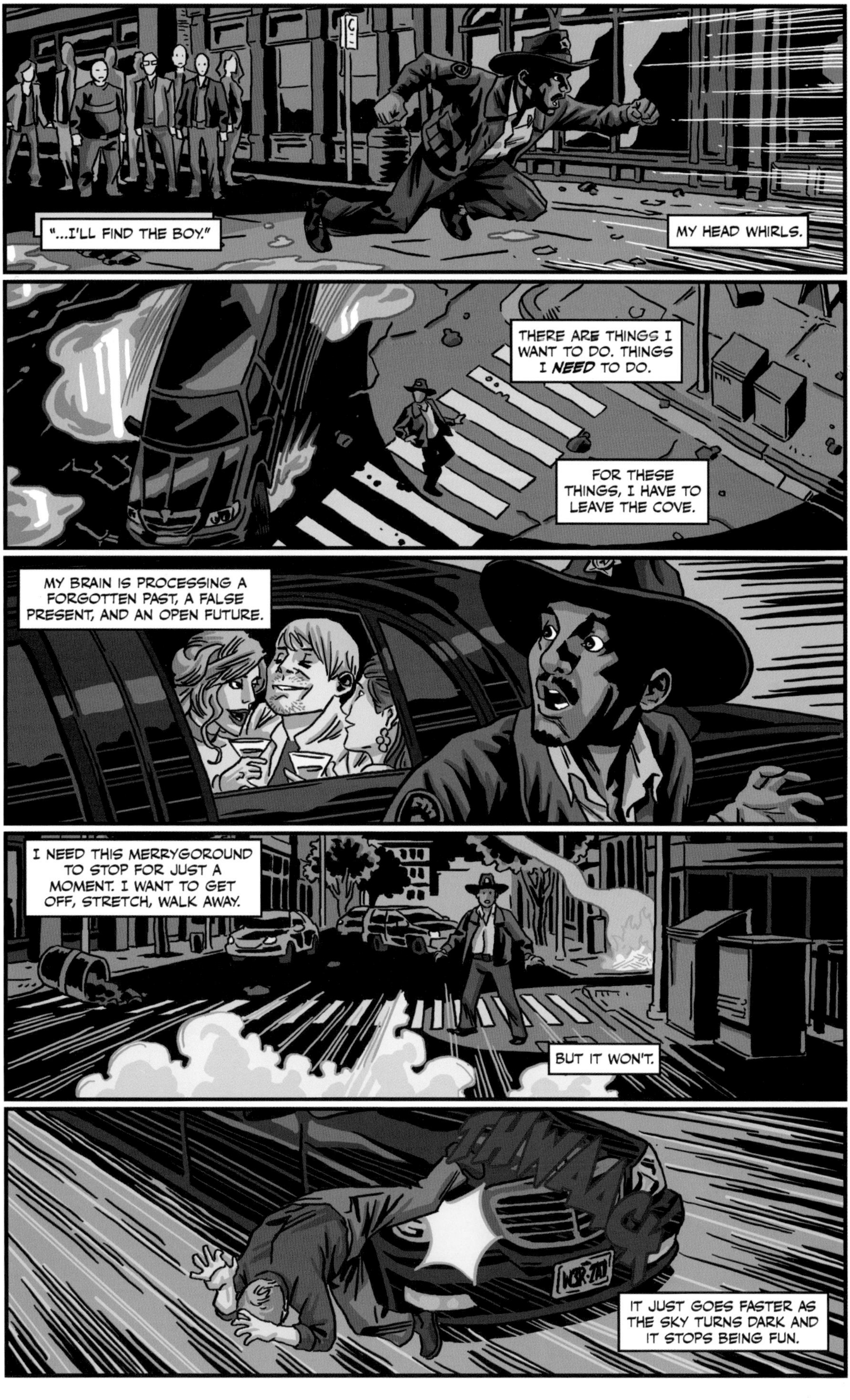
"...I'LL FIND THE BOY."
MY HEAD WHIRLS.
THERE ARE THINGS I WANT TO DO. THINGS I ***NEED*** TO DO.
FOR THESE THINGS, I HAVE TO LEAVE THE COVE.
MY BRAIN IS PROCESSING A FORGOTTEN PAST, A FALSE PRESENT, AND AN OPEN FUTURE.
I NEED THIS MERRYGOROUND TO STOP FOR JUST A MOMENT. I WANT TO GET OFF, STRETCH, WALK AWAY.
BUT IT WON'T.
IT JUST GOES FASTER AS THE SKY TURNS DARK AND IT STOPS BEING FUN.

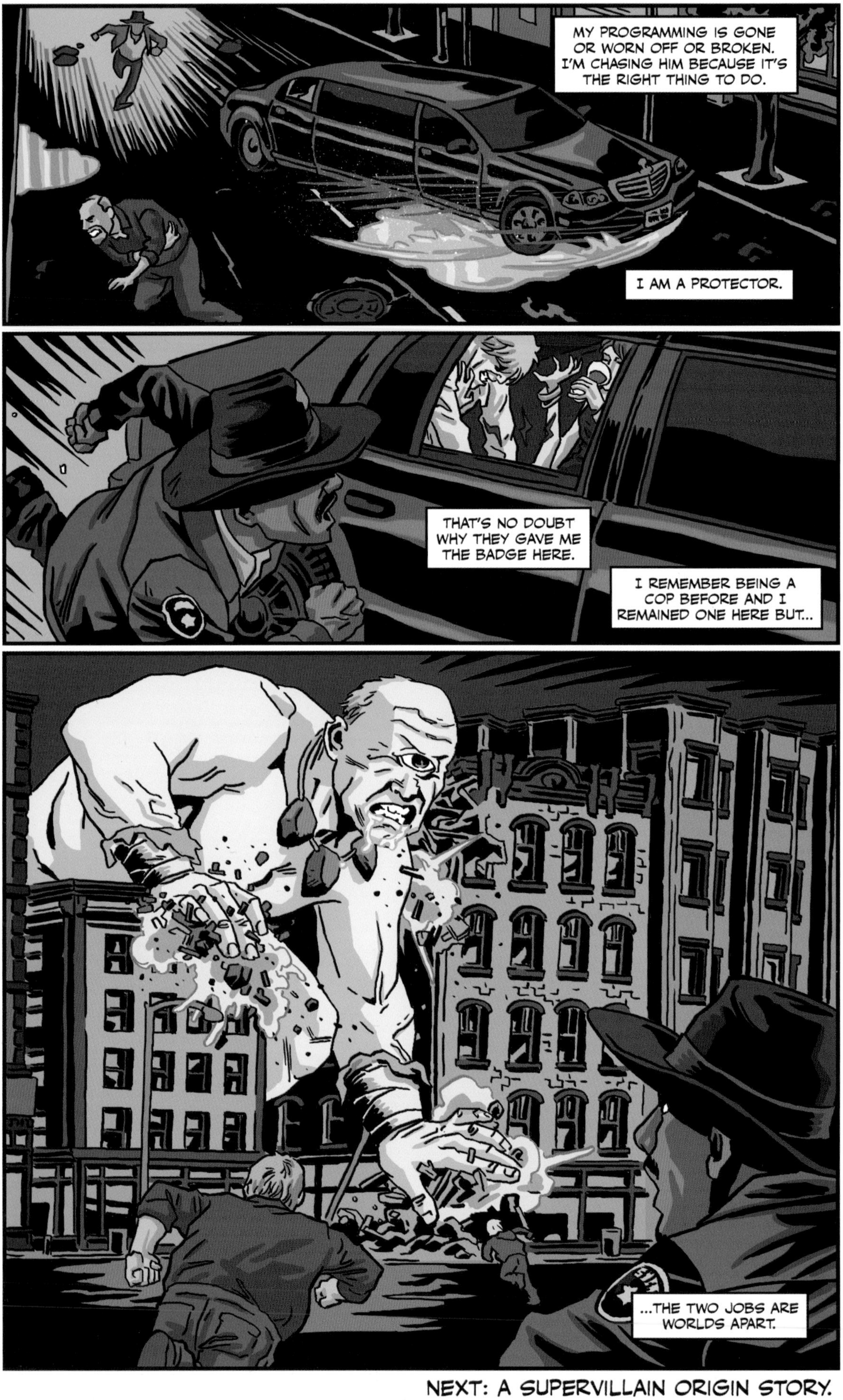
MY PROGRAMMING IS GONE OR WORN OFF OR BROKEN. I'M CHASING HIM BECAUSE IT'S THE RIGHT THING TO DO.
I AM A PROTECTOR.
THAT'S NO DOUBT WHY THEY GAVE ME THE BADGE HERE.
I REMEMBER BEING A COP BEFORE AND I REMAINED ONE HERE BUT...
...THE TWO JOBS ARE WORLDS APART.

NEXT: A SUPERVILLAIN ORIGIN STORY.

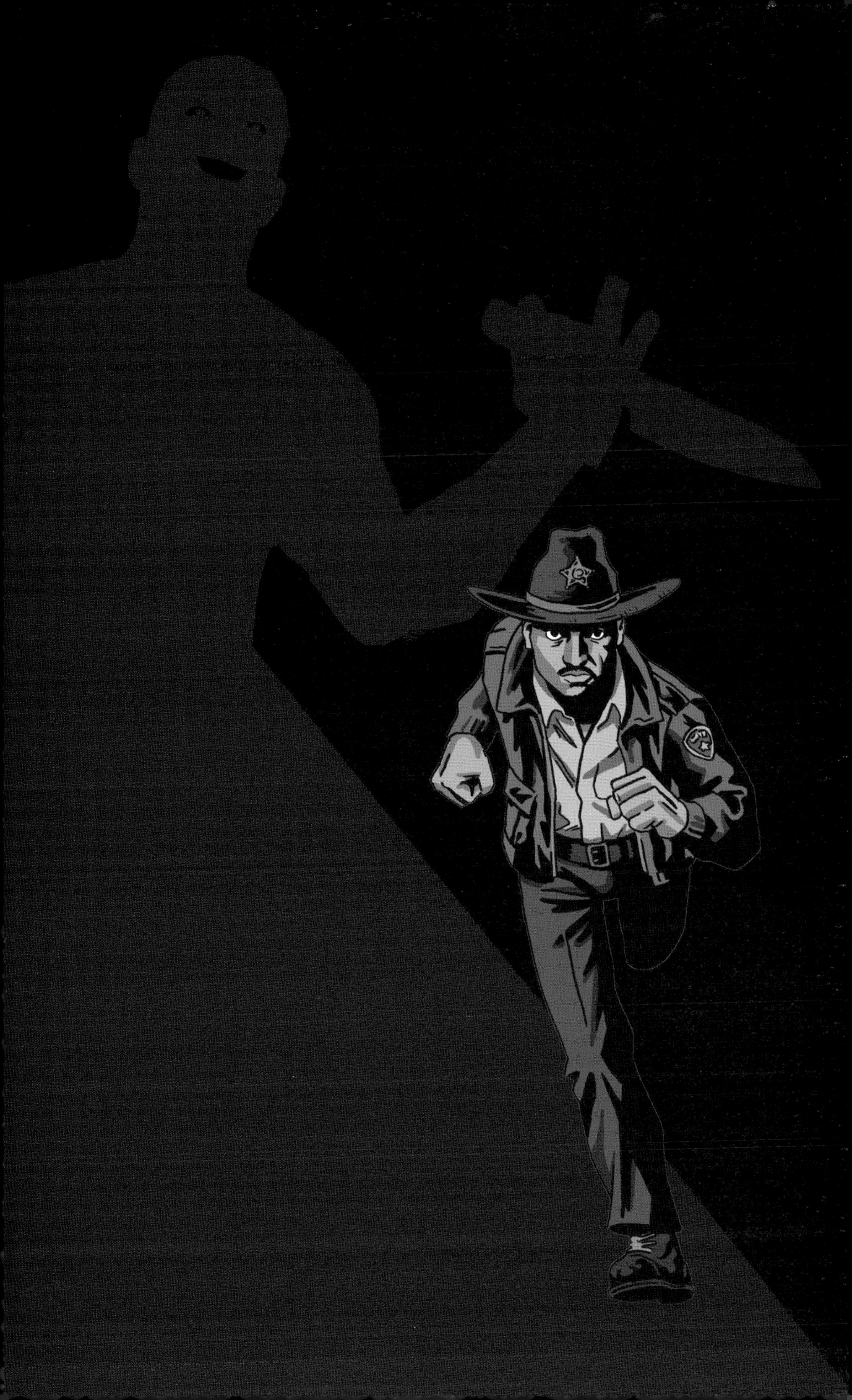

Chapter 4

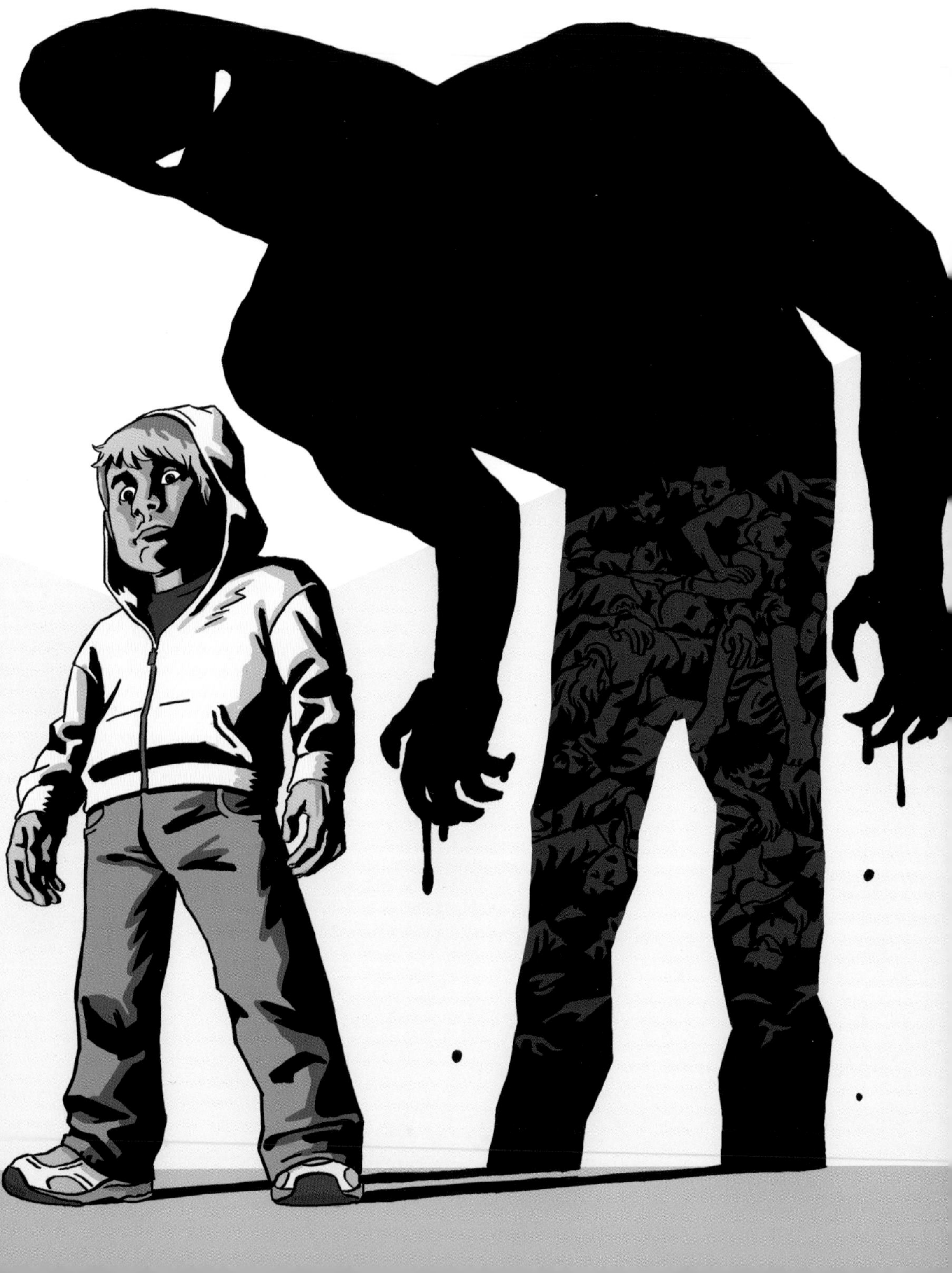

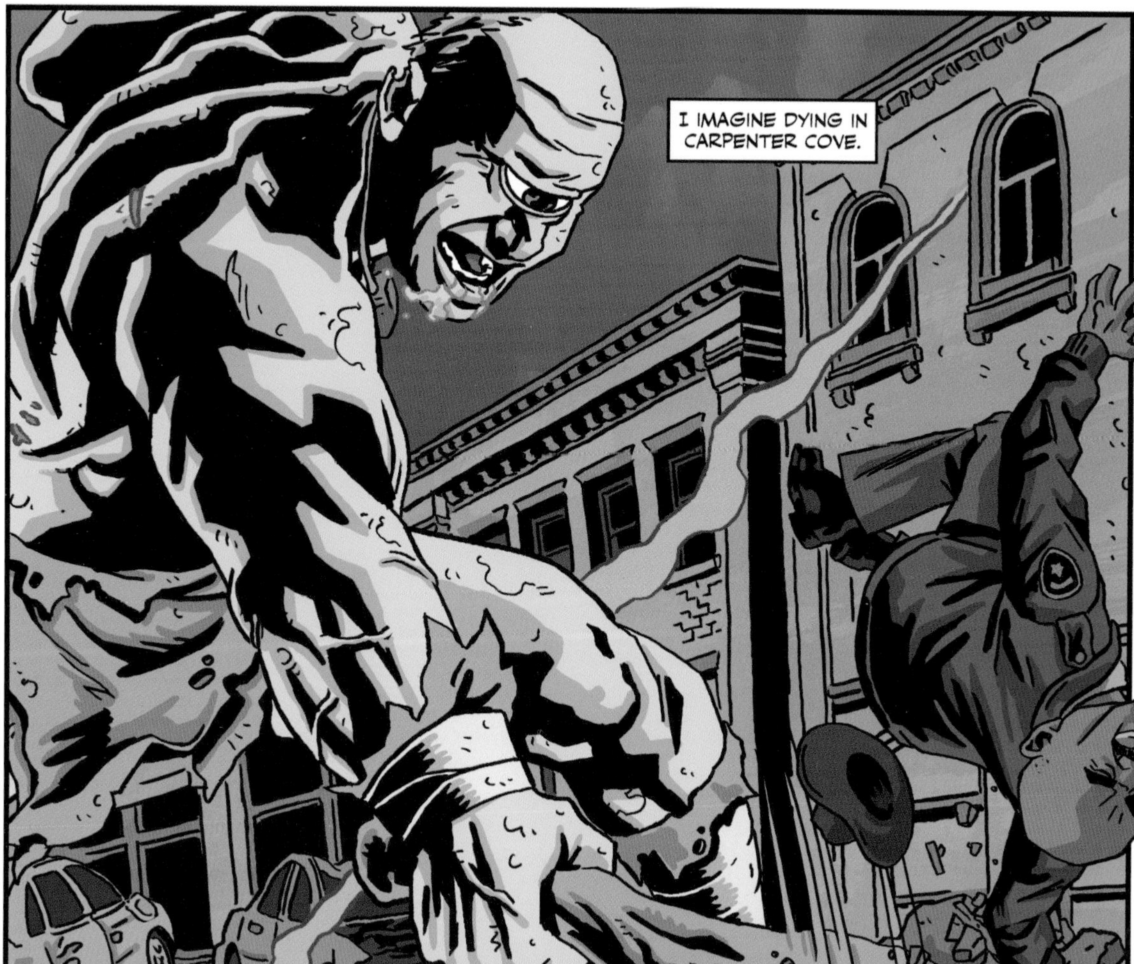
I IMAGINE DYING IN CARPENTER COVE.

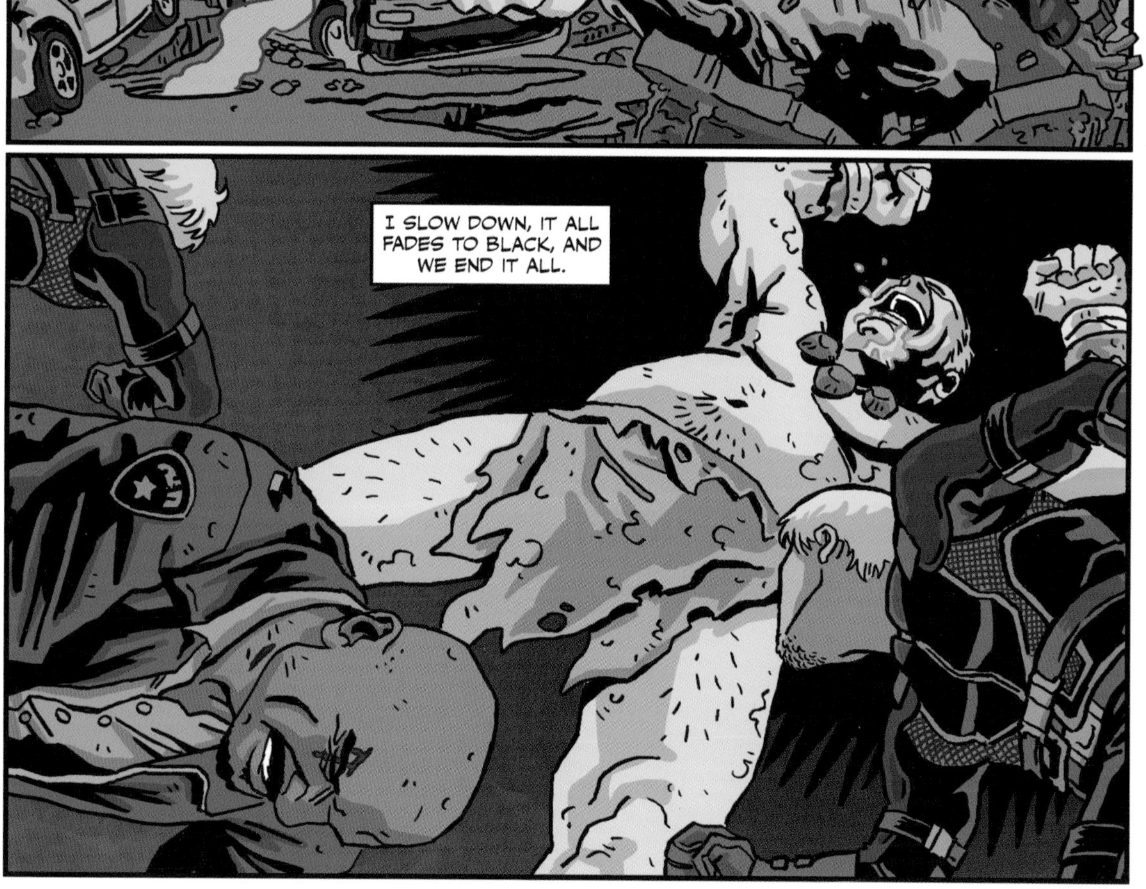
I SLOW DOWN, IT ALL FADES TO BLACK, AND WE END IT ALL.

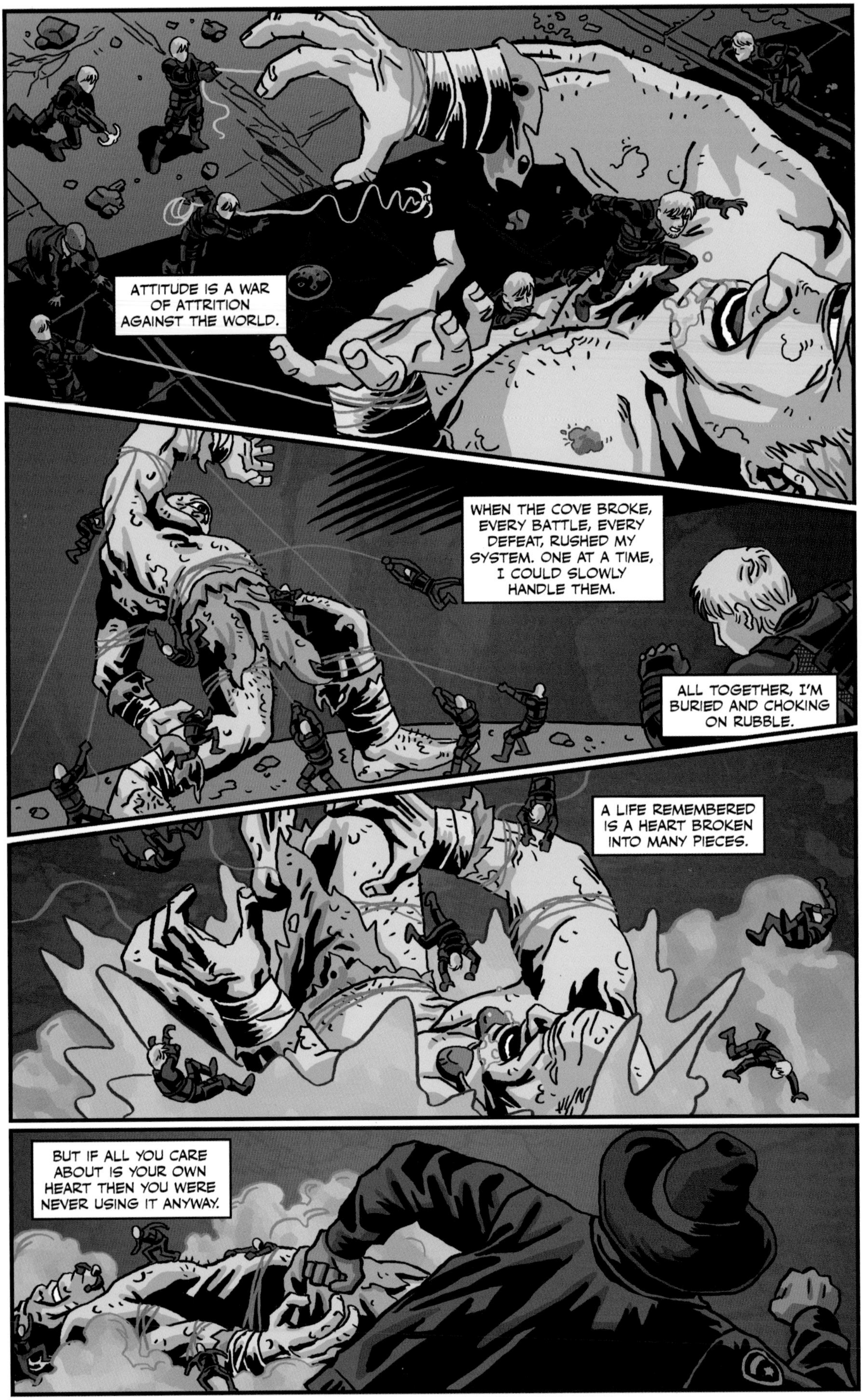
ATTITUDE IS A WAR OF ATTRITION AGAINST THE WORLD.
WHEN THE COVE BROKE, EVERY BATTLE, EVERY DEFEAT, RUSHED MY SYSTEM. ONE AT A TIME, I COULD SLOWLY HANDLE THEM.
ALL TOGETHER, I'M BURIED AND CHOKING ON RUBBLE.
A LIFE REMEMBERED IS A HEART BROKEN INTO MANY PIECES.
BUT IF ALL YOU CARE ABOUT IS YOUR OWN HEART THEN YOU WERE NEVER USING IT ANYWAY.

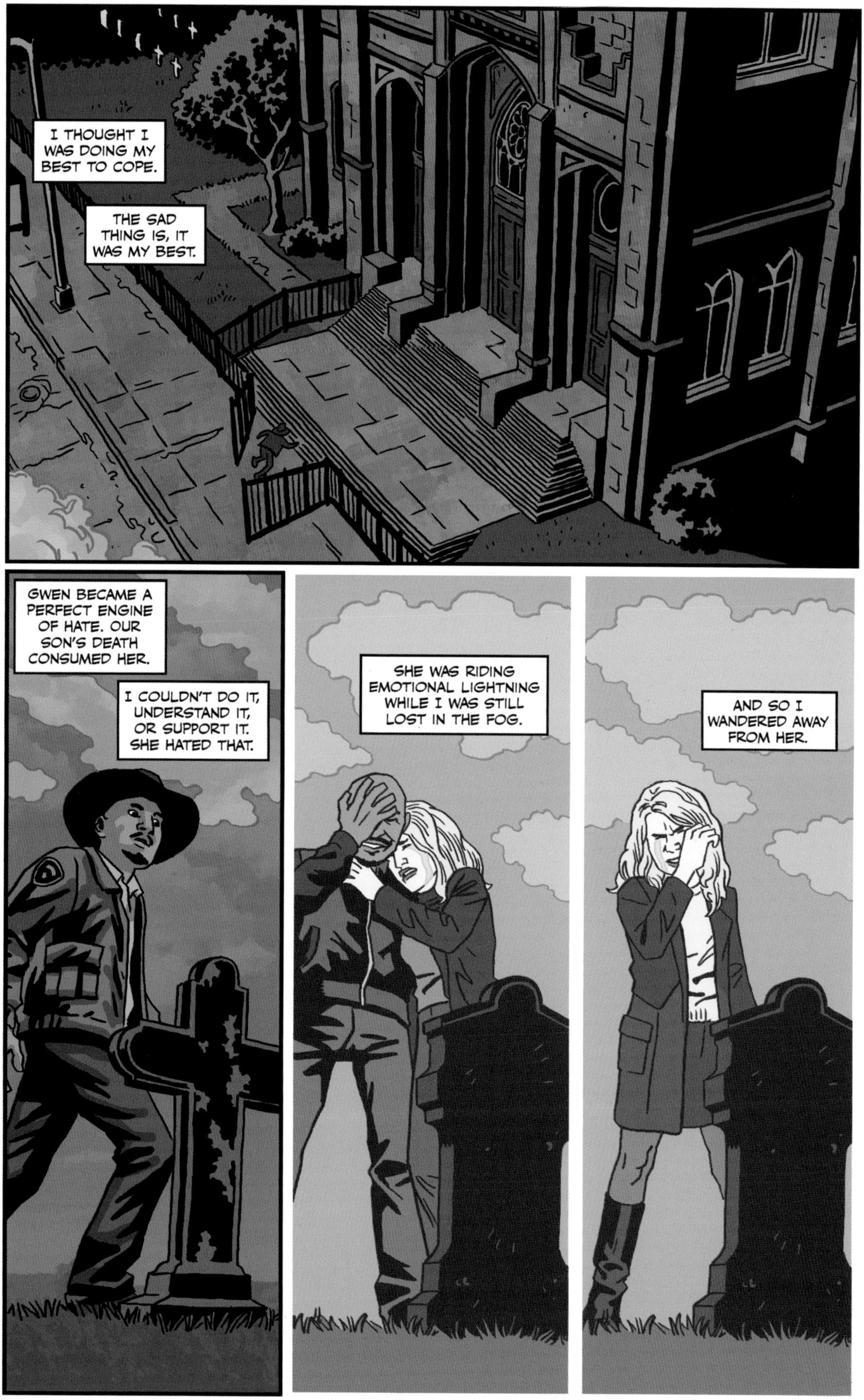
I THOUGHT I WAS DOING MY BEST TO COPE.
THE SAD THING IS, IT WAS MY BEST.
GWEN BECAME A PERFECT ENGINE OF HATE. OUR SON'S DEATH CONSUMED HER.
I COULDN'T DO IT, UNDERSTAND IT, OR SUPPORT IT. SHE HATED THAT.
SHE WAS RIDING EMOTIONAL LIGHTNING WHILE I WAS STILL LOST IN THE FOG.
AND SO I WANDERED AWAY FROM HER.

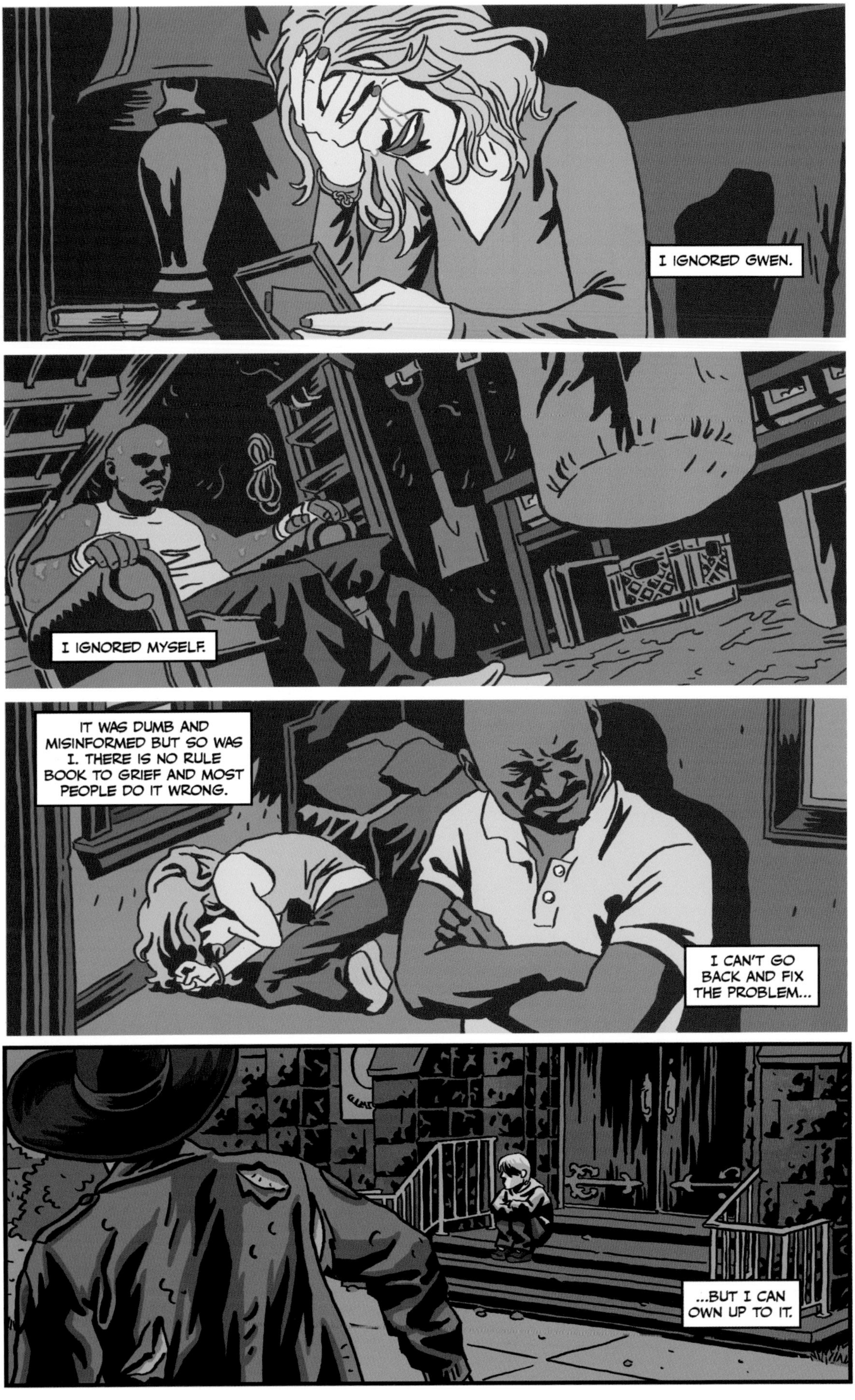
I IGNORED GWEN.
I IGNORED MYSELF.
IT WAS DUMB AND MISINFORMED BUT SO WAS I. THERE IS NO RULE BOOK TO GRIEF AND MOST PEOPLE DO IT WRONG.
I CAN'T GO BACK AND FIX THE PROBLEM...
...BUT I CAN OWN UP TO IT.

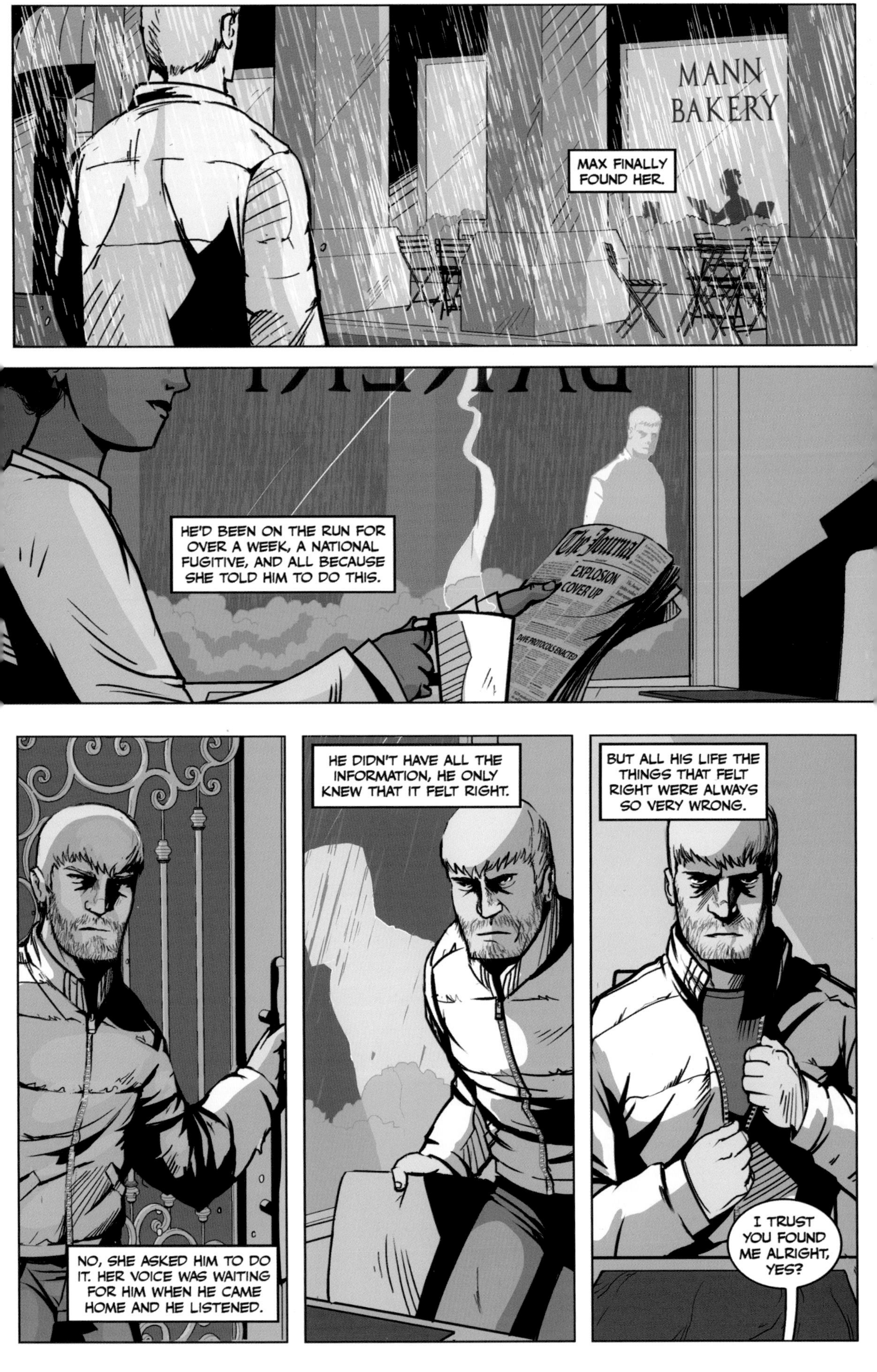
MANN BAKERY
MAX FINALLY FOUND HER.
HE'D BEEN ON THE RUN FOR OVER A WEEK, A NATIONAL FUGITIVE, AND ALL BECAUSE SHE TOLD HIM TO DO THIS.
The Journal
EXPLOSION COVER UP
NO, SHE ASKED HIM TO DO IT. HER VOICE WAS WAITING FOR HIM WHEN HE CAME HOME AND HE LISTENED.
HE DIDN'T HAVE ALL THE INFORMATION, HE ONLY KNEW THAT IT FELT RIGHT.
BUT ALL HIS LIFE THE THINGS THAT FELT RIGHT WERE ALWAYS SO VERY WRONG.
I TRUST YOU FOUND ME ALRIGHT, YES?

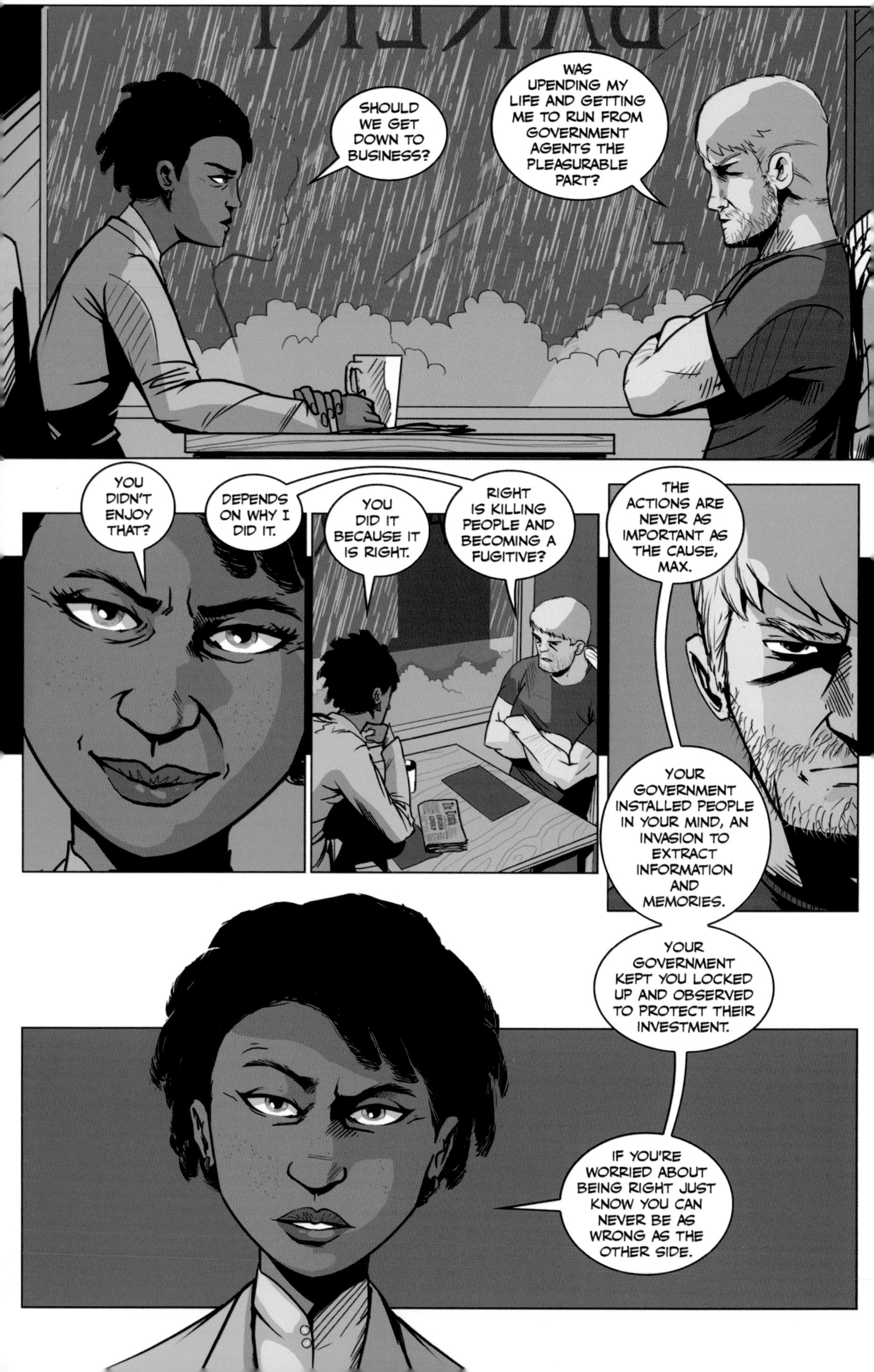
SHOULD WE GET DOWN TO BUSINESS?
WAS UPENDING MY LIFE AND GETTING ME TO RUN FROM GOVERNMENT AGENTS THE PLEASURABLE PART?
YOU DIDN'T ENJOY THAT?
DEPENDS ON WHY I DID IT.
YOU DID IT BECAUSE IT IS RIGHT.
RIGHT IS KILLING PEOPLE AND BECOMING A FUGITIVE?
THE ACTIONS ARE NEVER AS IMPORTANT AS THE CAUSE, MAX.
YOUR GOVERNMENT INSTALLED PEOPLE IN YOUR MIND, AN INVASION TO EXTRACT INFORMATION AND MEMORIES.
YOUR GOVERNMENT KEPT YOU LOCKED UP AND OBSERVED TO PROTECT THEIR INVESTMENT.
IF YOU'RE WORRIED ABOUT BEING RIGHT JUST KNOW YOU CAN NEVER BE AS WRONG AS THE OTHER SIDE.

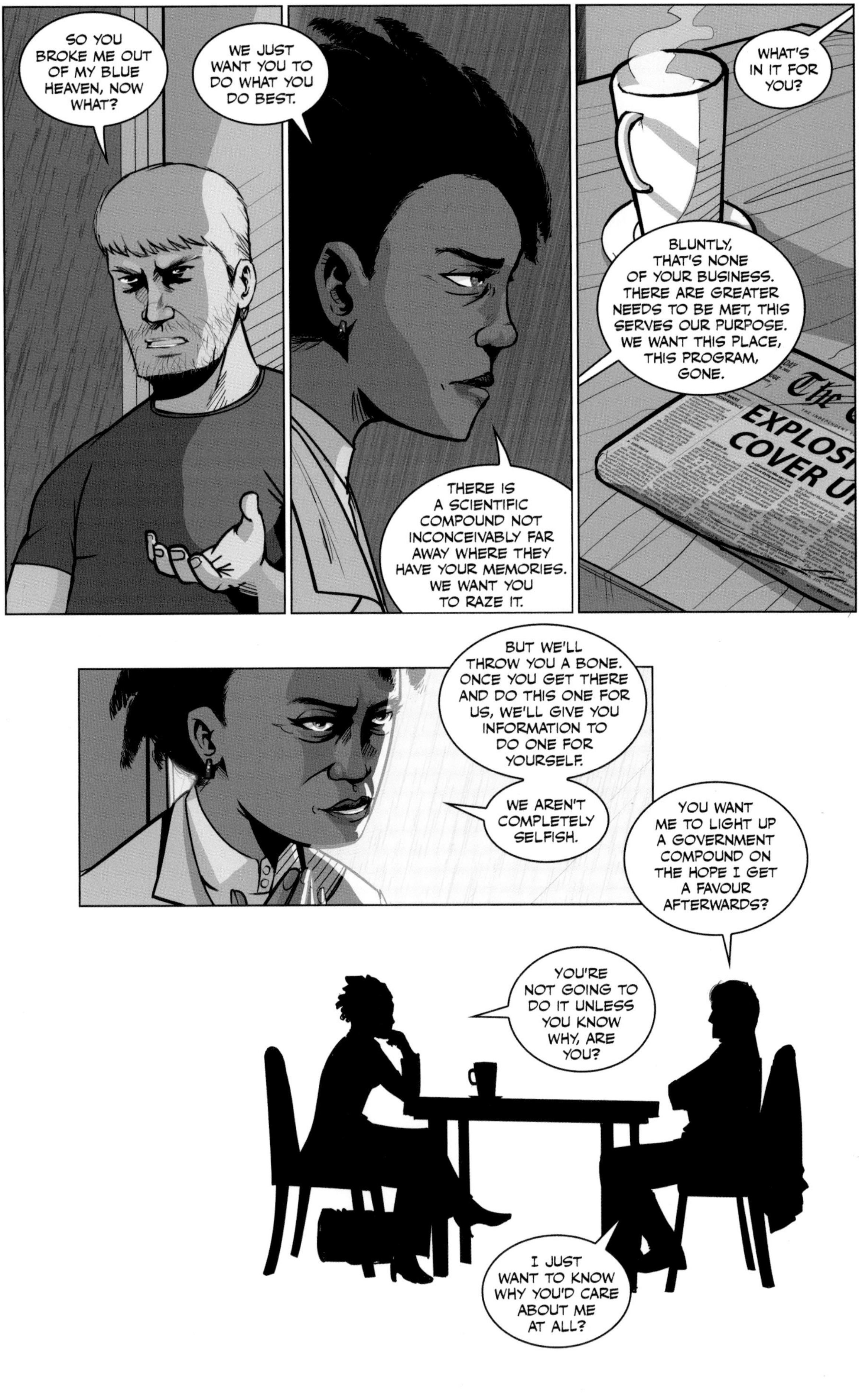
SO YOU BROKE ME OUT OF MY BLUE HEAVEN, NOW WHAT?
WE JUST WANT YOU TO DO WHAT YOU DO BEST.
THERE IS A SCIENTIFIC COMPOUND NOT INCONCEIVABLY FAR AWAY WHERE THEY HAVE YOUR MEMORIES. WE WANT YOU TO RAZE IT.
WHAT'S IN IT FOR YOU?
BLUNTLY, THAT'S NONE OF YOUR BUSINESS. THERE ARE GREATER NEEDS TO BE MET, THIS SERVES OUR PURPOSE. WE WANT THIS PLACE, THIS PROGRAM, GONE.
BUT WE'LL THROW YOU A BONE. ONCE YOU GET THERE AND DO THIS ONE FOR US, WE'LL GIVE YOU INFORMATION TO DO ONE FOR YOURSELF.
WE AREN'T COMPLETELY SELFISH.
YOU WANT ME TO LIGHT UP A GOVERNMENT COMPOUND ON THE HOPE I GET A FAVOUR AFTERWARDS?
YOU'RE NOT GOING TO DO IT UNLESS YOU KNOW WHY, ARE YOU?
I JUST WANT TO KNOW WHY YOU'D CARE ABOUT ME AT ALL?

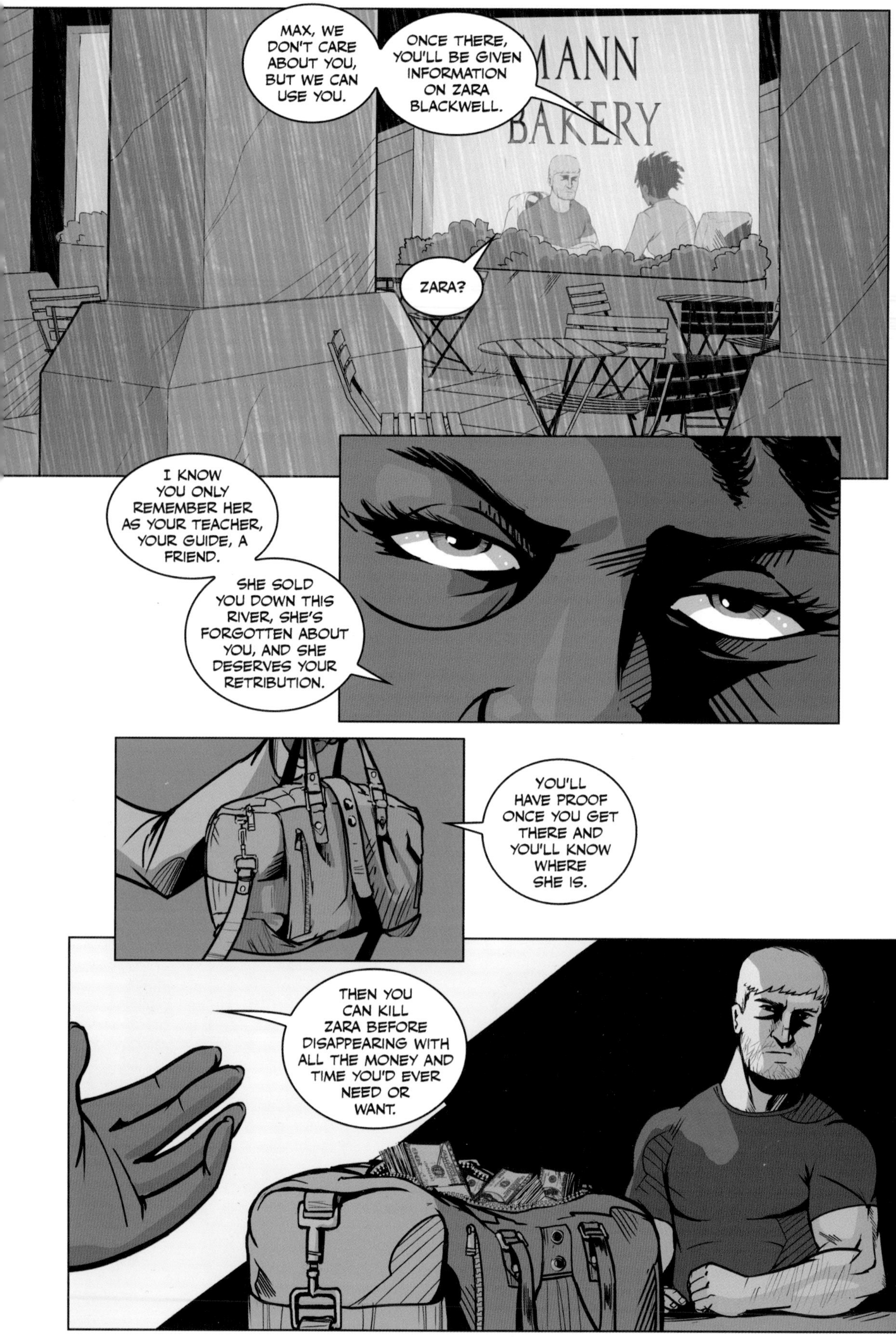

MAX, WE DON'T CARE ABOUT YOU, BUT WE CAN USE YOU.
ONCE THERE, YOU'LL BE GIVEN INFORMATION ON ZARA BLACKWELL.
MANN BAKERY
ZARA?
I KNOW YOU ONLY REMEMBER HER AS YOUR TEACHER, YOUR GUIDE, A FRIEND.
SHE SOLD YOU DOWN THIS RIVER, SHE'S FORGOTTEN ABOUT YOU, AND SHE DESERVES YOUR RETRIBUTION.
YOU'LL HAVE PROOF ONCE YOU GET THERE AND YOU'LL KNOW WHERE SHE IS.
THEN YOU CAN KILL ZARA BEFORE DISAPPEARING WITH ALL THE MONEY AND TIME YOU'D EVER NEED OR WANT.

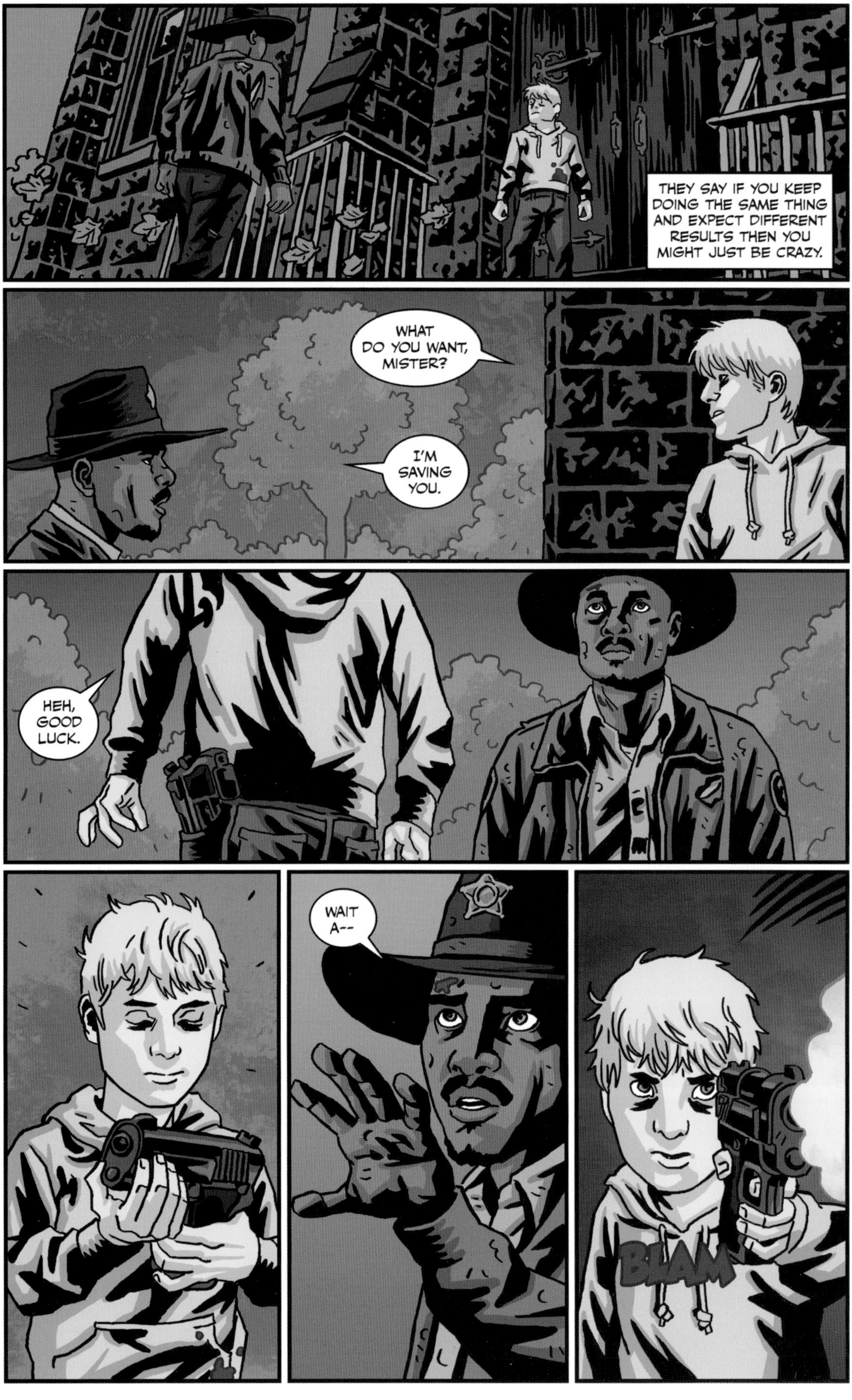
THEY SAY IF YOU KEEP DOING THE SAME THING AND EXPECT DIFFERENT RESULTS THEN YOU MIGHT JUST BE CRAZY.
WHAT DO YOU WANT, MISTER?
I'M SAVING YOU.
HEH, GOOD LUCK.
WAIT A--
BLAM

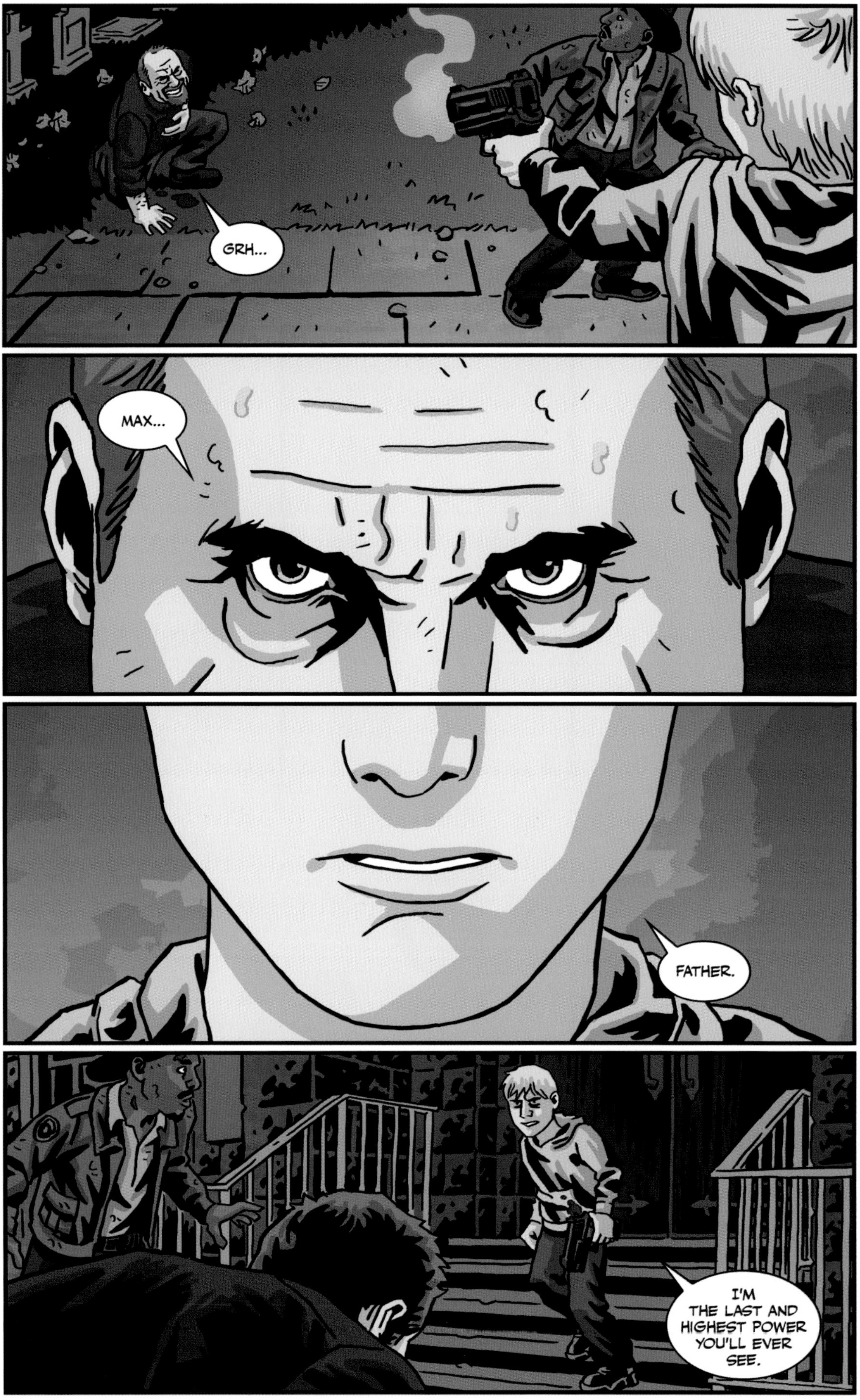
GRH...
MAX...
FATHER.
I'M THE LAST AND HIGHEST POWER YOU'LL EVER SEE.

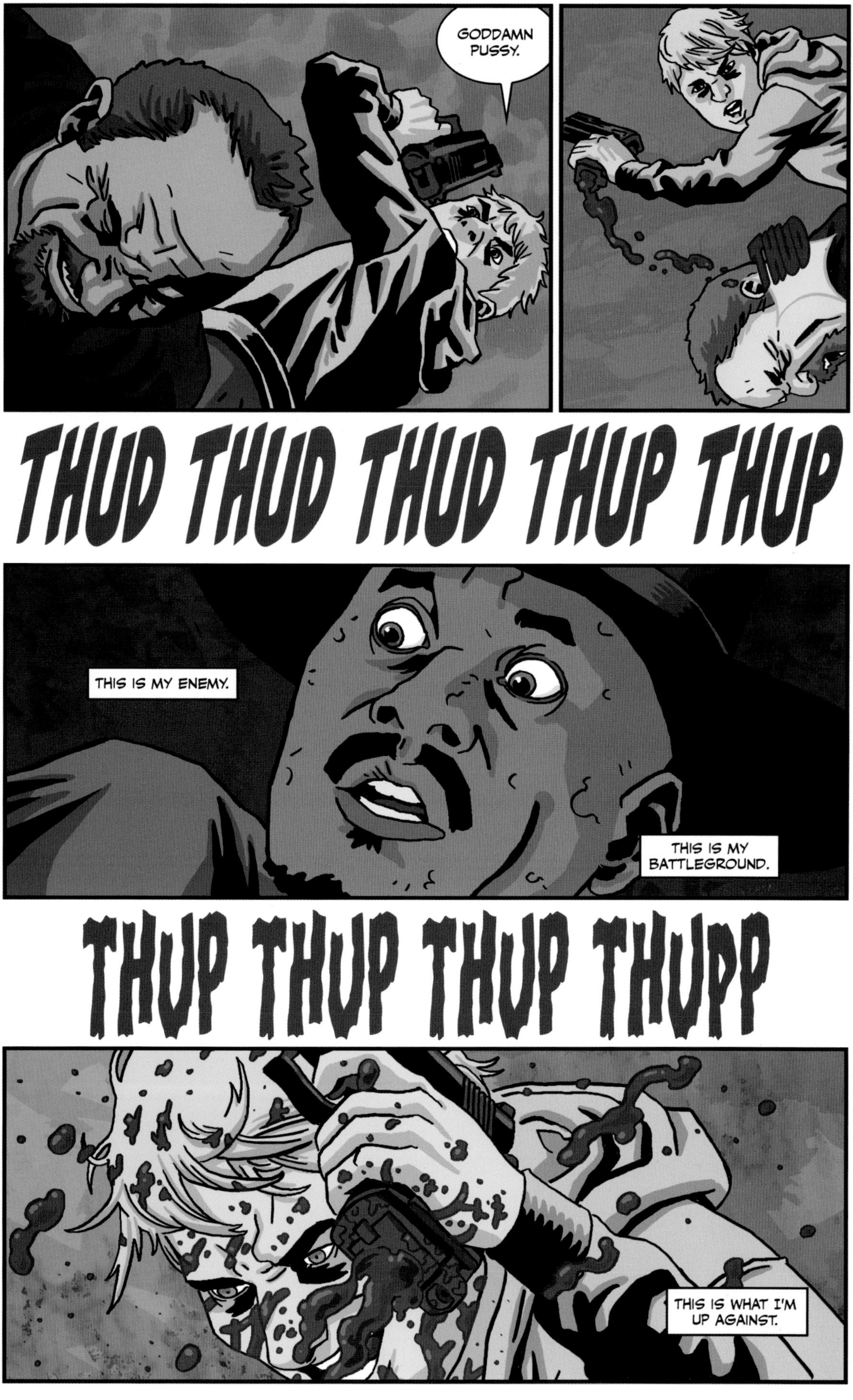
GODDAMN PUSSY.
THUD THUD THUD THUP THUP
THIS IS MY ENEMY.
THIS IS MY BATTLEGROUND.
THUP THUP THUP THUPP
THIS IS WHAT I'M UP AGAINST.

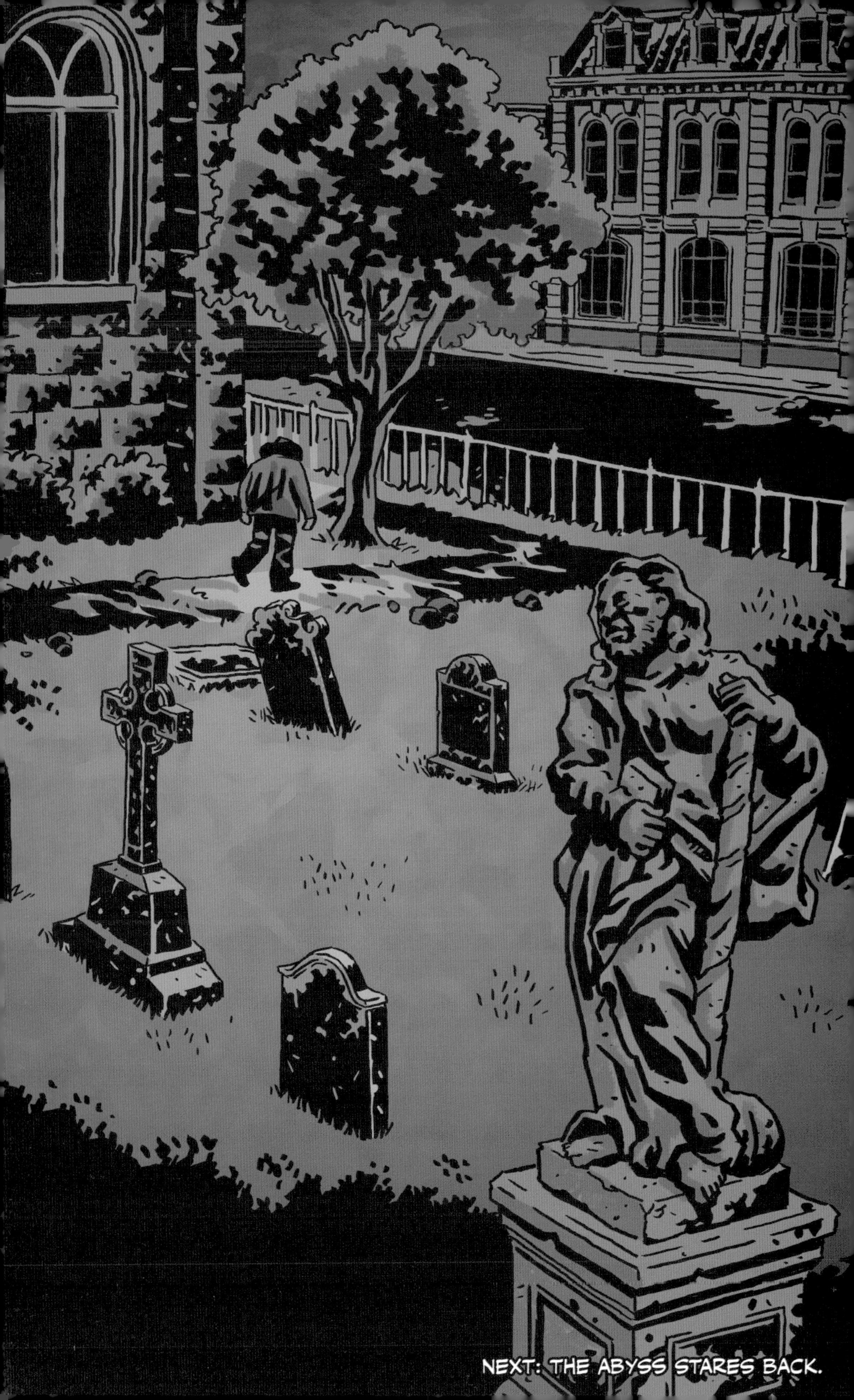
NEXT: THE ABYSS STARES BACK.

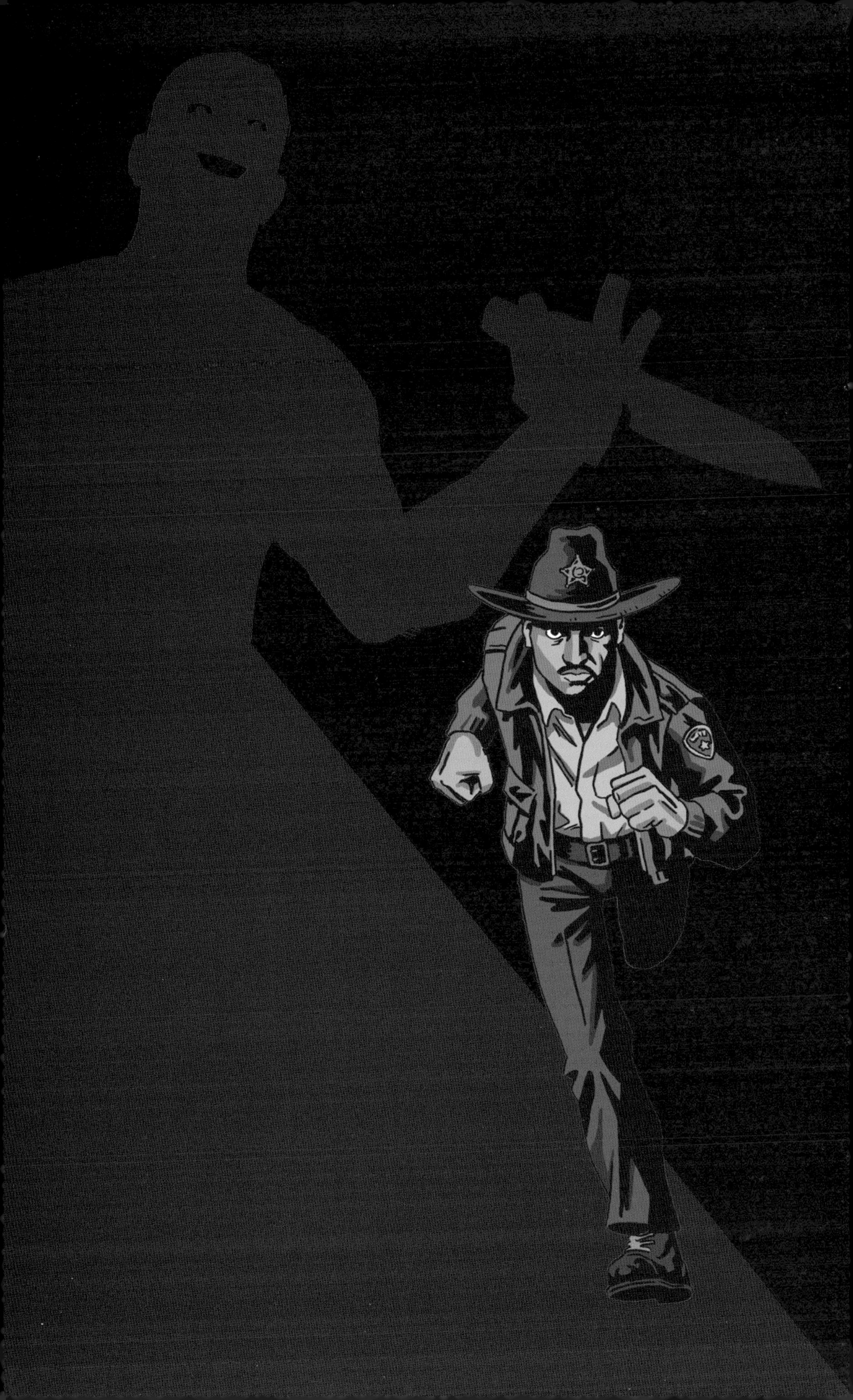

Chapter 5

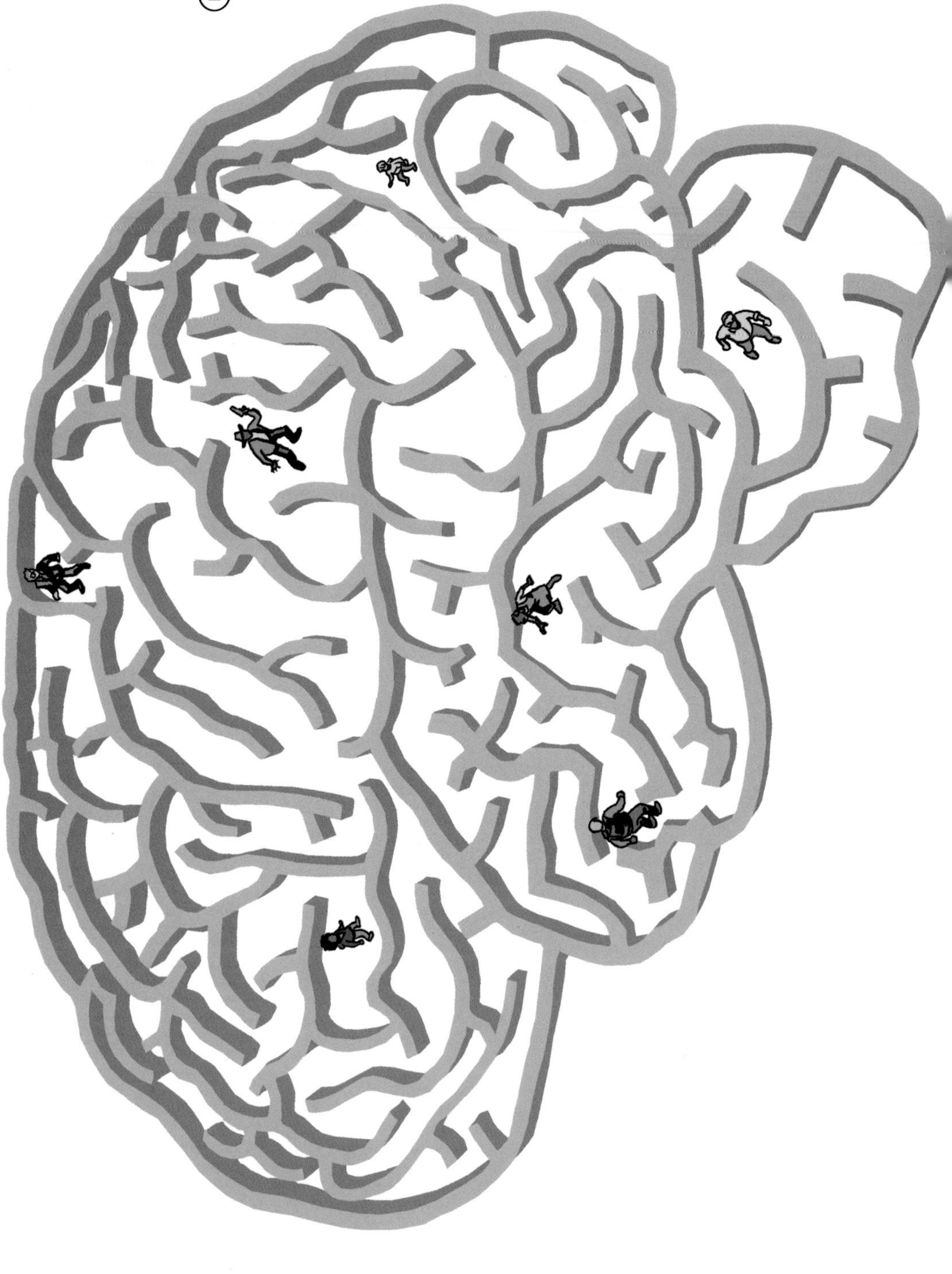

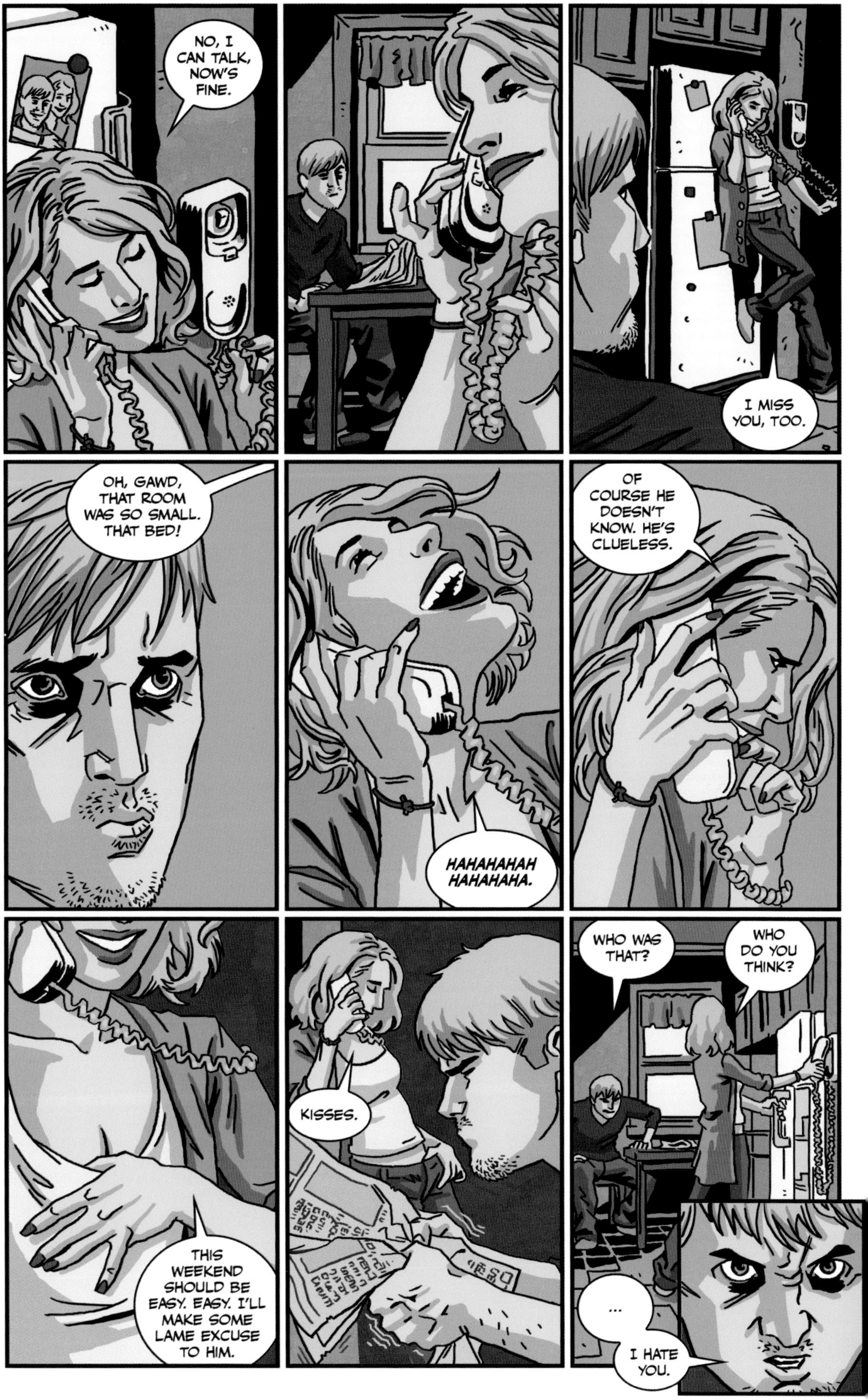
NO, I CAN TALK, NOW'S FINE.
I MISS YOU, TOO.
OH, GAWD, THAT ROOM WAS SO SMALL. THAT BED!
HAHAHAHAH HAHAHAHA.
OF COURSE HE DOESN'T KNOW. HE'S CLUELESS.
THIS WEEKEND SHOULD BE EASY. EASY. I'LL MAKE SOME LAME EXCUSE TO HIM.
KISSES.
WHO WAS THAT?
WHO DO YOU THINK?
...
I HATE YOU.

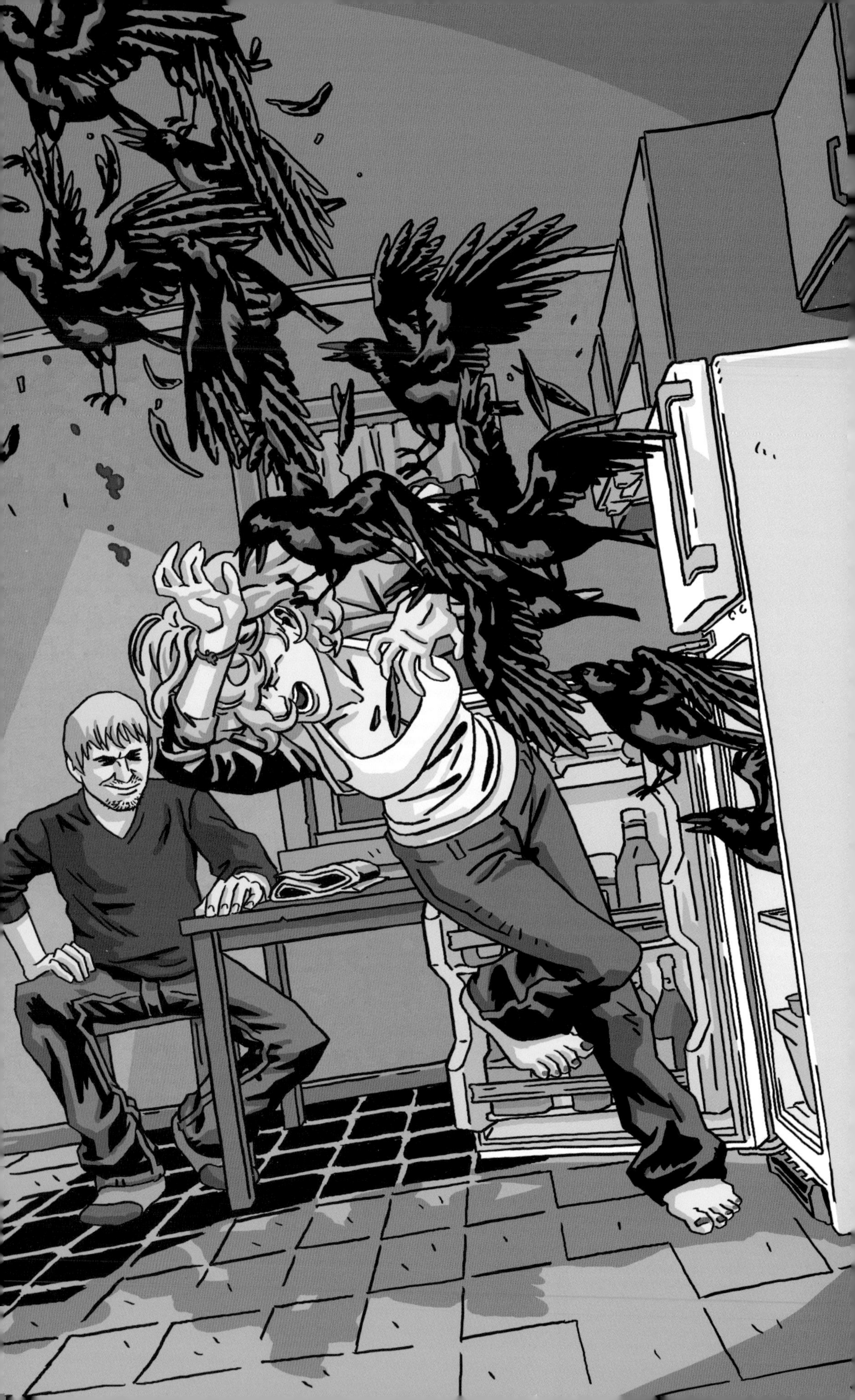

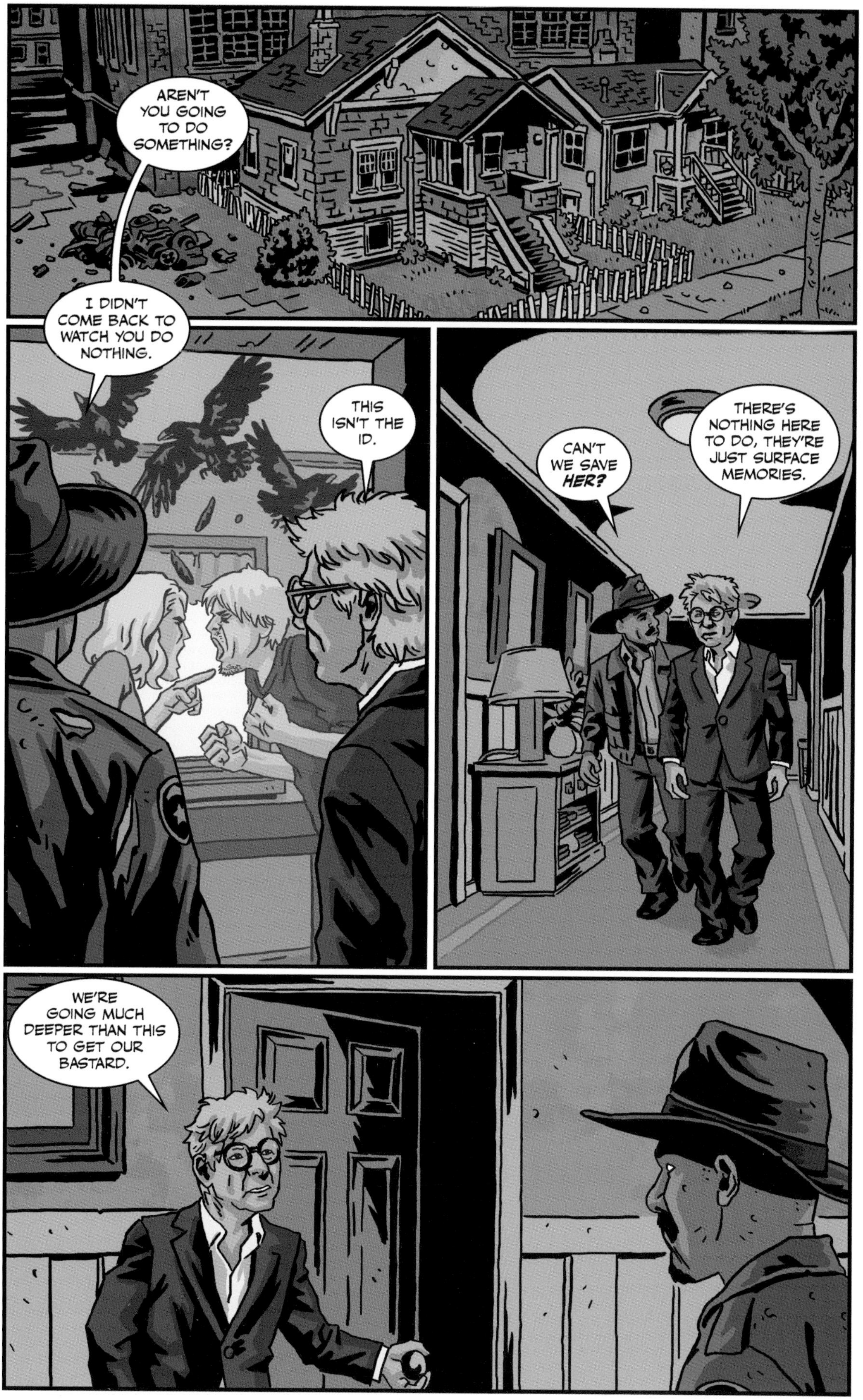
AREN'T YOU GOING TO DO SOMETHING?
I DIDN'T COME BACK TO WATCH YOU DO NOTHING.
THIS ISN'T THE ID.
CAN'T WE SAVE HER?
THERE'S NOTHING HERE TO DO, THEY'RE JUST SURFACE MEMORIES.
WE'RE GOING MUCH DEEPER THAN THIS TO GET OUR BASTARD.

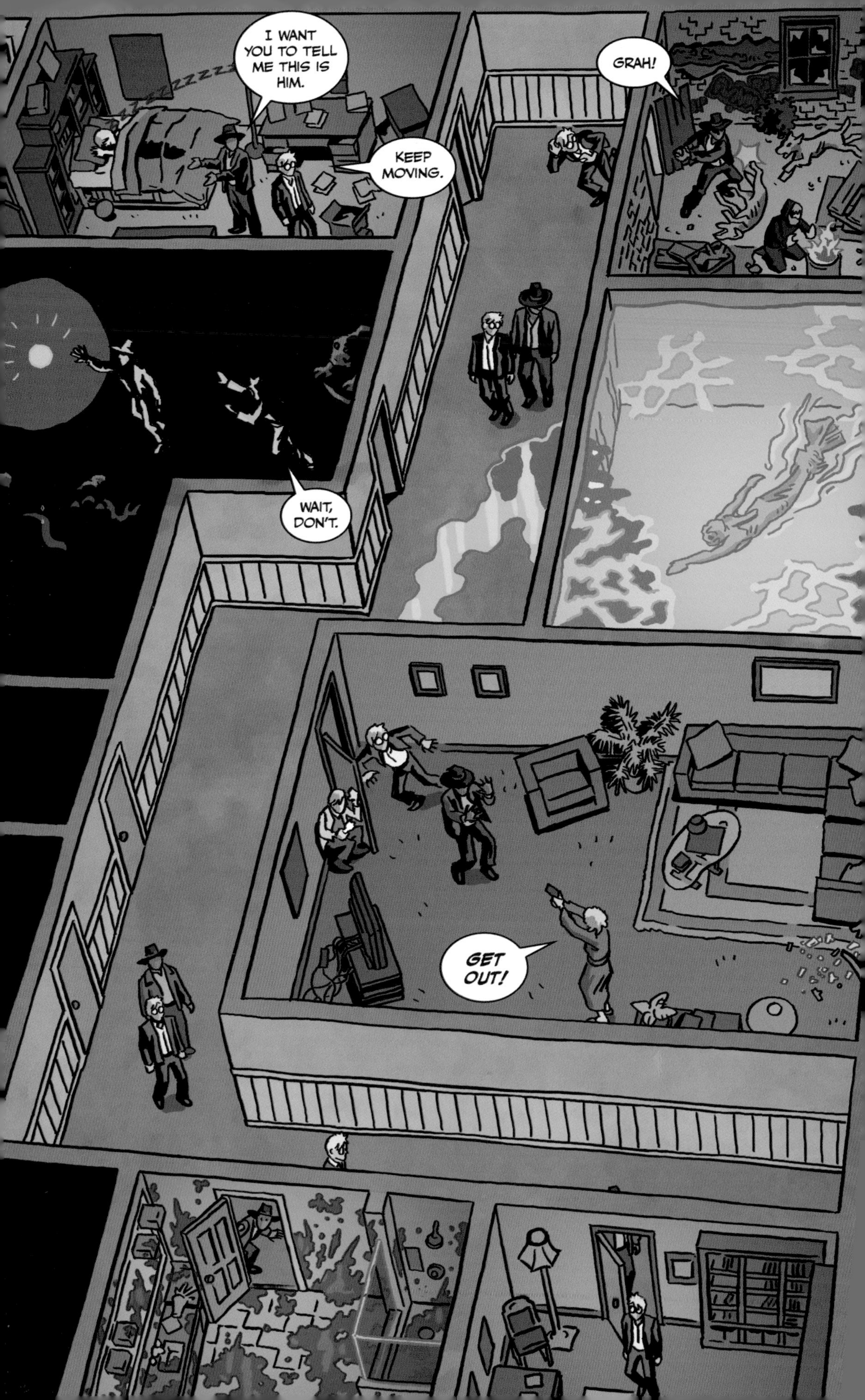
I WANT YOU TO TELL ME THIS IS HIM.
KEEP MOVING.
GRAH!
WAIT, DON'T.
GET OUT!

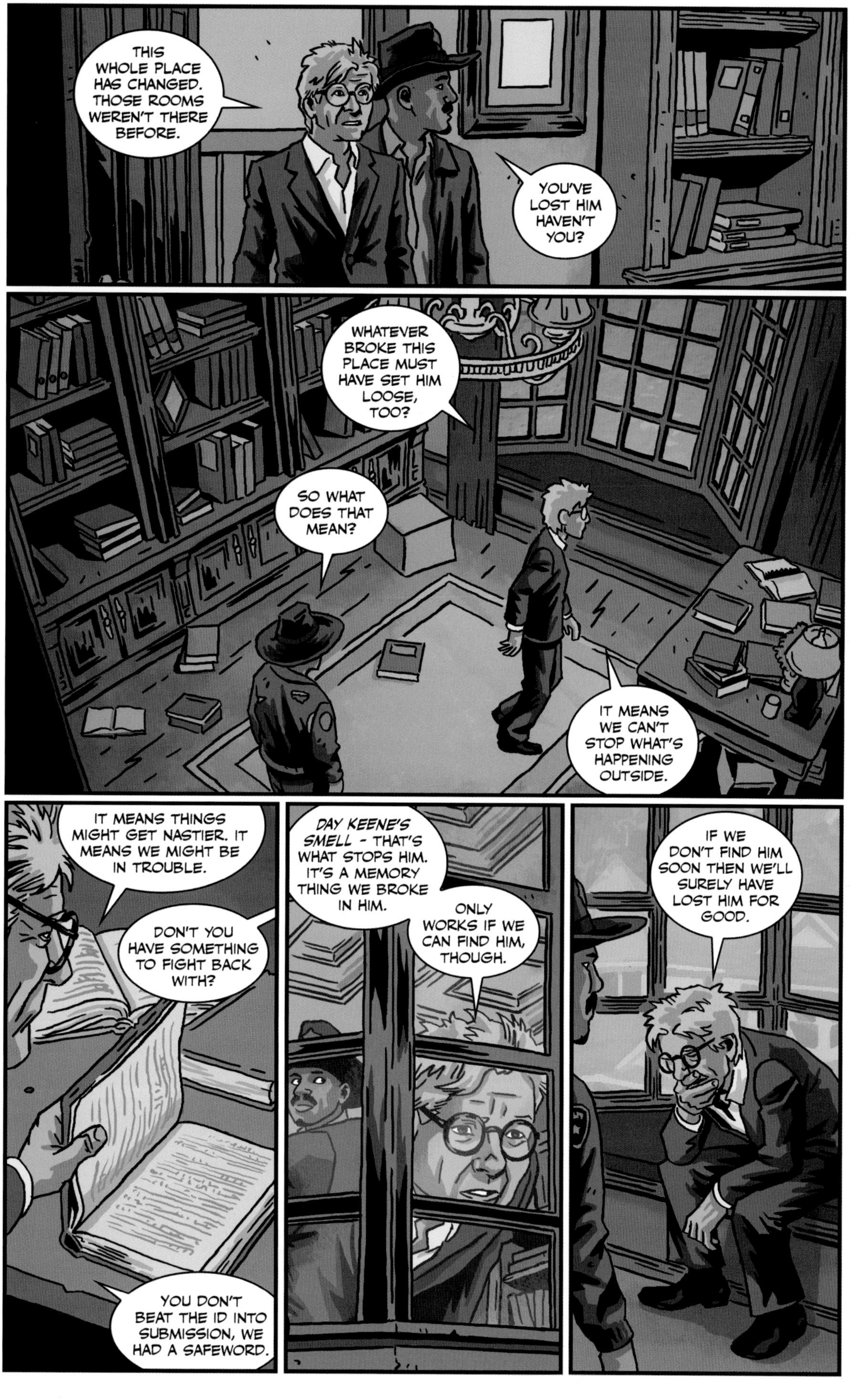
THIS WHOLE PLACE HAS CHANGED. THOSE ROOMS WEREN'T THERE BEFORE.
YOU'VE LOST HIM HAVEN'T YOU?
WHATEVER BROKE THIS PLACE MUST HAVE SET HIM LOOSE, TOO?
SO WHAT DOES THAT MEAN?
IT MEANS WE CAN'T STOP WHAT'S HAPPENING OUTSIDE.
IT MEANS THINGS MIGHT GET NASTIER. IT MEANS WE MIGHT BE IN TROUBLE.
DON'T YOU HAVE SOMETHING TO FIGHT BACK WITH?
YOU DON'T BEAT THE ID INTO SUBMISSION, WE HAD A SAFEWORD.
DAY KEENE'S SMELL - THAT'S WHAT STOPS HIM. IT'S A MEMORY THING WE BROKE IN HIM.
ONLY WORKS IF WE CAN FIND HIM, THOUGH.
IF WE DON'T FIND HIM SOON THEN WE'LL SURELY HAVE LOST HIM FOR GOOD.

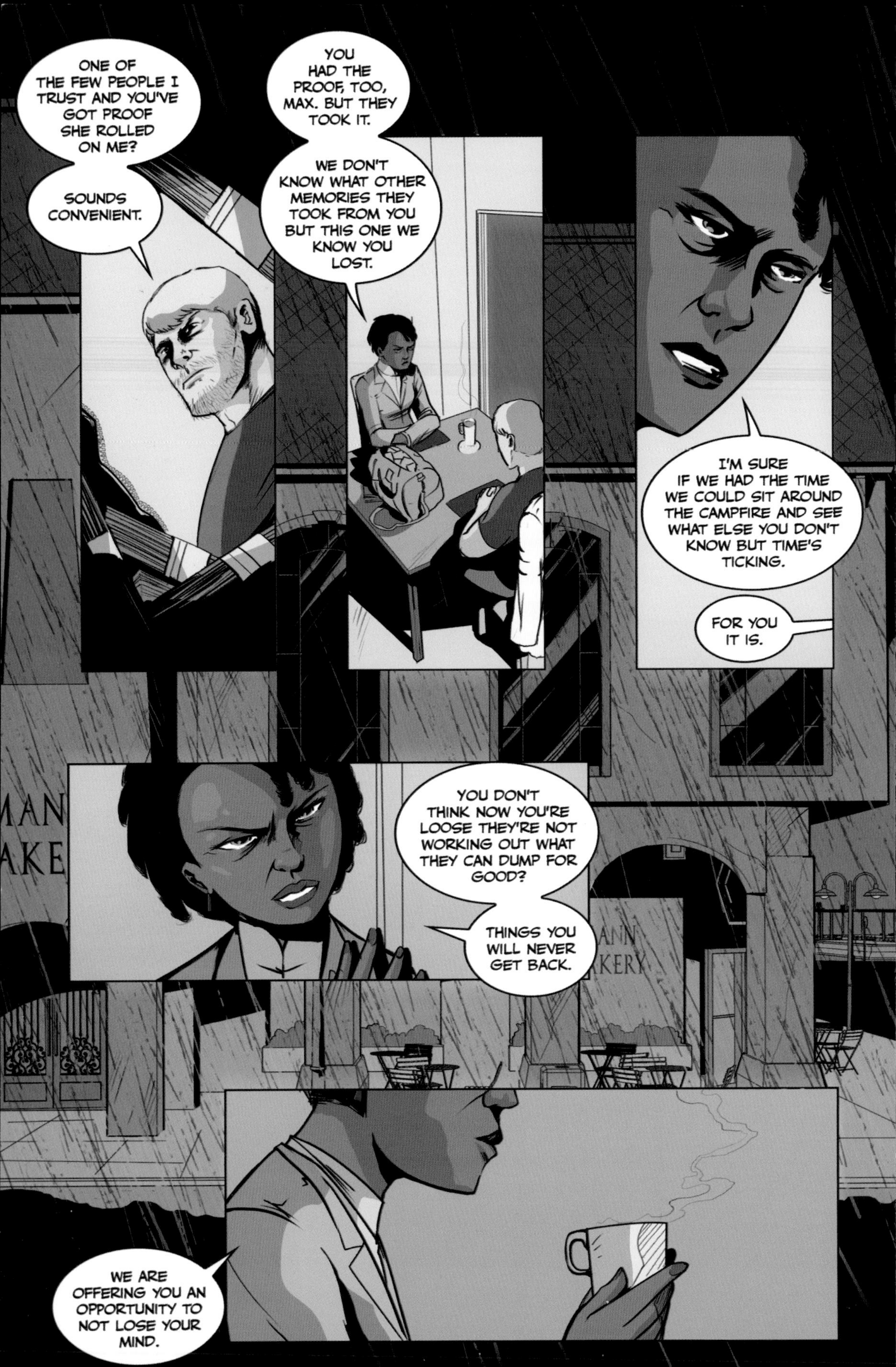
ONE OF THE FEW PEOPLE I TRUST AND YOU'VE GOT PROOF SHE ROLLED ON ME?
SOUNDS CONVENIENT.
YOU HAD THE PROOF, TOO, MAX. BUT THEY TOOK IT.
WE DON'T KNOW WHAT OTHER MEMORIES THEY TOOK FROM YOU BUT THIS ONE WE KNOW YOU LOST.
I'M SURE IF WE HAD THE TIME WE COULD SIT AROUND THE CAMPFIRE AND SEE WHAT ELSE YOU DON'T KNOW BUT TIME'S TICKING.
FOR YOU IT IS.
YOU DON'T THINK NOW YOU'RE LOOSE THEY'RE NOT WORKING OUT WHAT THEY CAN DUMP FOR GOOD?
THINGS YOU WILL NEVER GET BACK.
WE ARE OFFERING YOU AN OPPORTUNITY TO NOT LOSE YOUR MIND.

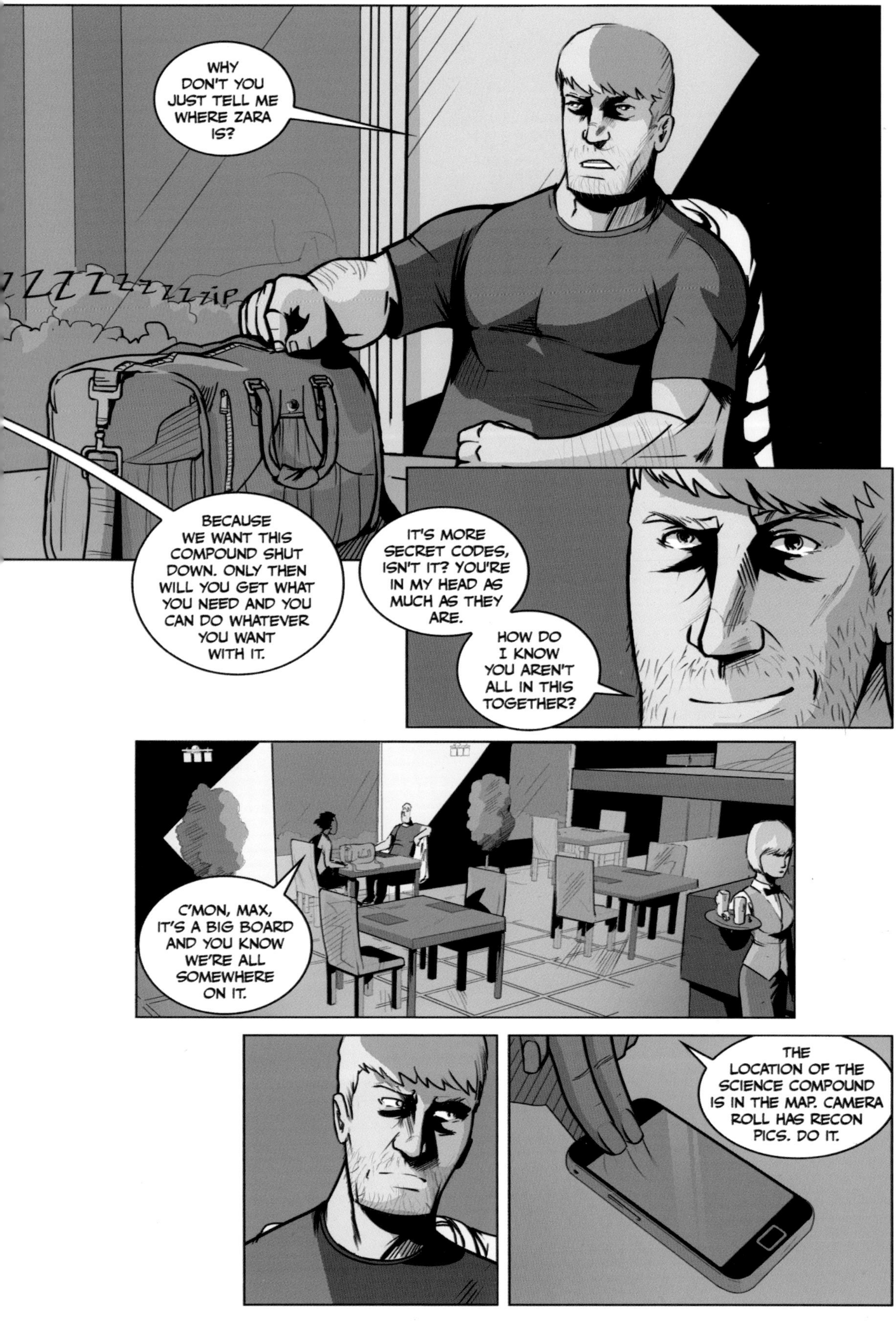
WHY DON'T YOU JUST TELL ME WHERE ZARA IS?
ZZZZZzzzzzip
BECAUSE WE WANT THIS COMPOUND SHUT DOWN. ONLY THEN WILL YOU GET WHAT YOU NEED AND YOU CAN DO WHATEVER YOU WANT WITH IT.
IT'S MORE SECRET CODES, ISN'T IT? YOU'RE IN MY HEAD AS MUCH AS THEY ARE.
HOW DO I KNOW YOU AREN'T ALL IN THIS TOGETHER?
C'MON, MAX, IT'S A BIG BOARD AND YOU KNOW WE'RE ALL SOMEWHERE ON IT.
THE LOCATION OF THE SCIENCE COMPOUND IS IN THE MAP. CAMERA ROLL HAS RECON PICS. DO IT.

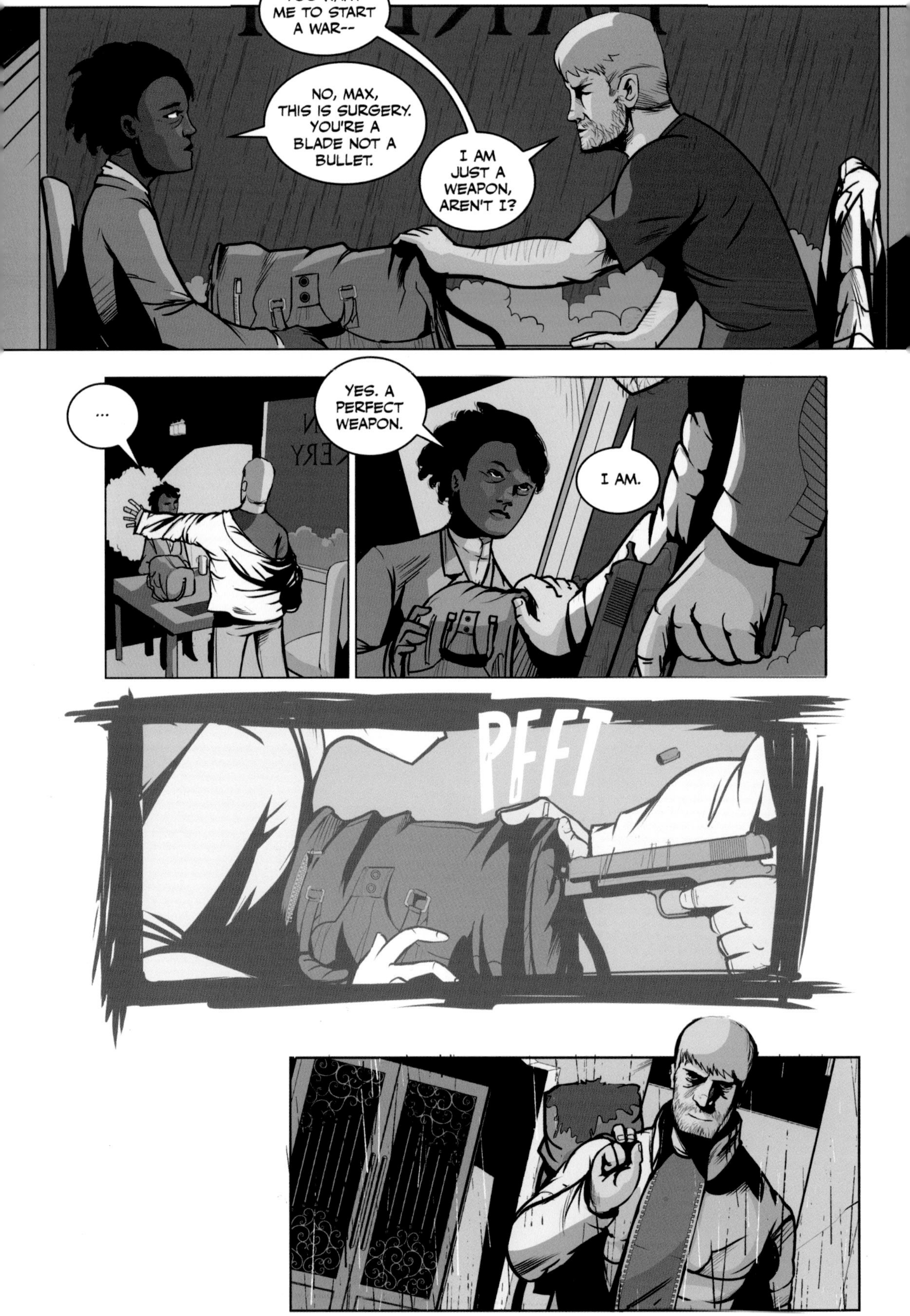
YOU WANT ME TO START A WAR--
NO, MAX, THIS IS SURGERY. YOU'RE A BLADE NOT A BULLET.
I AM JUST A WEAPON, AREN'T I?
...
YES. A PERFECT WEAPON.
I AM.
PFFT

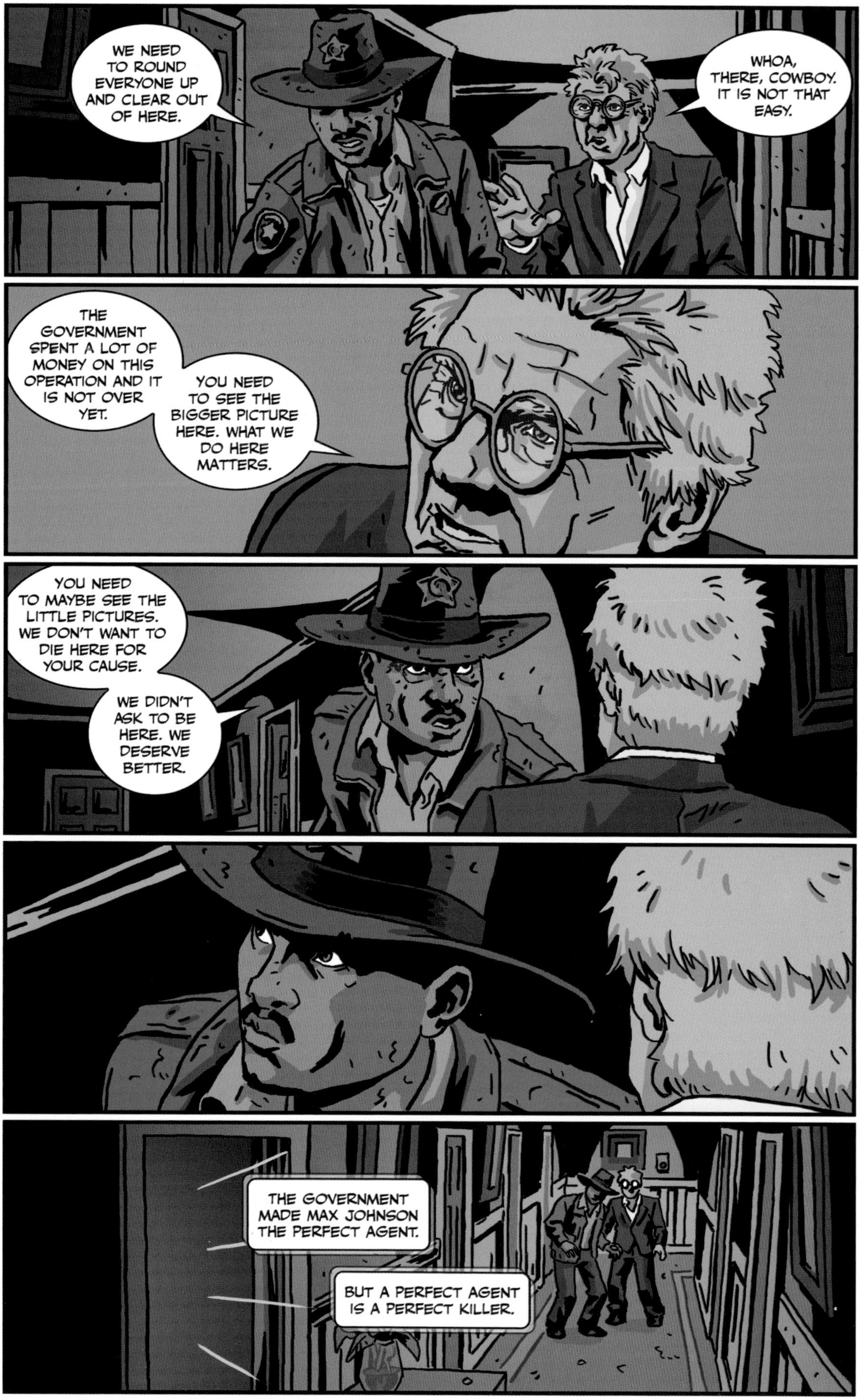
WE NEED TO ROUND EVERYONE UP AND CLEAR OUT OF HERE.
WHOA, THERE, COWBOY. IT IS NOT THAT EASY.
THE GOVERNMENT SPENT A LOT OF MONEY ON THIS OPERATION AND IT IS NOT OVER YET.
YOU NEED TO SEE THE BIGGER PICTURE HERE. WHAT WE DO HERE MATTERS.
YOU NEED TO MAYBE SEE THE LITTLE PICTURES. WE DON'T WANT TO DIE HERE FOR YOUR CAUSE.
WE DIDN'T ASK TO BE HERE. WE DESERVE BETTER.
THE GOVERNMENT MADE MAX JOHNSON THE PERFECT AGENT.
BUT A PERFECT AGENT IS A PERFECT KILLER.

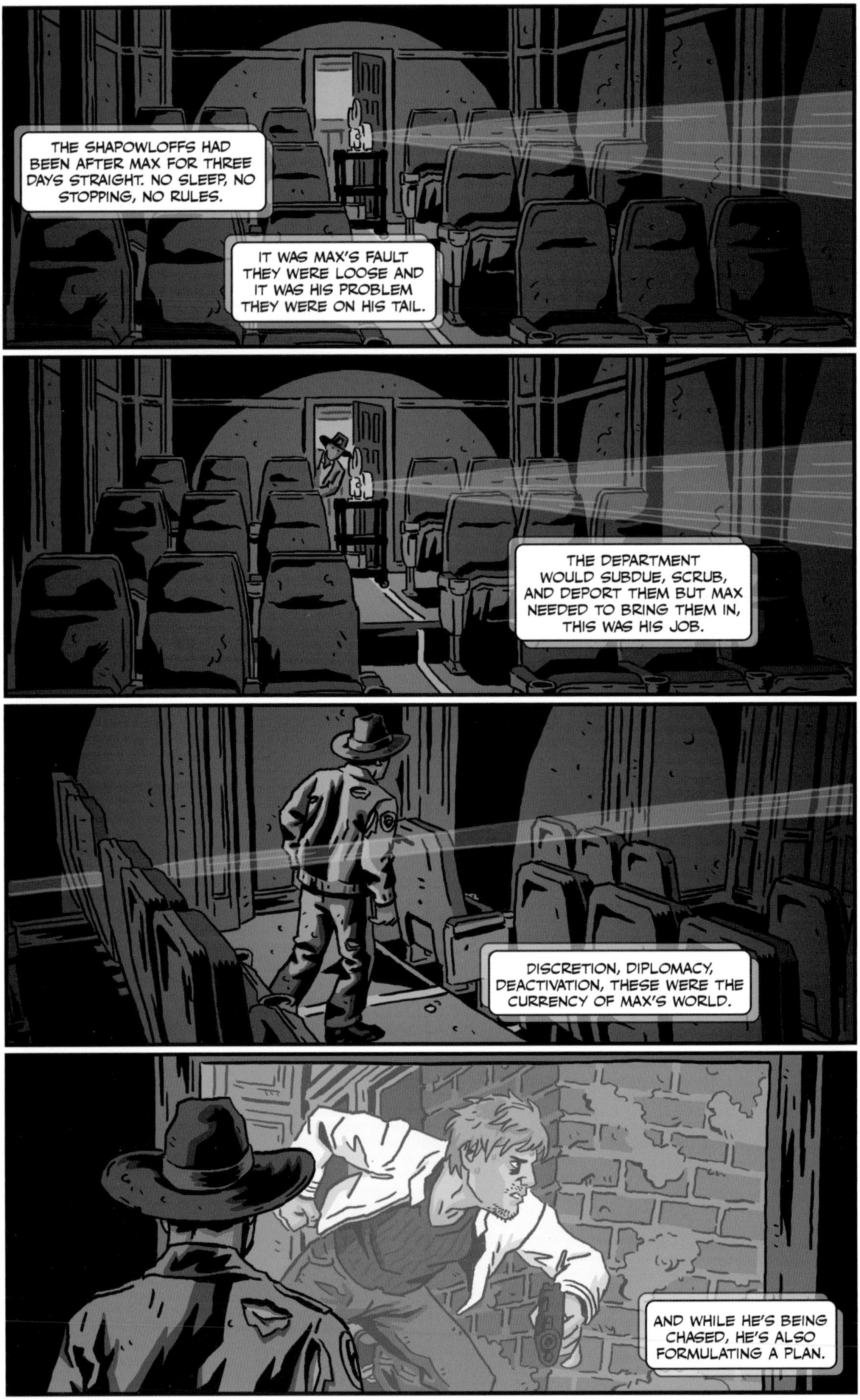
THE SHAPOWLOFFS HAD BEEN AFTER MAX FOR THREE DAYS STRAIGHT. NO SLEEP, NO STOPPING, NO RULES.
IT WAS MAX'S FAULT THEY WERE LOOSE AND IT WAS HIS PROBLEM THEY WERE ON HIS TAIL.
THE DEPARTMENT WOULD SUBDUE, SCRUB, AND DEPORT THEM BUT MAX NEEDED TO BRING THEM IN, THIS WAS HIS JOB.
DISCRETION, DIPLOMACY, DEACTIVATION, THESE WERE THE CURRENCY OF MAX'S WORLD.
AND WHILE HE'S BEING CHASED, HE'S ALSO FORMULATING A PLAN.

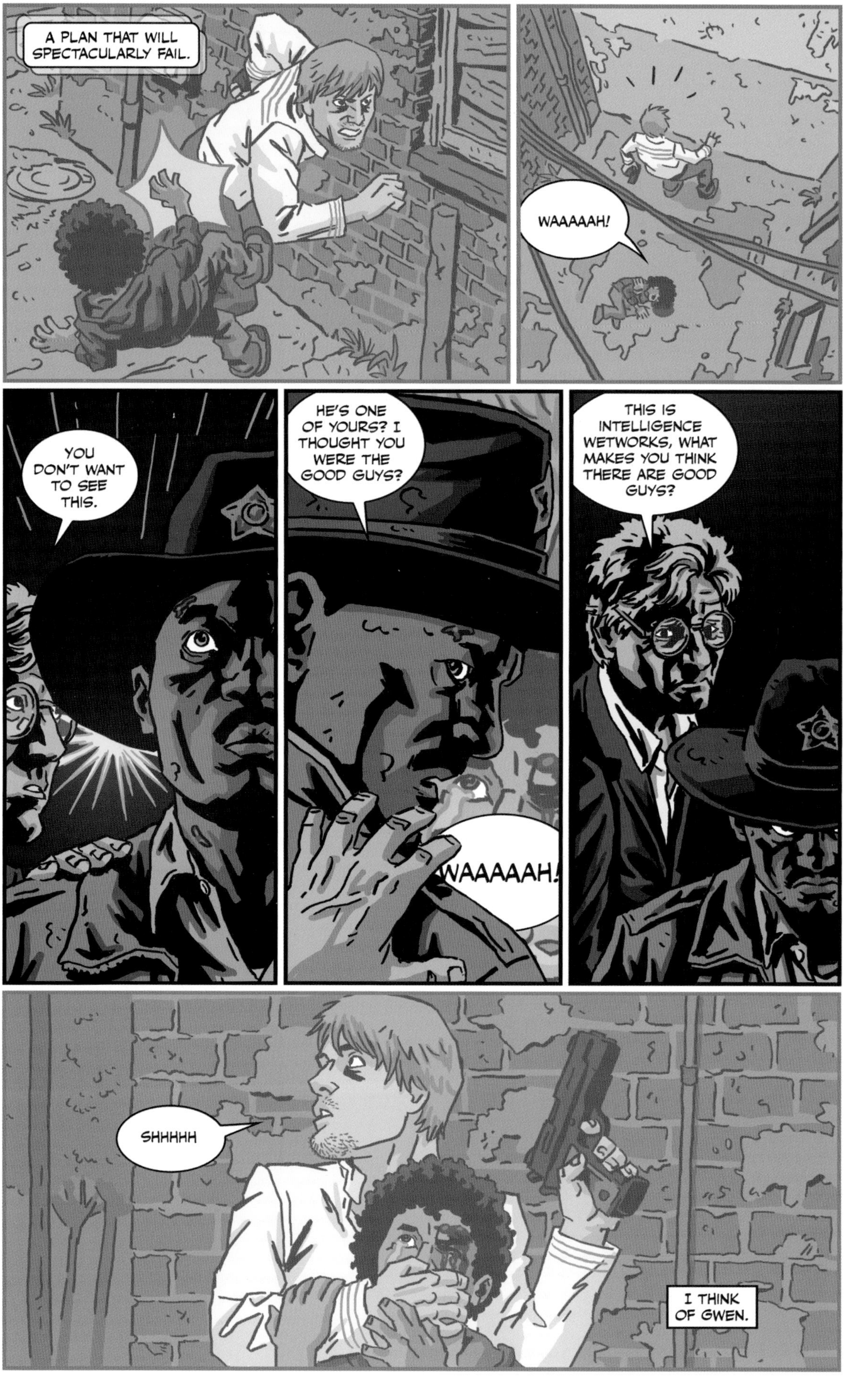
A PLAN THAT WILL SPECTACULARLY FAIL.
WAAAAAH!
YOU DON'T WANT TO SEE THIS.
HE'S ONE OF YOURS? I THOUGHT YOU WERE THE GOOD GUYS?
WAAAAAH!
THIS IS INTELLIGENCE WETWORKS, WHAT MAKES YOU THINK THERE ARE GOOD GUYS?
SHHHHH
I THINK OF GWEN.

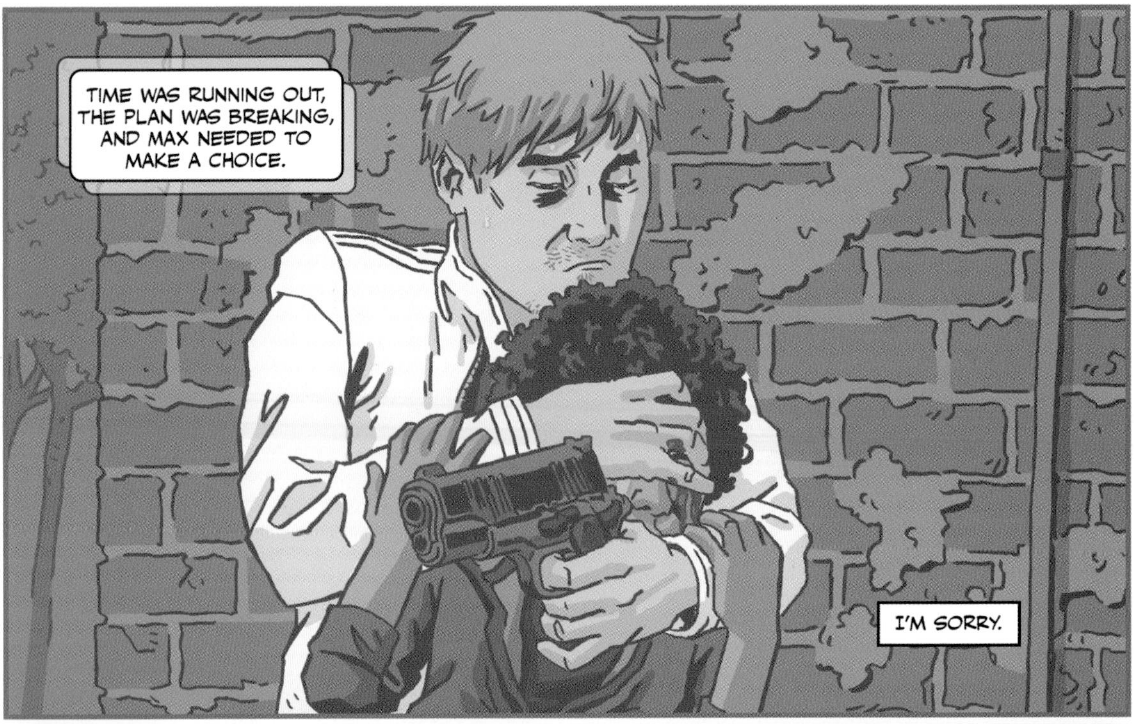
TIME WAS RUNNING OUT, THE PLAN WAS BREAKING, AND MAX NEEDED TO MAKE A CHOICE.
I'M SORRY.

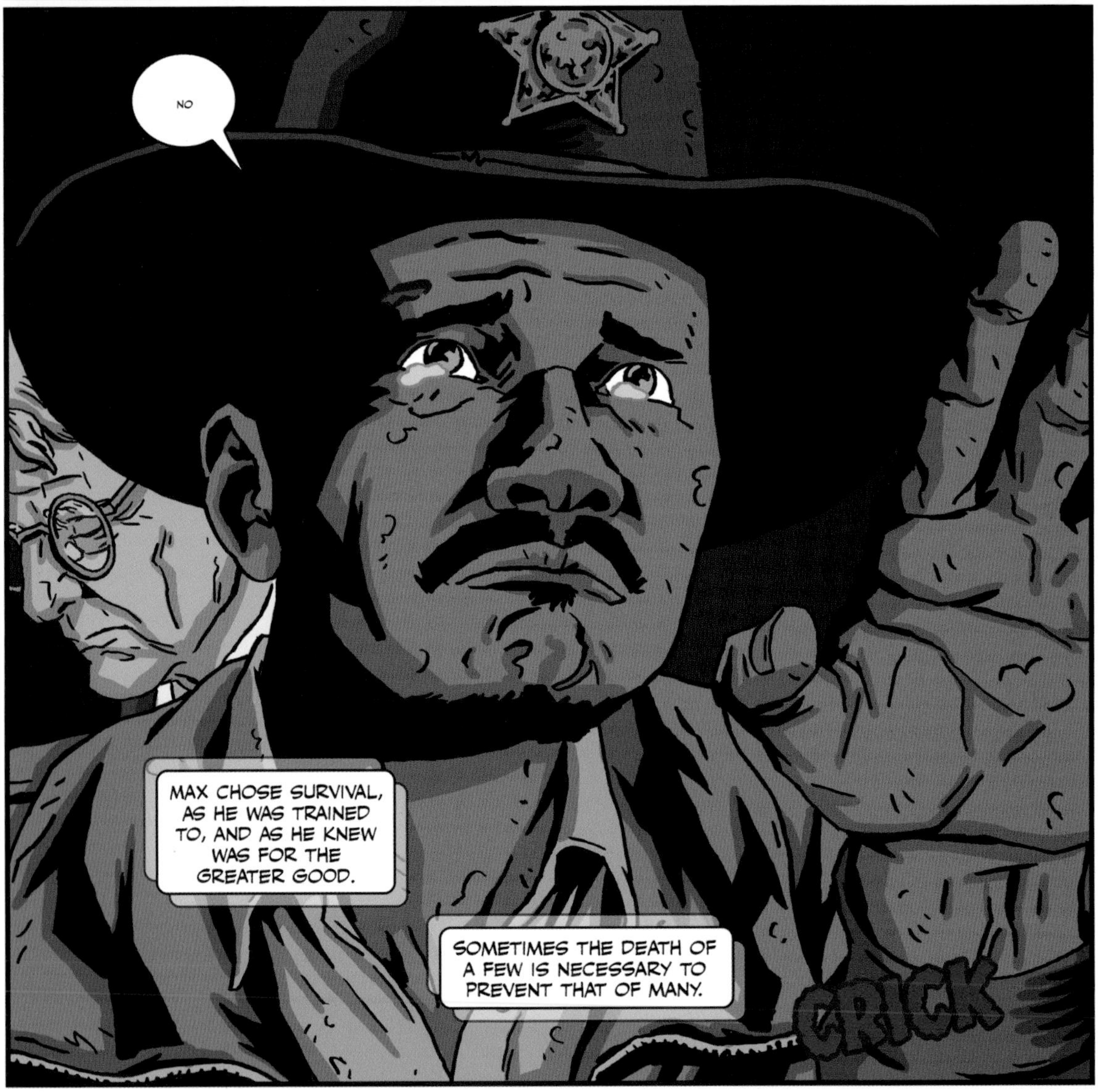
NO
MAX CHOSE SURVIVAL, AS HE WAS TRAINED TO, AND AS HE KNEW WAS FOR THE GREATER GOOD.
SOMETIMES THE DEATH OF A FEW IS NECESSARY TO PREVENT THAT OF MANY.
CRICK

NEXT: SHANE LEAVES THE COVE

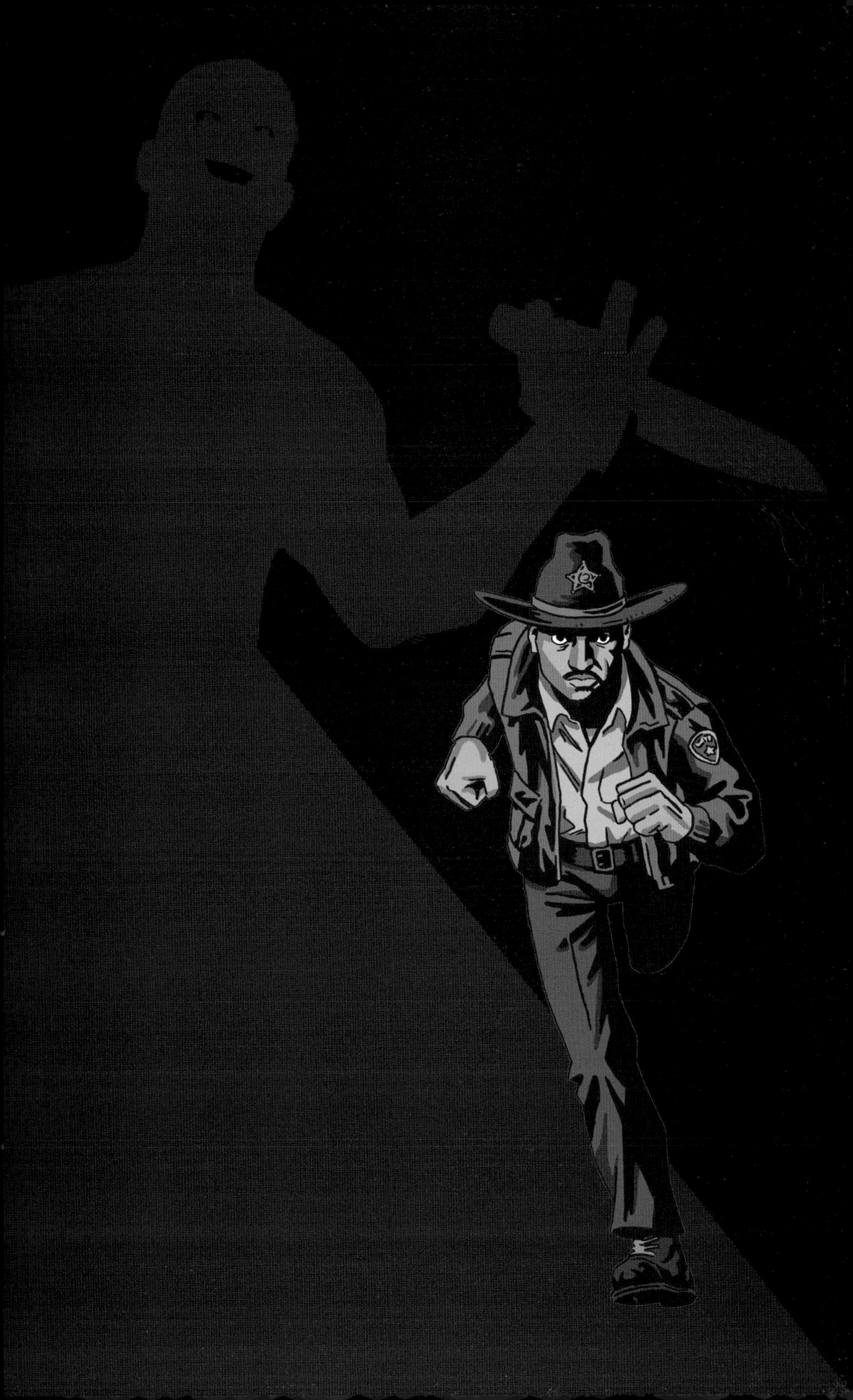

Chapter 6

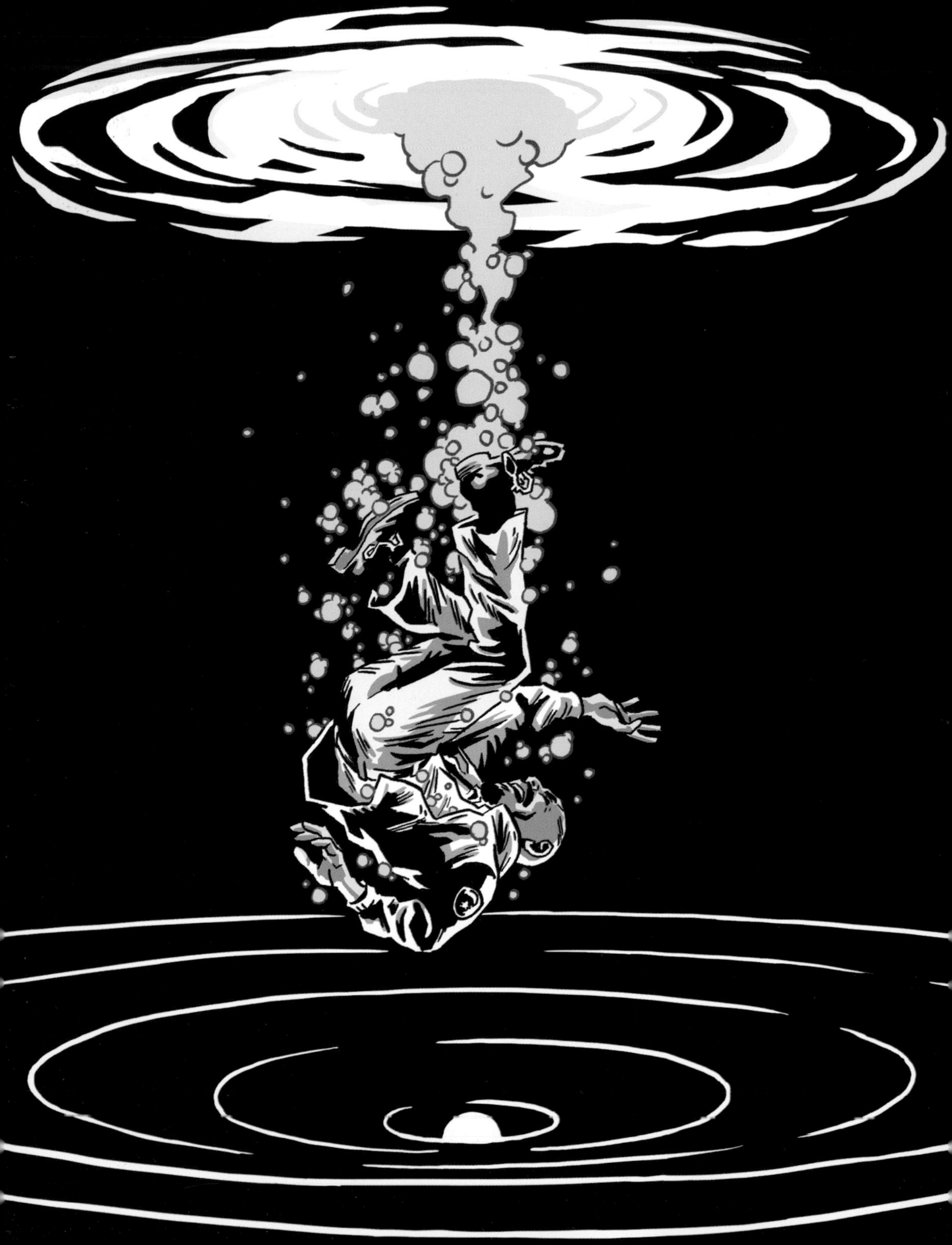

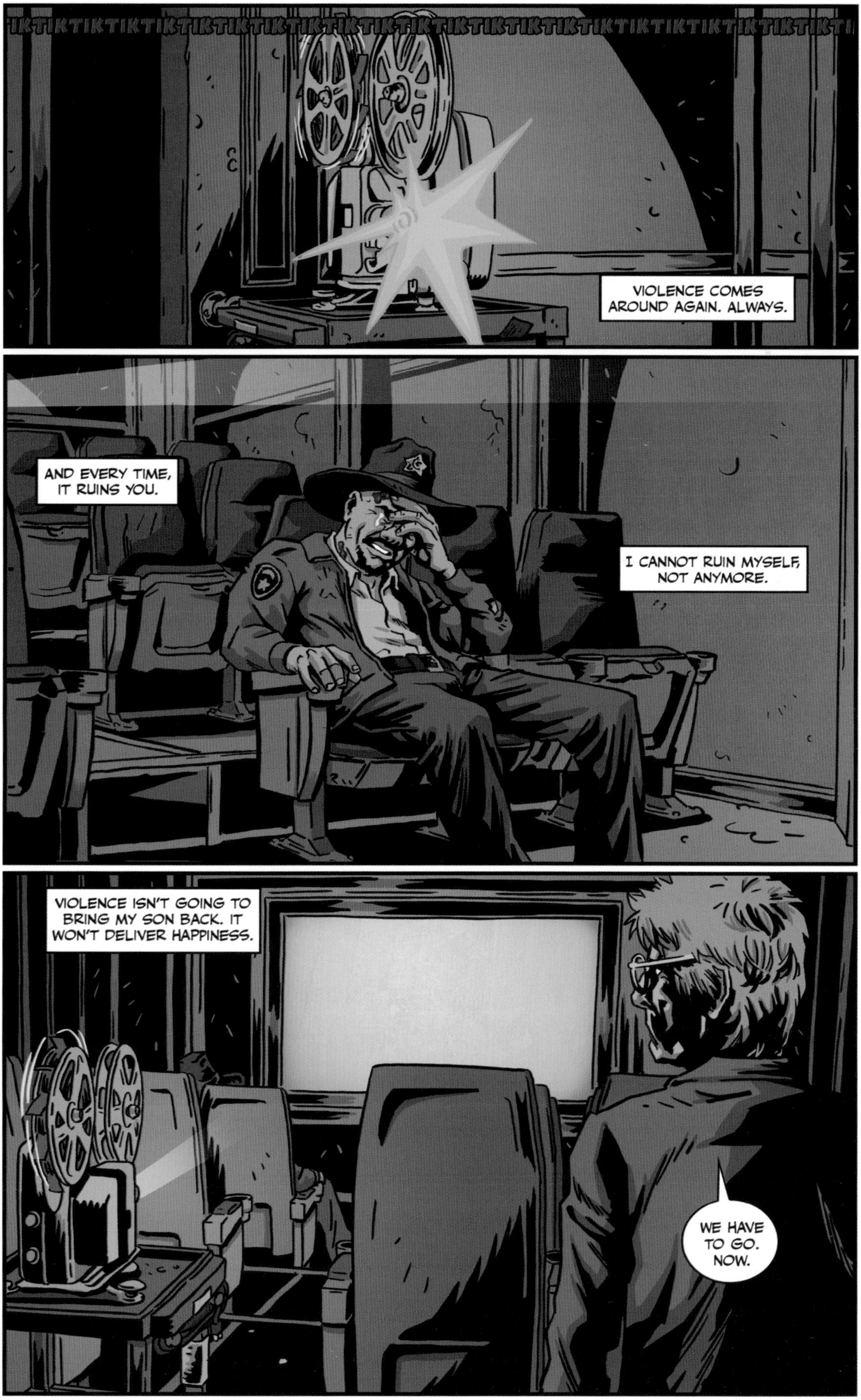
TIKTIKTIKTIKTIKTIKTIKTIKTIKTIKTIKTIKTIKTIKTIKTIKTIKTIKTIKTIKTI
VIOLENCE COMES AROUND AGAIN. ALWAYS.
AND EVERY TIME, IT RUINS YOU.
I CANNOT RUIN MYSELF, NOT ANYMORE.
VIOLENCE ISN'T GOING TO BRING MY SON BACK. IT WON'T DELIVER HAPPINESS.
WE HAVE TO GO. NOW.

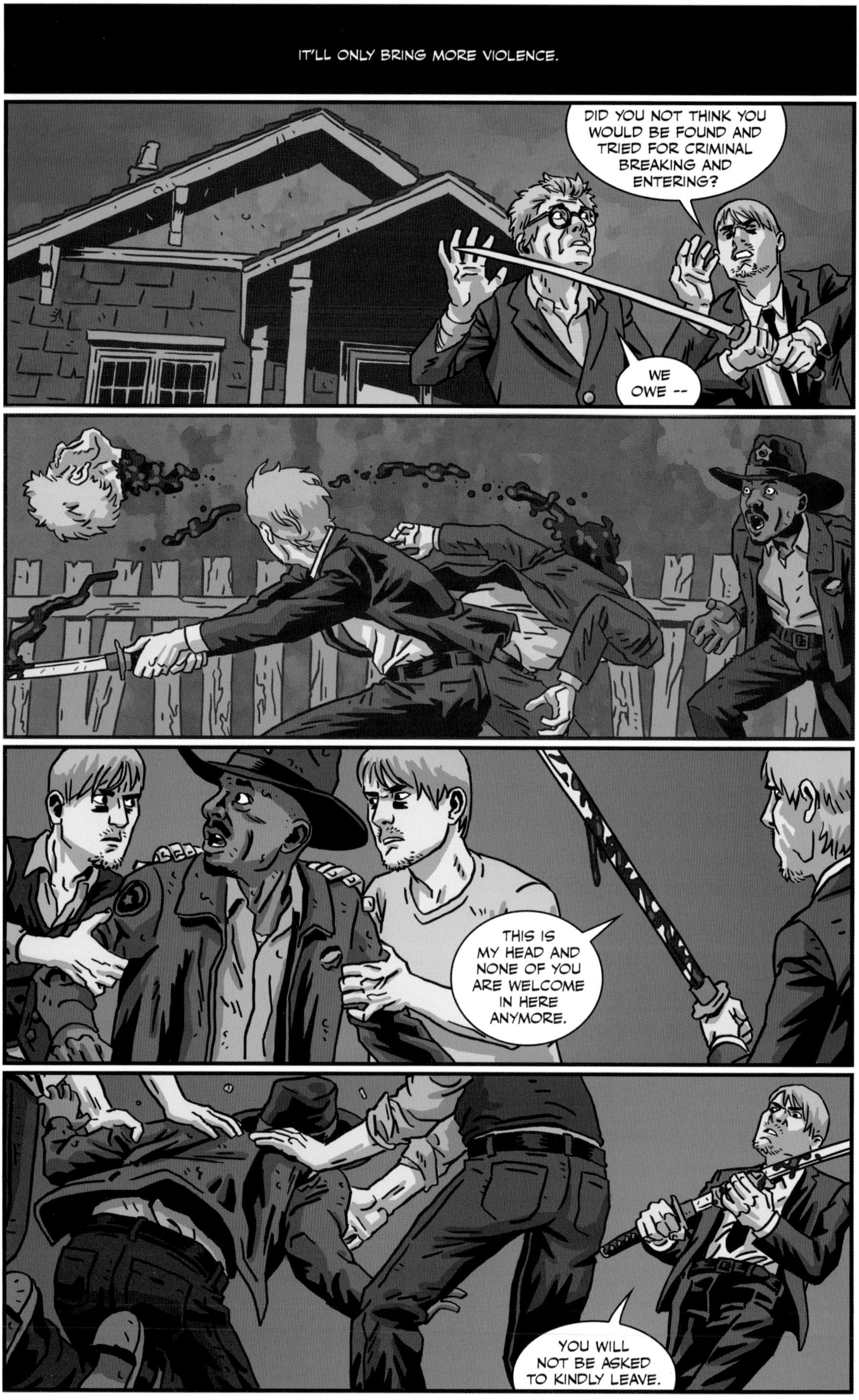
IT'LL ONLY BRING MORE VIOLENCE.
DID YOU NOT THINK YOU WOULD BE FOUND AND TRIED FOR CRIMINAL BREAKING AND ENTERING?
WE OWE --
THIS IS MY HEAD AND NONE OF YOU ARE WELCOME IN HERE ANYMORE.
YOU WILL NOT BE ASKED TO KINDLY LEAVE.

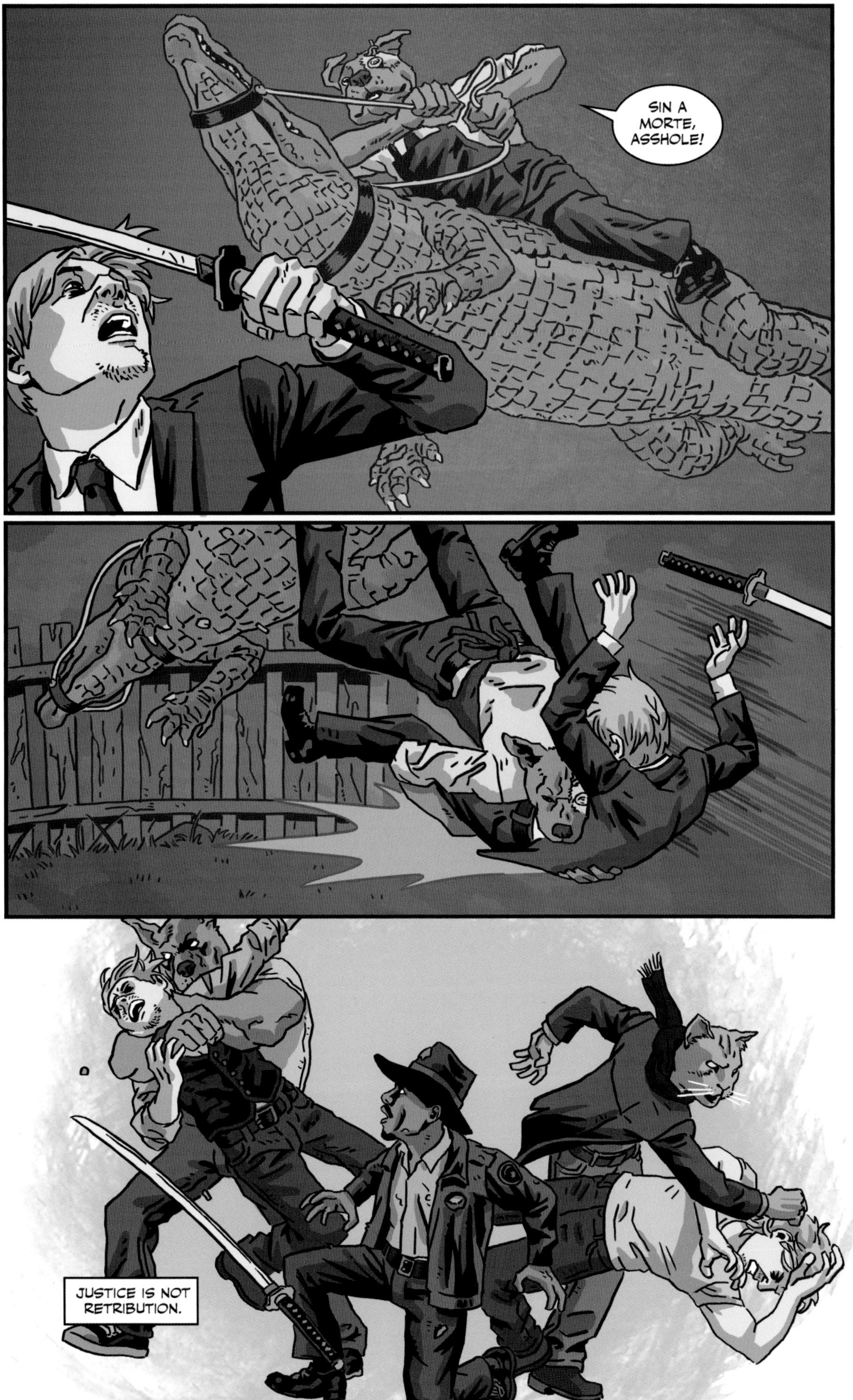
SIN A MORTE, ASSHOLE!
JUSTICE IS NOT RETRIBUTION.

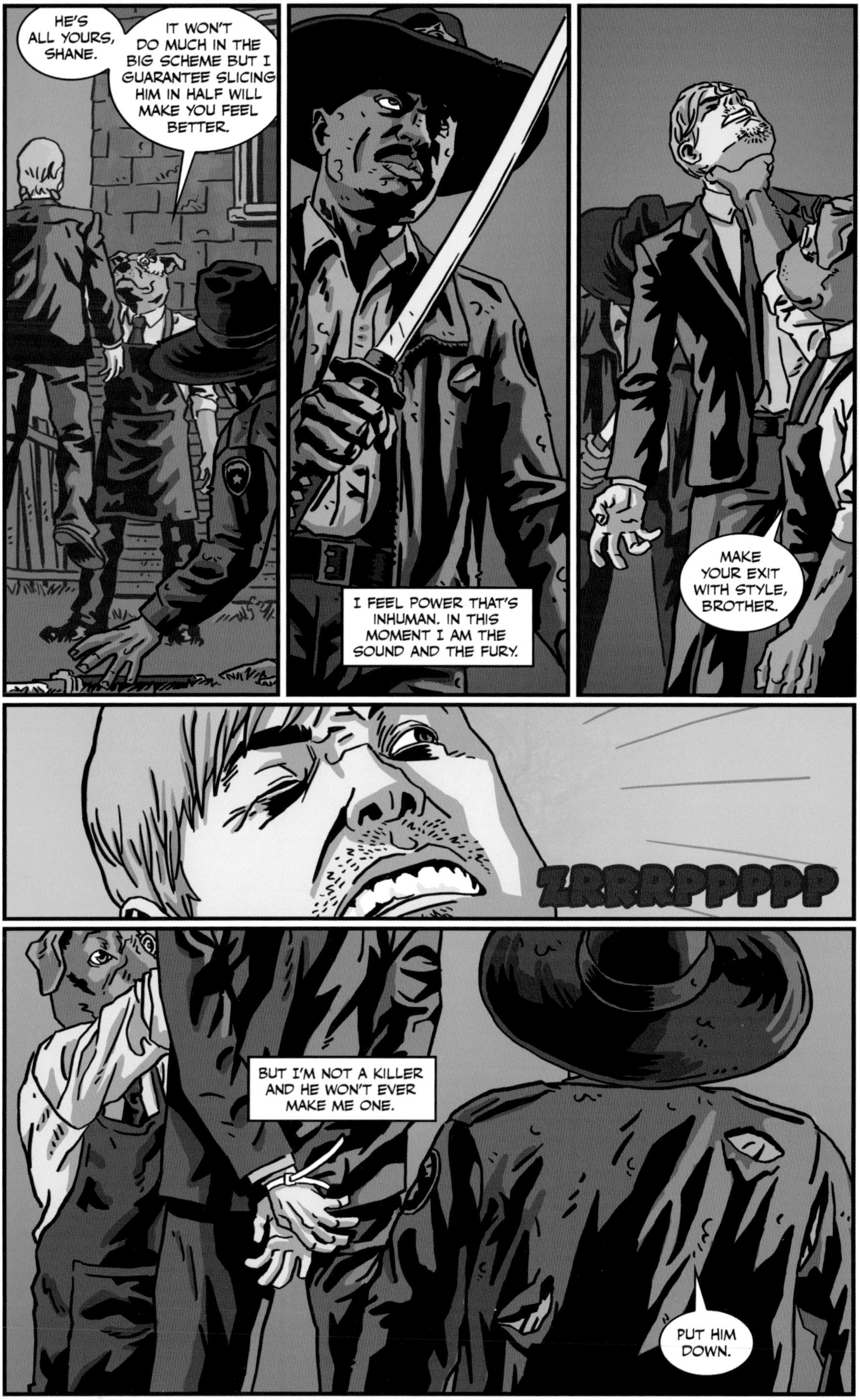
HE'S ALL YOURS, SHANE.
IT WON'T DO MUCH IN THE BIG SCHEME BUT I GUARANTEE SLICING HIM IN HALF WILL MAKE YOU FEEL BETTER.
I FEEL POWER THAT'S INHUMAN. IN THIS MOMENT I AM THE SOUND AND THE FURY.
MAKE YOUR EXIT WITH STYLE, BROTHER.
ZRRRPPPPP
BUT I'M NOT A KILLER AND HE WON'T EVER MAKE ME ONE.
PUT HIM DOWN.

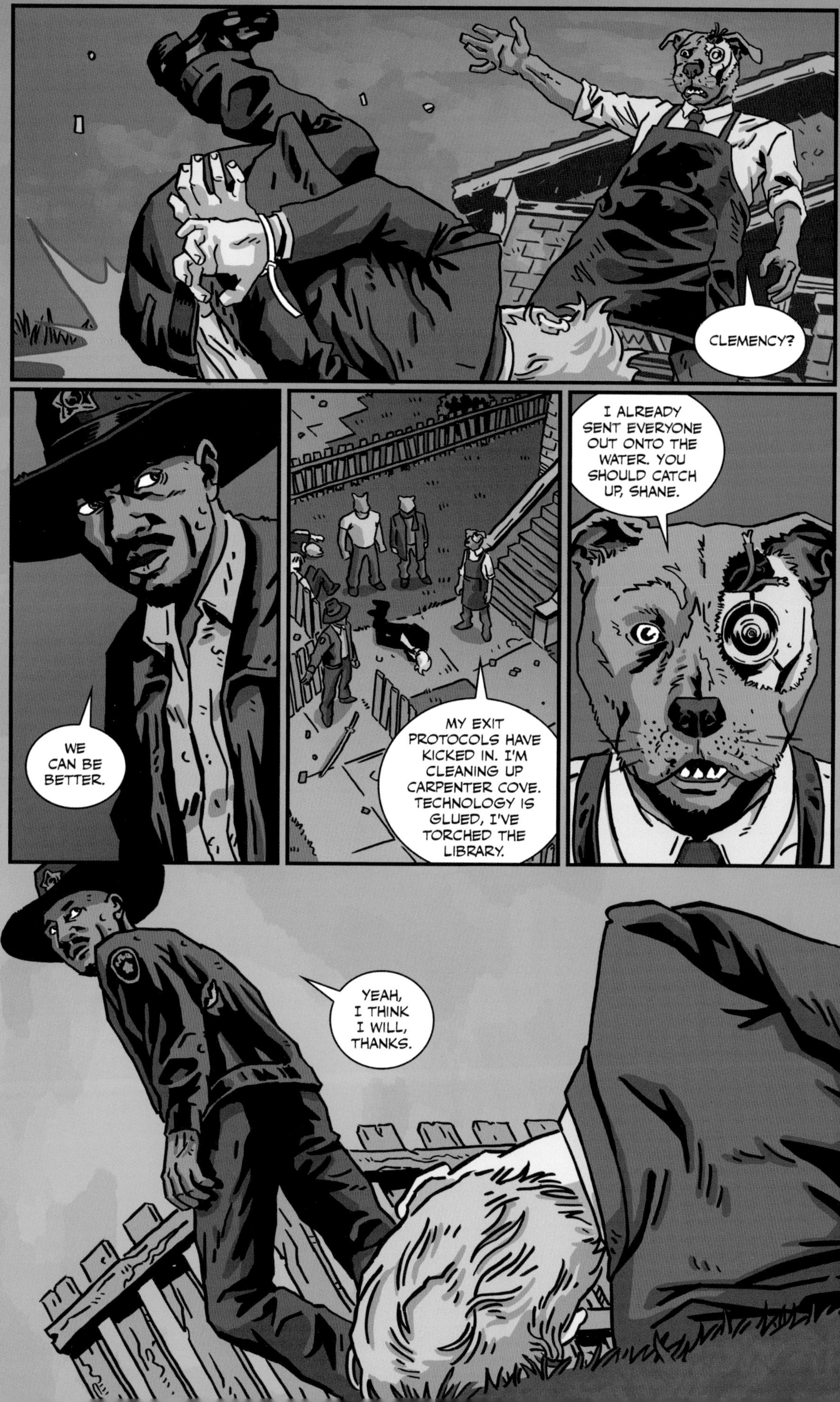
CLEMENCY?
WE CAN BE BETTER.
MY EXIT PROTOCOLS HAVE KICKED IN. I'M CLEANING UP CARPENTER COVE. TECHNOLOGY IS GLUED, I'VE TORCHED THE LIBRARY.
I ALREADY SENT EVERYONE OUT ONTO THE WATER. YOU SHOULD CATCH UP, SHANE.
YEAH, I THINK I WILL, THANKS.

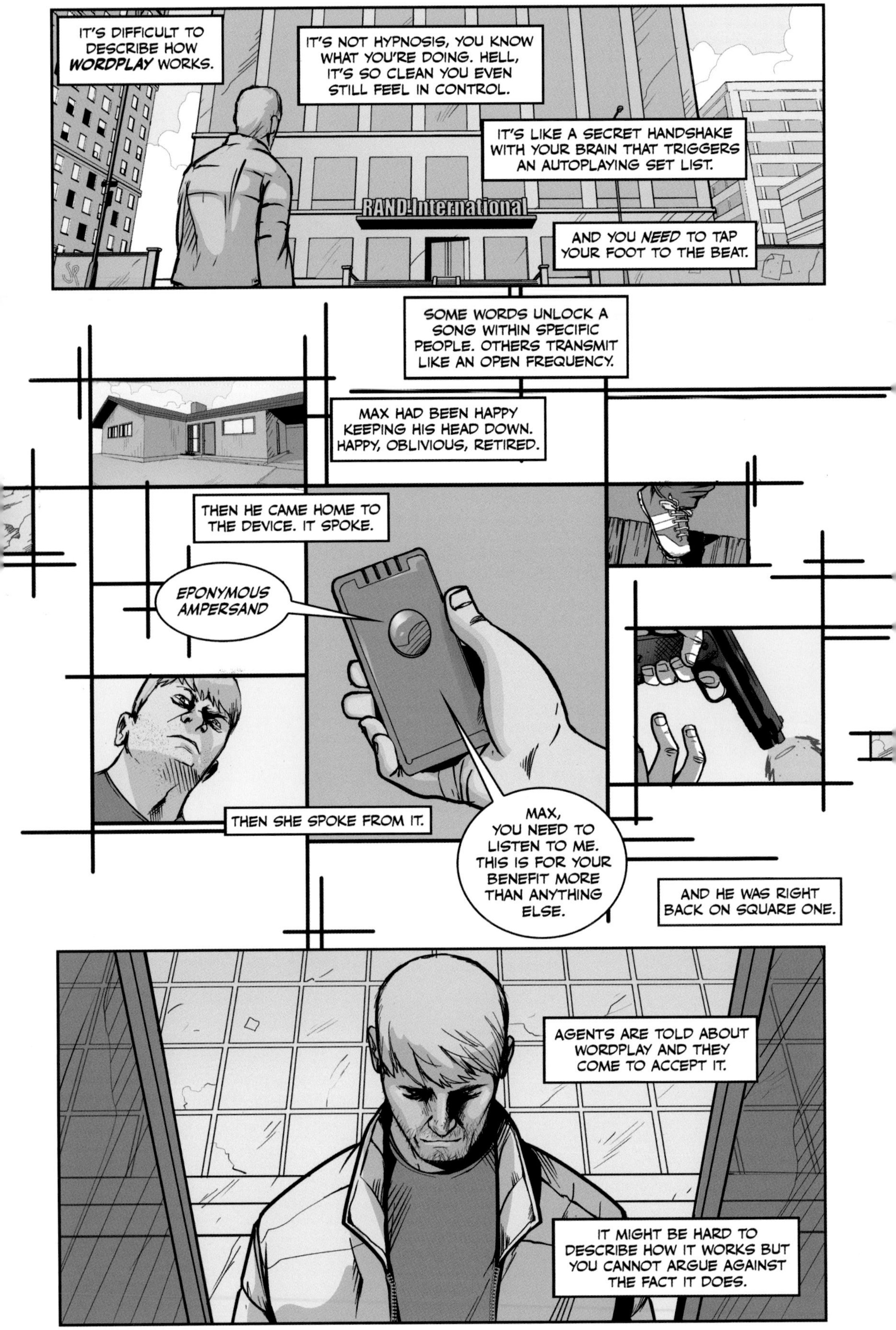

IT'S DIFFICULT TO DESCRIBE HOW *WORDPLAY* WORKS.
IT'S NOT HYPNOSIS, YOU KNOW WHAT YOU'RE DOING. HELL, IT'S SO CLEAN YOU EVEN STILL FEEL IN CONTROL.
IT'S LIKE A SECRET HANDSHAKE WITH YOUR BRAIN THAT TRIGGERS AN AUTOPLAYING SET LIST.
RAND-International
AND YOU *NEED* TO TAP YOUR FOOT TO THE BEAT.
SOME WORDS UNLOCK A SONG WITHIN SPECIFIC PEOPLE. OTHERS TRANSMIT LIKE AN OPEN FREQUENCY.
MAX HAD BEEN HAPPY KEEPING HIS HEAD DOWN. HAPPY, OBLIVIOUS, RETIRED.
THEN HE CAME HOME TO THE DEVICE. IT SPOKE.
EPONYMOUS AMPERSAND
THEN SHE SPOKE FROM IT.
MAX, YOU NEED TO LISTEN TO ME. THIS IS FOR YOUR BENEFIT MORE THAN ANYTHING ELSE.
AND HE WAS RIGHT BACK ON SQUARE ONE.
AGENTS ARE TOLD ABOUT WORDPLAY AND THEY COME TO ACCEPT IT.
IT MIGHT BE HARD TO DESCRIBE HOW IT WORKS BUT YOU CANNOT ARGUE AGAINST THE FACT IT DOES.

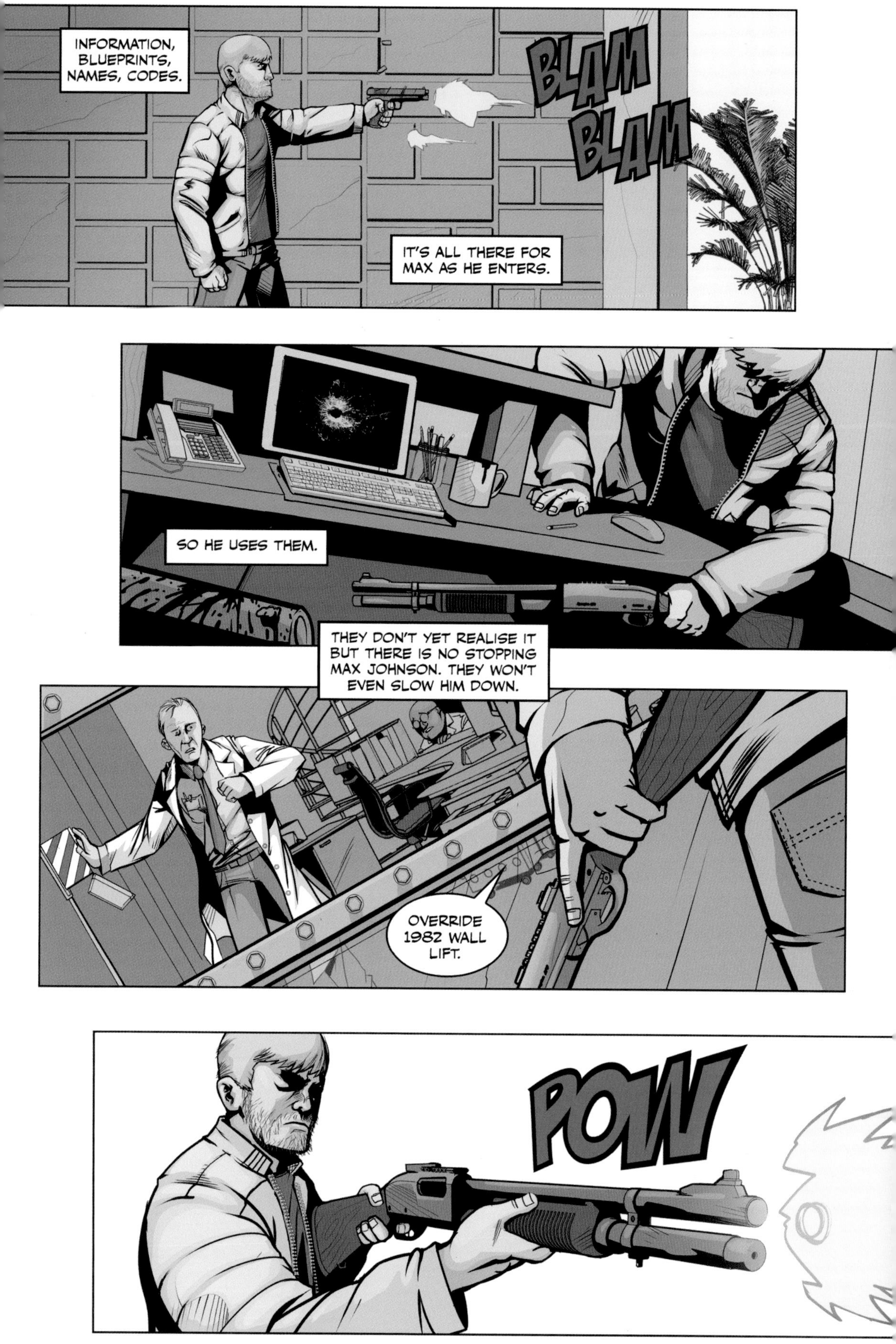
INFORMATION, BLUEPRINTS, NAMES, CODES.
BLAM BLAM
IT'S ALL THERE FOR MAX AS HE ENTERS.
SO HE USES THEM.
THEY DON'T YET REALISE IT BUT THERE IS NO STOPPING MAX JOHNSON. THEY WON'T EVEN SLOW HIM DOWN.
OVERRIDE 1982 WALL LIFT.
POW

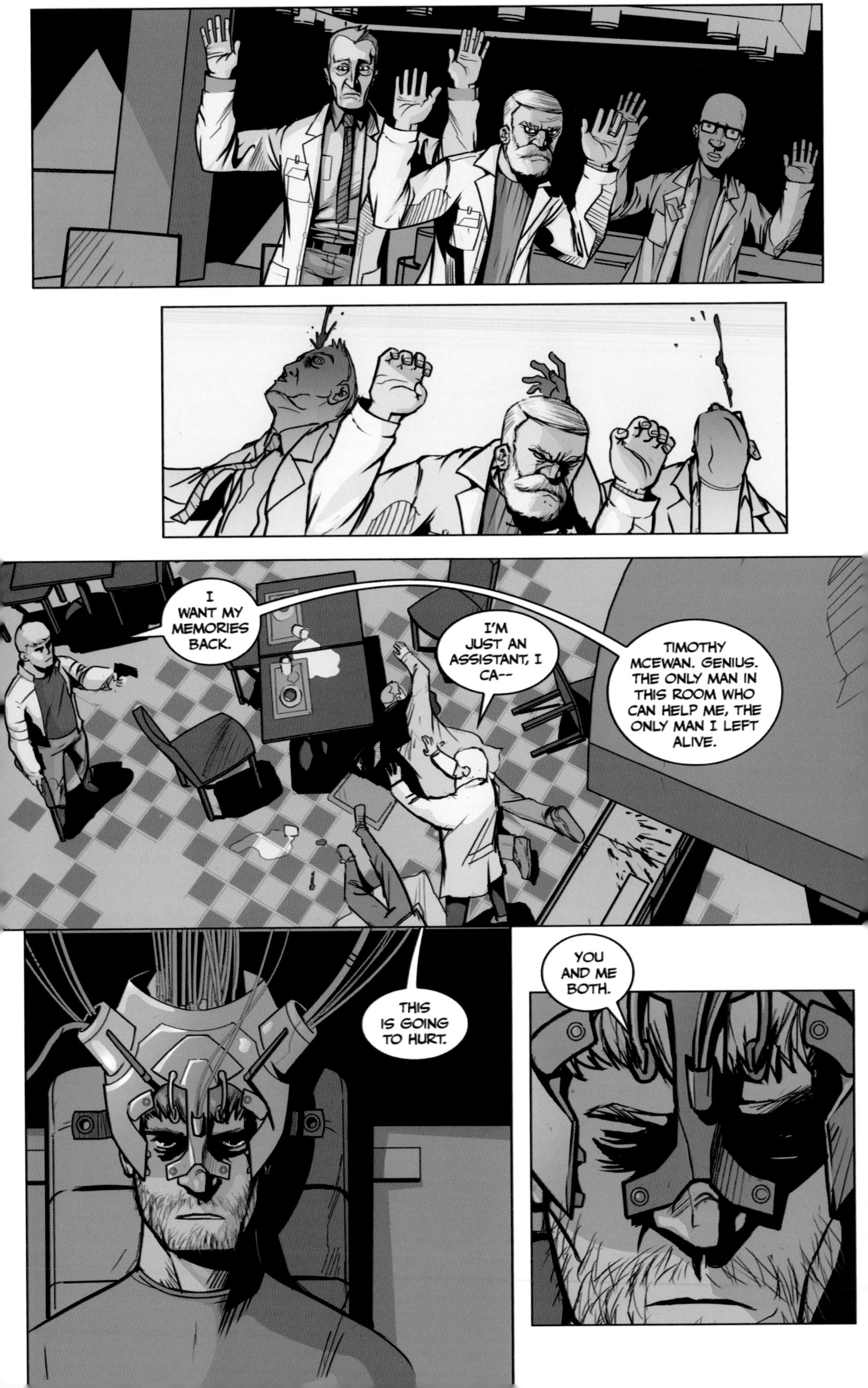
I WANT MY MEMORIES BACK.
I'M JUST AN ASSISTANT, I CA--
TIMOTHY MCEWAN. GENIUS. THE ONLY MAN IN THIS ROOM WHO CAN HELP ME, THE ONLY MAN I LEFT ALIVE.
THIS IS GOING TO HURT.
YOU AND ME BOTH.

IT'S OKAY, YOU'RE BACK NOW. IT'S ALL OVER.

...I'LL NEVER NEED THIS AGAIN.

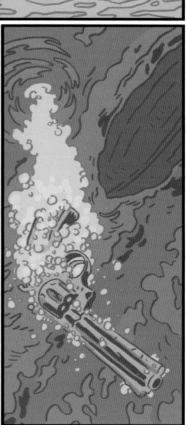

THAT'S A GRAND GESTURE, I KNOW YOU DON'T THINK OF YOURSELF AS A KILLER...

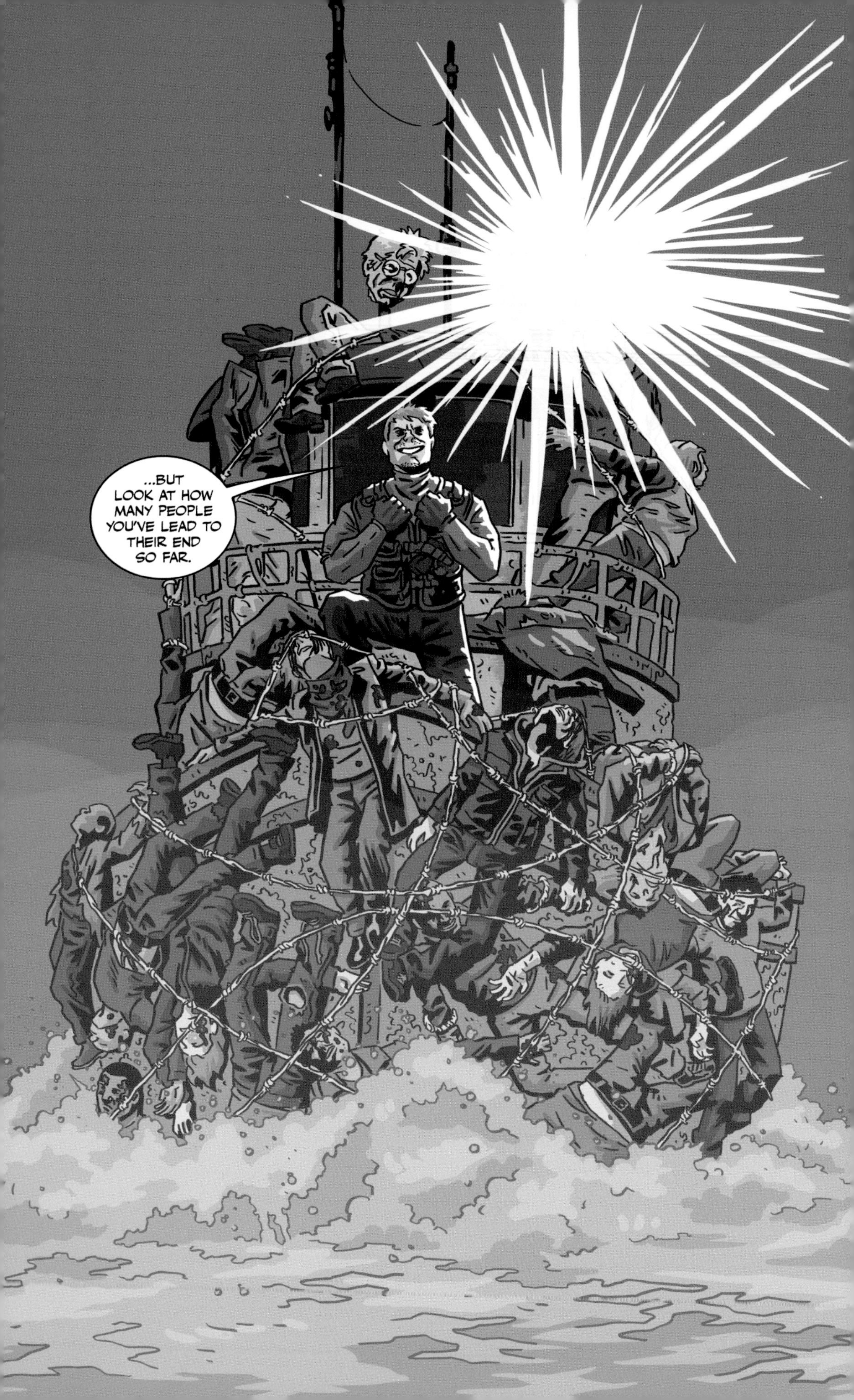
...BUT LOOK AT HOW MANY PEOPLE YOU'VE LEAD TO THEIR END SO FAR.

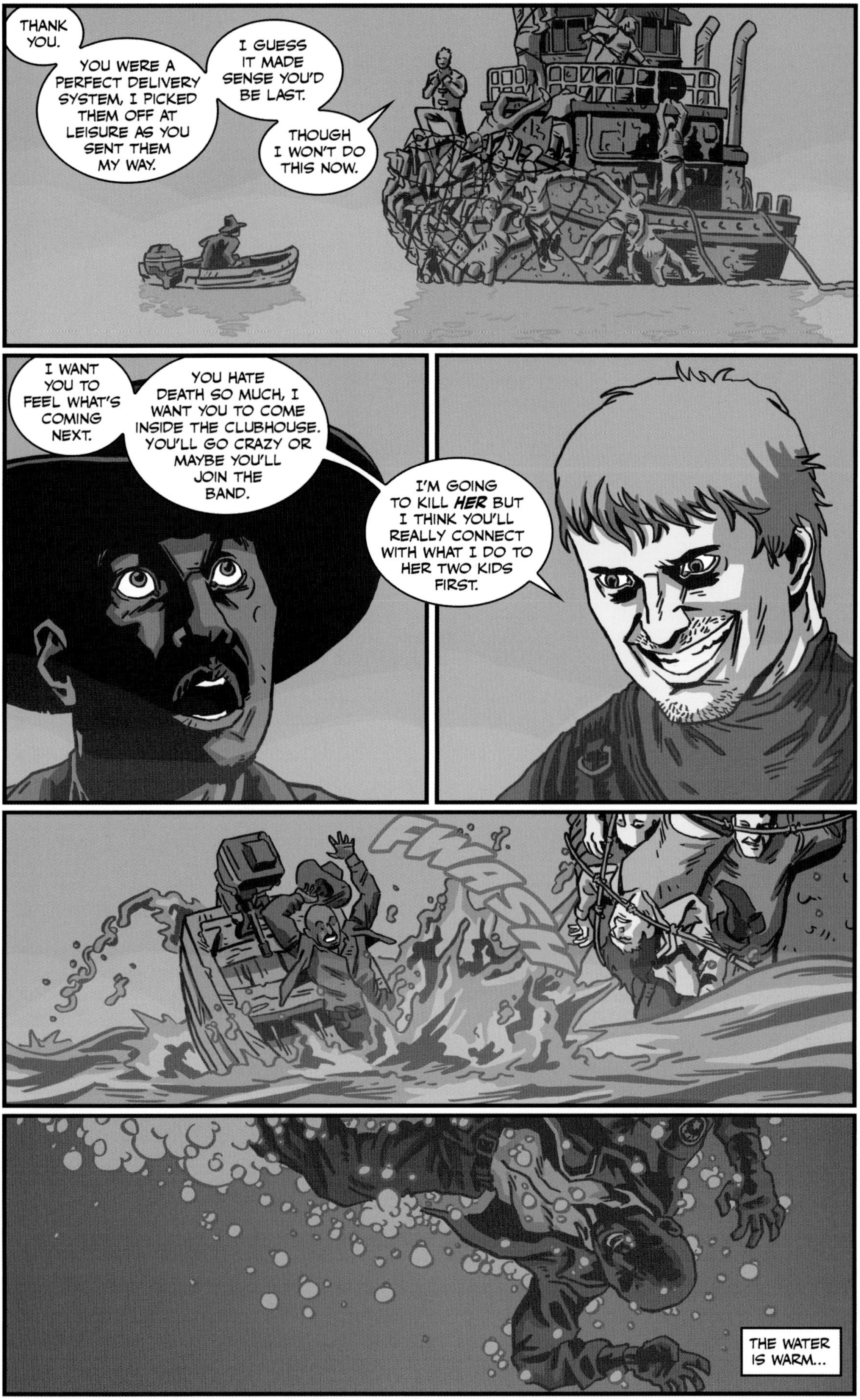
THANK YOU.
YOU WERE A PERFECT DELIVERY SYSTEM, I PICKED THEM OFF AT LEISURE AS YOU SENT THEM MY WAY.
I GUESS IT MADE SENSE YOU'D BE LAST.
THOUGH I WON'T DO THIS NOW.
I WANT YOU TO FEEL WHAT'S COMING NEXT.
YOU HATE DEATH SO MUCH, I WANT YOU TO COME INSIDE THE CLUBHOUSE. YOU'LL GO CRAZY OR MAYBE YOU'LL JOIN THE BAND.
I'M GOING TO KILL *HER* BUT I THINK YOU'LL REALLY CONNECT WITH WHAT I DO TO HER TWO KIDS FIRST.
FWASH
THE WATER IS WARM...

...I MIGHT BE HEADING DOWN TO HELL.

BUT INSTEAD I FIND SALVATION...

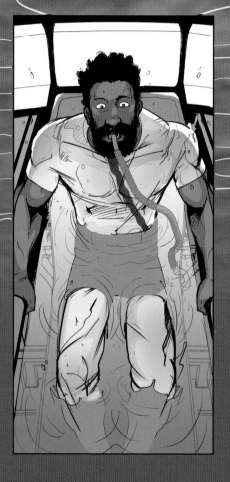

IT'S OKAY, YOU'RE BACK NOW. IT'S ALL OVER.

NEXT: FREEDOM

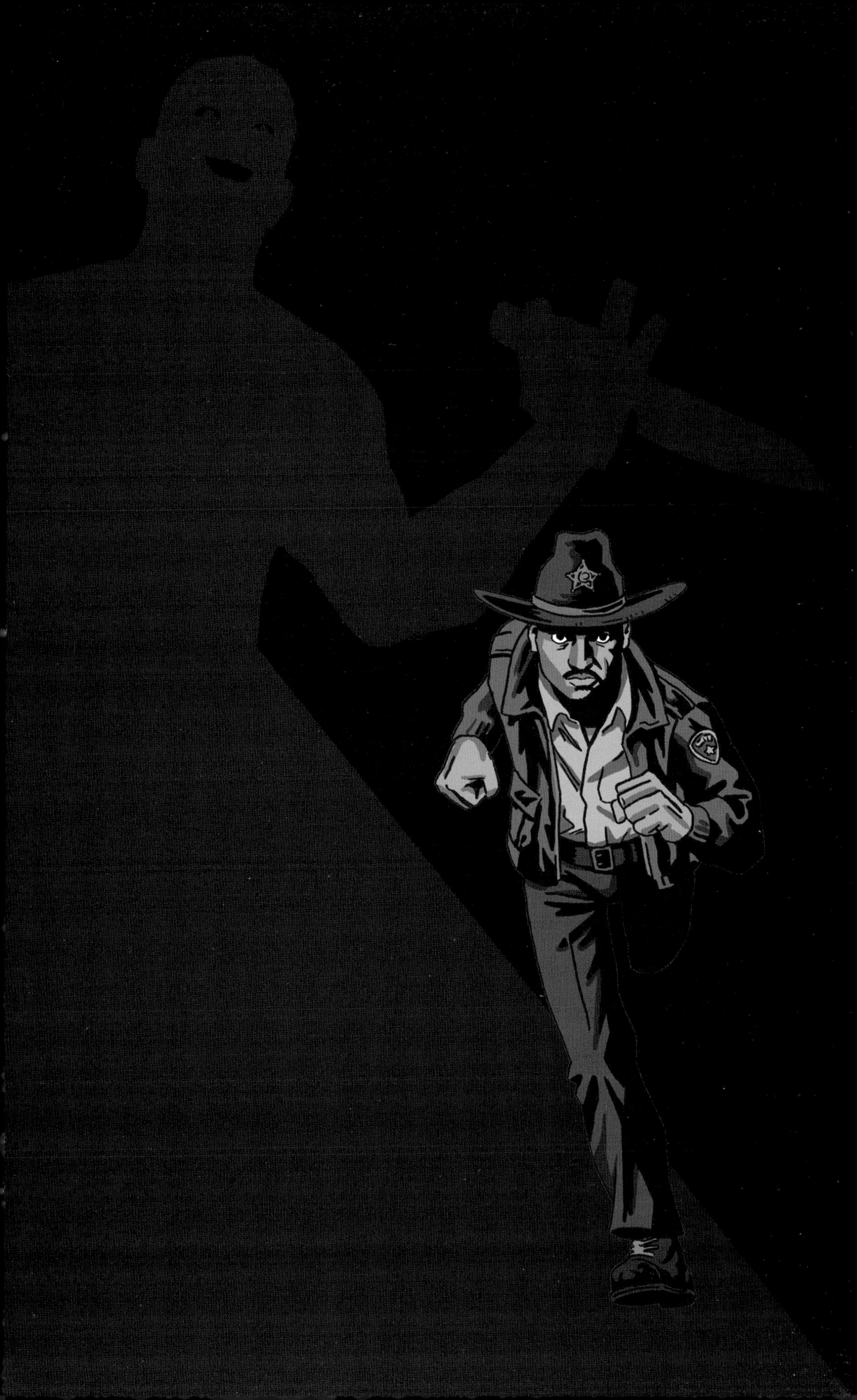

Chapter 7

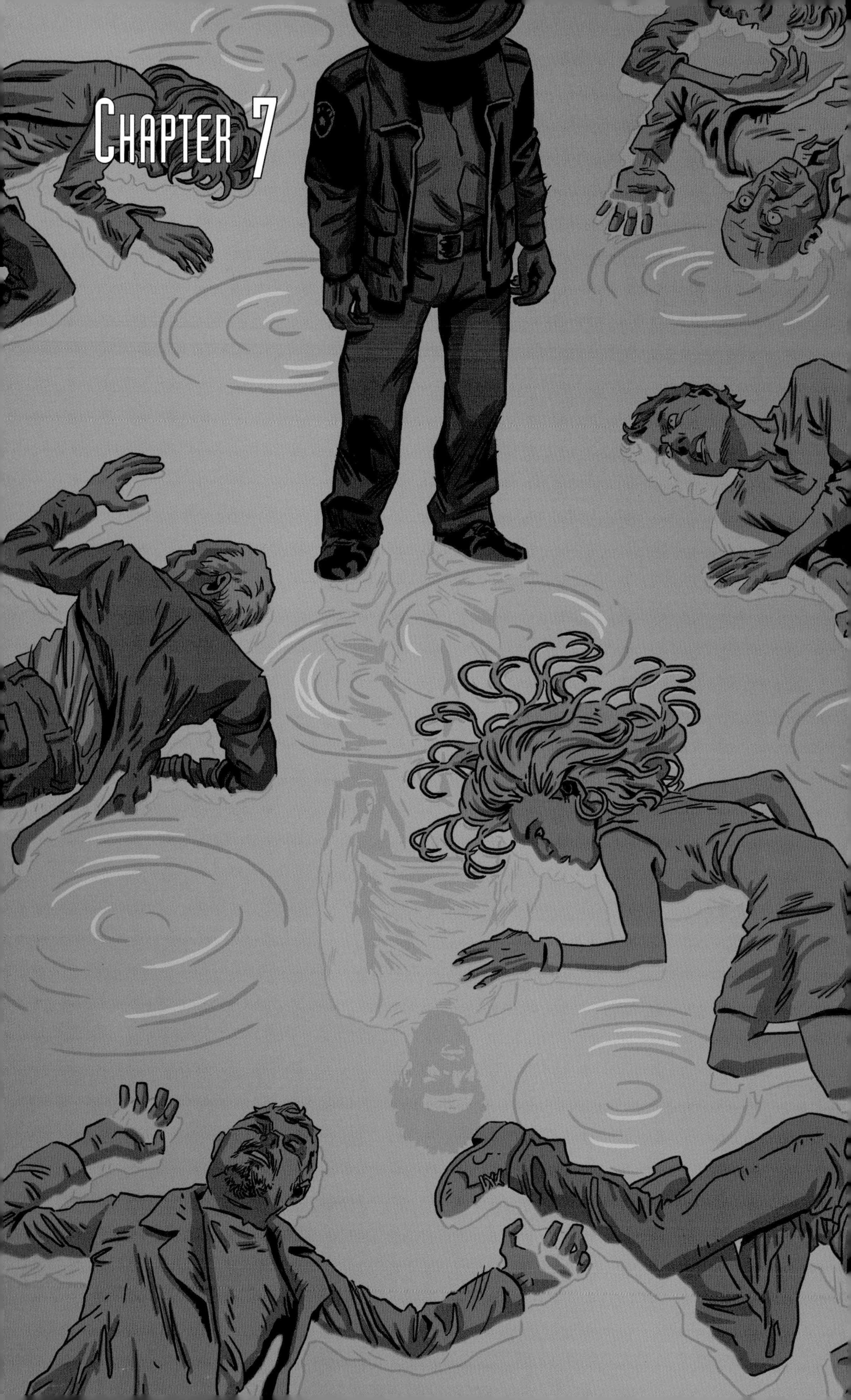

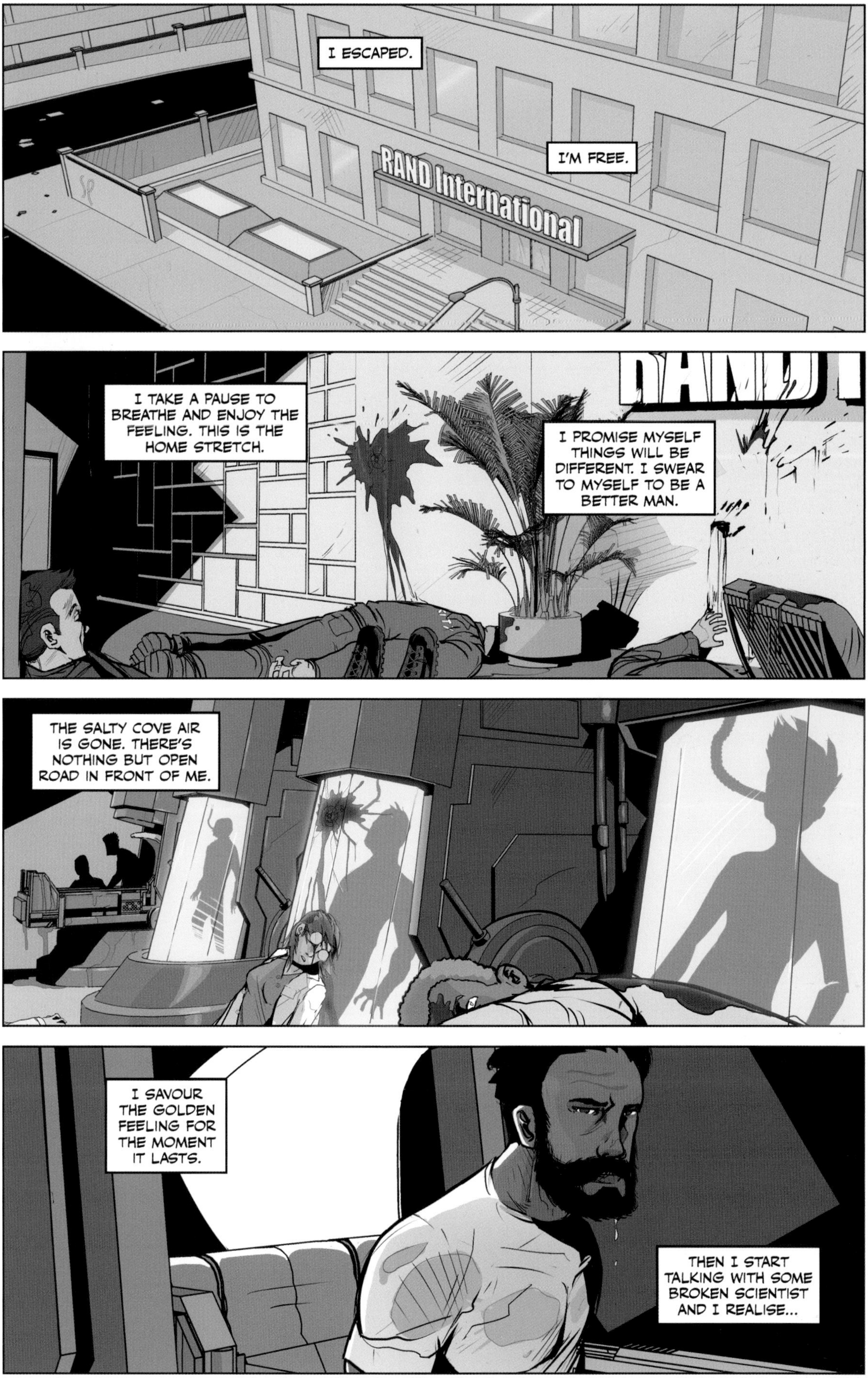
I ESCAPED.
I'M FREE.
RAND International
I TAKE A PAUSE TO BREATHE AND ENJOY THE FEELING. THIS IS THE HOME STRETCH.
I PROMISE MYSELF THINGS WILL BE DIFFERENT. I SWEAR TO MYSELF TO BE A BETTER MAN.
THE SALTY COVE AIR IS GONE. THERE'S NOTHING BUT OPEN ROAD IN FRONT OF ME.
I SAVOUR THE GOLDEN FEELING FOR THE MOMENT IT LASTS.
THEN I START TALKING WITH SOME BROKEN SCIENTIST AND I REALISE...

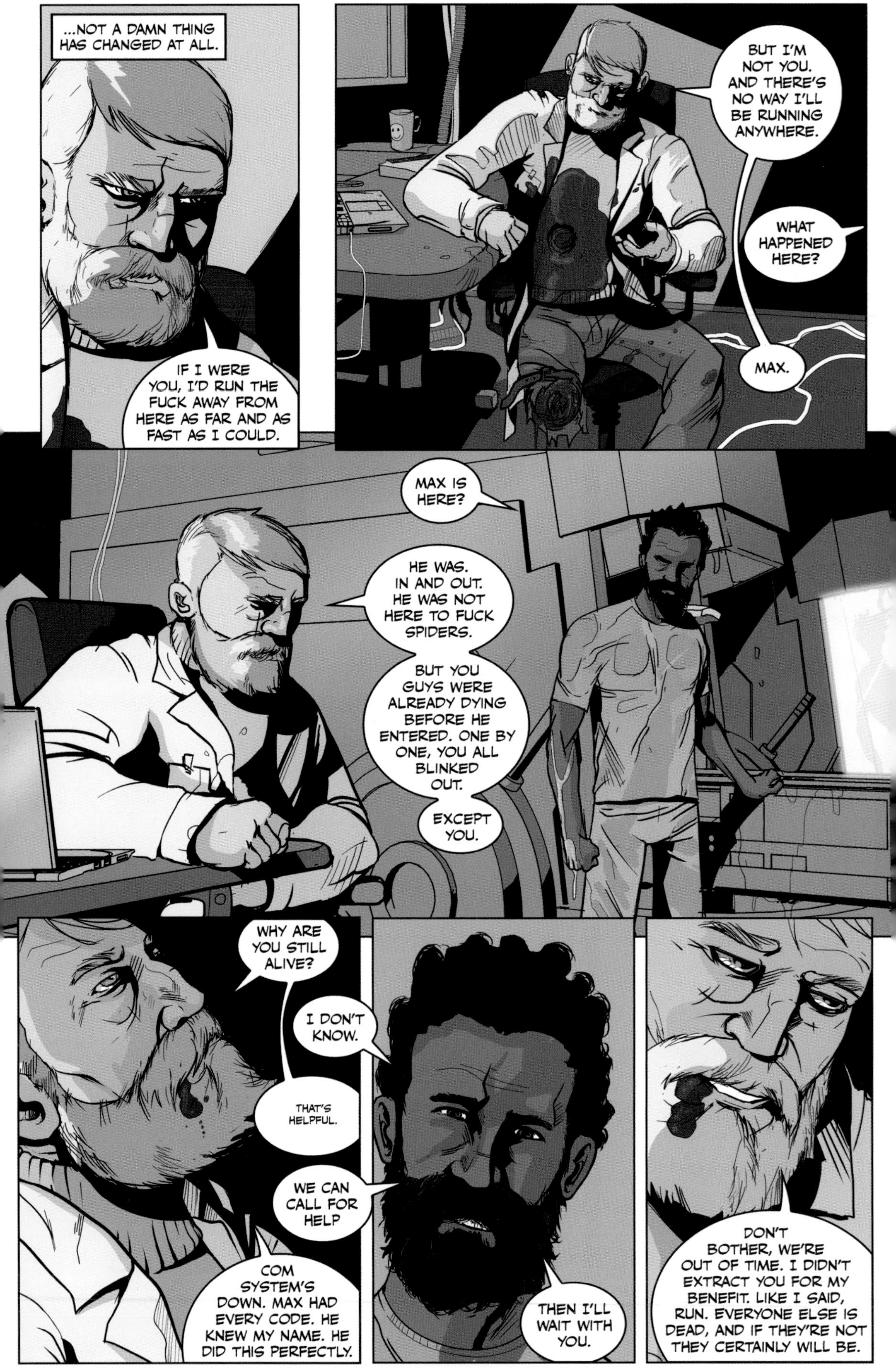

...NOT A DAMN THING HAS CHANGED AT ALL.
IF I WERE YOU, I'D RUN THE FUCK AWAY FROM HERE AS FAR AND AS FAST AS I COULD.
BUT I'M NOT YOU. AND THERE'S NO WAY I'LL BE RUNNING ANYWHERE.
WHAT HAPPENED HERE?
MAX.
MAX IS HERE?
HE WAS. IN AND OUT. HE WAS NOT HERE TO FUCK SPIDERS.
BUT YOU GUYS WERE ALREADY DYING BEFORE HE ENTERED. ONE BY ONE, YOU ALL BLINKED OUT.
EXCEPT YOU.
WHY ARE YOU STILL ALIVE?
I DON'T KNOW.
THAT'S HELPFUL.
WE CAN CALL FOR HELP
COM SYSTEM'S DOWN. MAX HAD EVERY CODE. HE KNEW MY NAME. HE DID THIS PERFECTLY.
THEN I'LL WAIT WITH YOU.
DON'T BOTHER, WE'RE OUT OF TIME. I DIDN'T EXTRACT YOU FOR MY BENEFIT. LIKE I SAID, RUN. EVERYONE ELSE IS DEAD, AND IF THEY'RE NOT THEY CERTAINLY WILL BE.

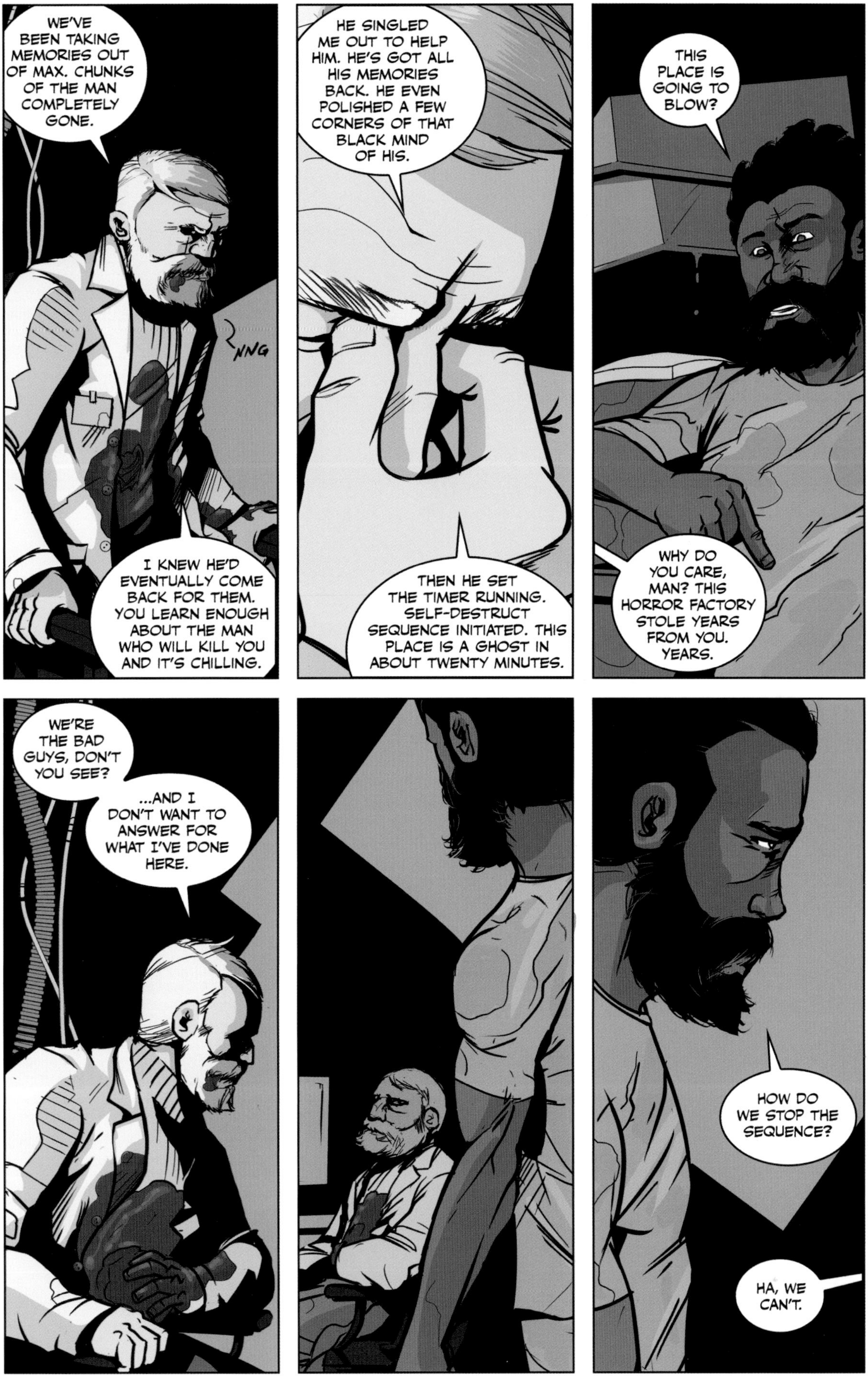
WE'VE BEEN TAKING MEMORIES OUT OF MAX. CHUNKS OF THE MAN COMPLETELY GONE.
NNG
I KNEW HE'D EVENTUALLY COME BACK FOR THEM. YOU LEARN ENOUGH ABOUT THE MAN WHO WILL KILL YOU AND IT'S CHILLING.
HE SINGLED ME OUT TO HELP HIM. HE'S GOT ALL HIS MEMORIES BACK. HE EVEN POLISHED A FEW CORNERS OF THAT BLACK MIND OF HIS.
THEN HE SET THE TIMER RUNNING. SELF-DESTRUCT SEQUENCE INITIATED. THIS PLACE IS A GHOST IN ABOUT TWENTY MINUTES.
THIS PLACE IS GOING TO BLOW?
WHY DO YOU CARE, MAN? THIS HORROR FACTORY STOLE YEARS FROM YOU. YEARS.
WE'RE THE BAD GUYS, DON'T YOU SEE?
...AND I DON'T WANT TO ANSWER FOR WHAT I'VE DONE HERE.
HOW DO WE STOP THE SEQUENCE?
HA, WE CAN'T.

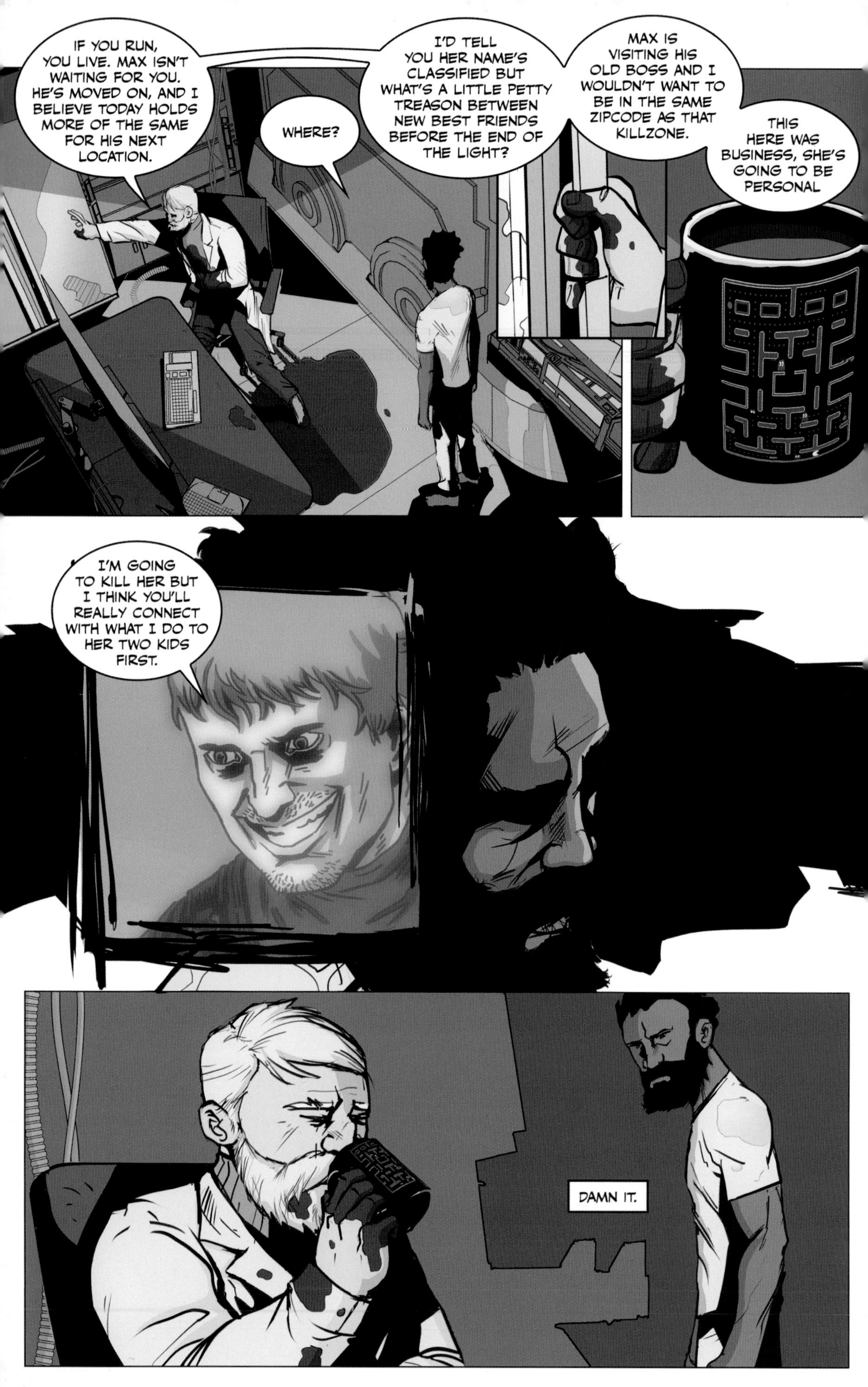
IF YOU RUN, YOU LIVE. MAX ISN'T WAITING FOR YOU. HE'S MOVED ON, AND I BELIEVE TODAY HOLDS MORE OF THE SAME FOR HIS NEXT LOCATION.
WHERE?
I'D TELL YOU HER NAME'S CLASSIFIED BUT WHAT'S A LITTLE PETTY TREASON BETWEEN NEW BEST FRIENDS BEFORE THE END OF THE LIGHT?
MAX IS VISITING HIS OLD BOSS AND I WOULDN'T WANT TO BE IN THE SAME ZIPCODE AS THAT KILLZONE.
THIS HERE WAS BUSINESS, SHE'S GOING TO BE PERSONAL
I'M GOING TO KILL HER BUT I THINK YOU'LL REALLY CONNECT WITH WHAT I DO TO HER TWO KIDS FIRST.
DAMN IT.

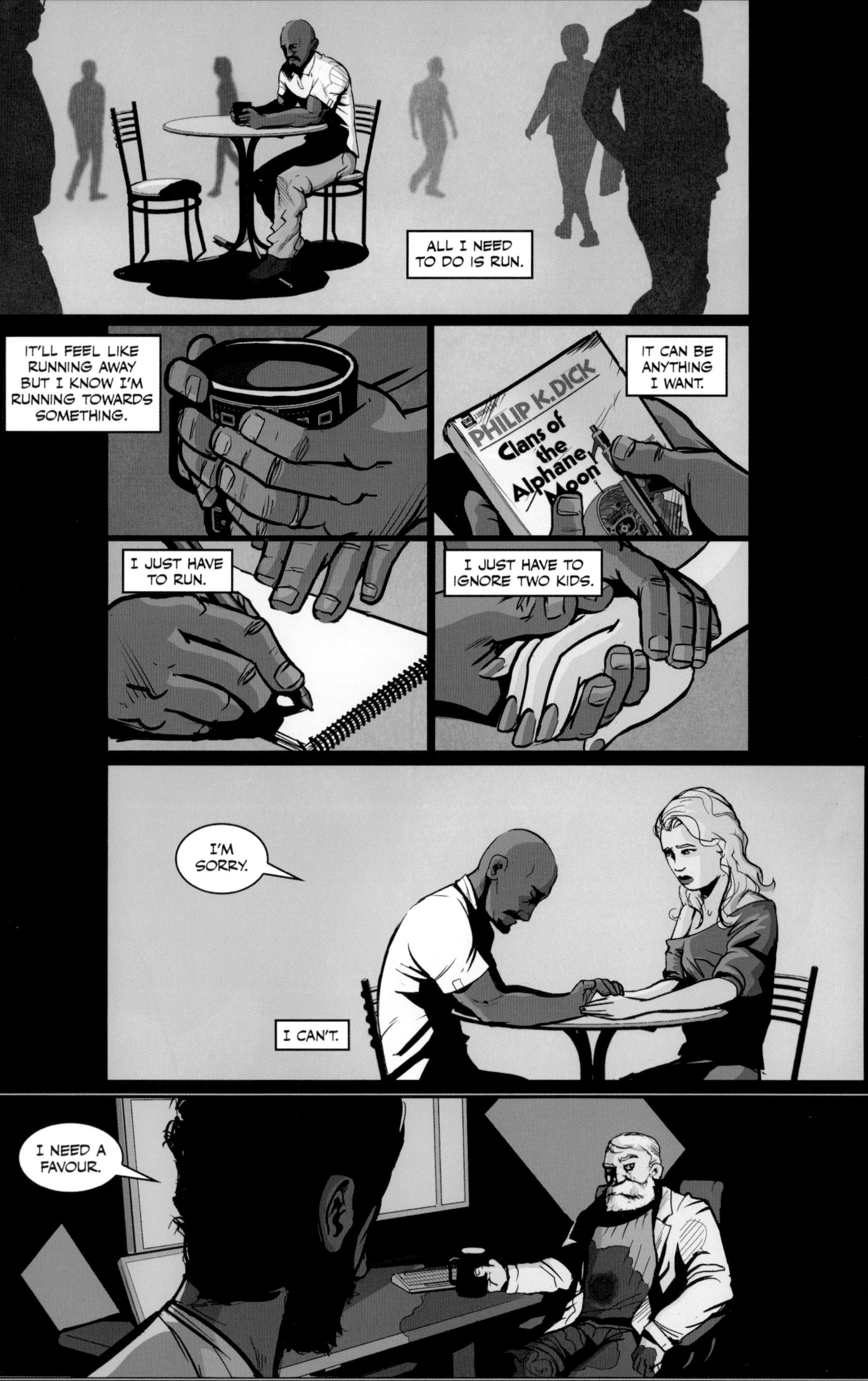
ALL I NEED TO DO IS RUN.
IT'LL FEEL LIKE RUNNING AWAY BUT I KNOW I'M RUNNING TOWARDS SOMETHING.
IT CAN BE ANYTHING I WANT.
PHILIP K. DICK
Clans of the Alphane Moon
I JUST HAVE TO RUN.
I JUST HAVE TO IGNORE TWO KIDS.
I'M SORRY.
I CAN'T.
I NEED A FAVOUR.

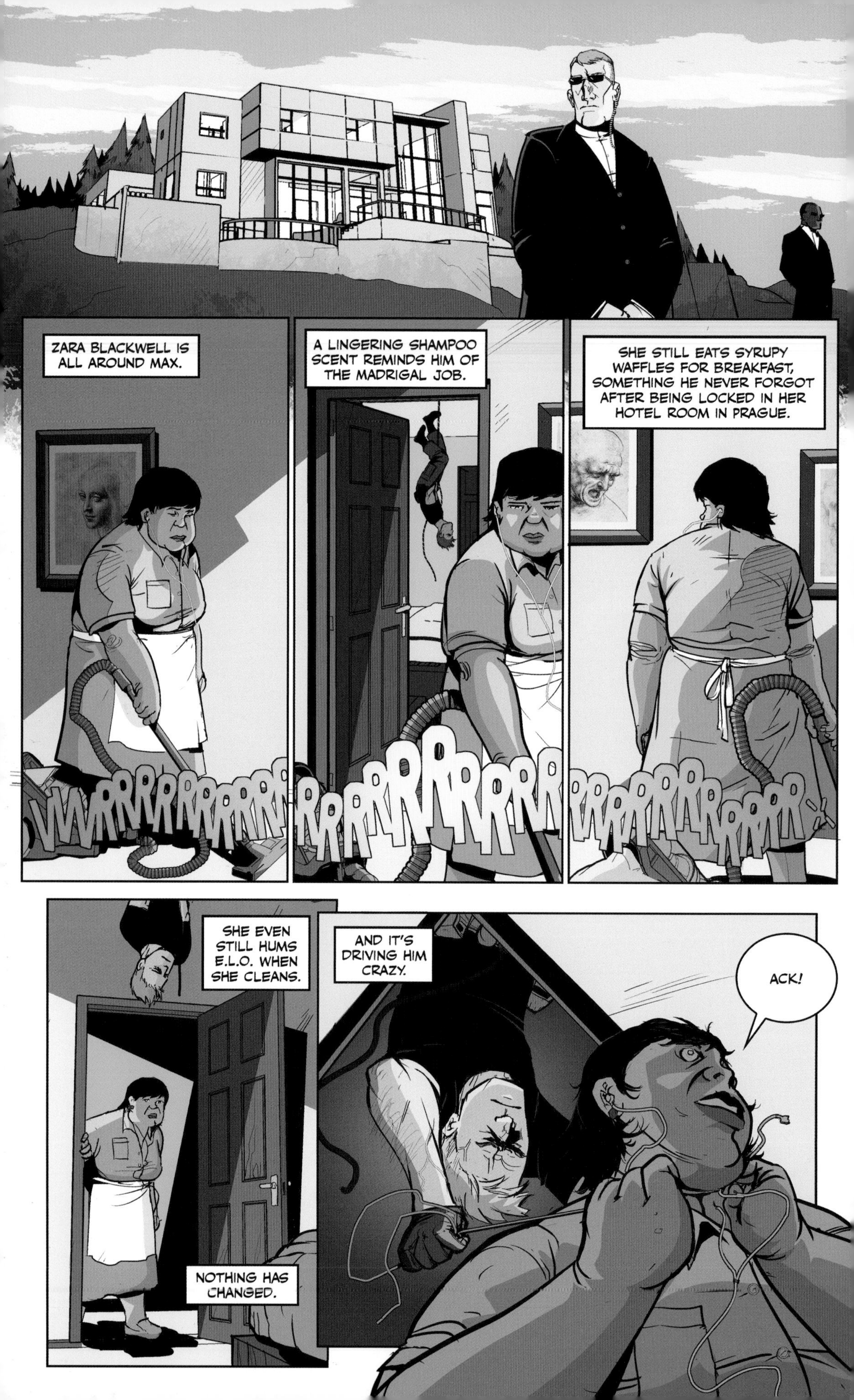
ZARA BLACKWELL IS ALL AROUND MAX.
VWRRRRRRRRRRR
A LINGERING SHAMPOO SCENT REMINDS HIM OF THE MADRIGAL JOB.
RRRRRRRRRRRRR
SHE STILL EATS SYRUPY WAFFLES FOR BREAKFAST, SOMETHING HE NEVER FORGOT AFTER BEING LOCKED IN HER HOTEL ROOM IN PRAGUE.
RRRRRRRRRRRRR-
SHE EVEN STILL HUMS E.L.O. WHEN SHE CLEANS.
NOTHING HAS CHANGED.
AND IT'S DRIVING HIM CRAZY.
ACK!

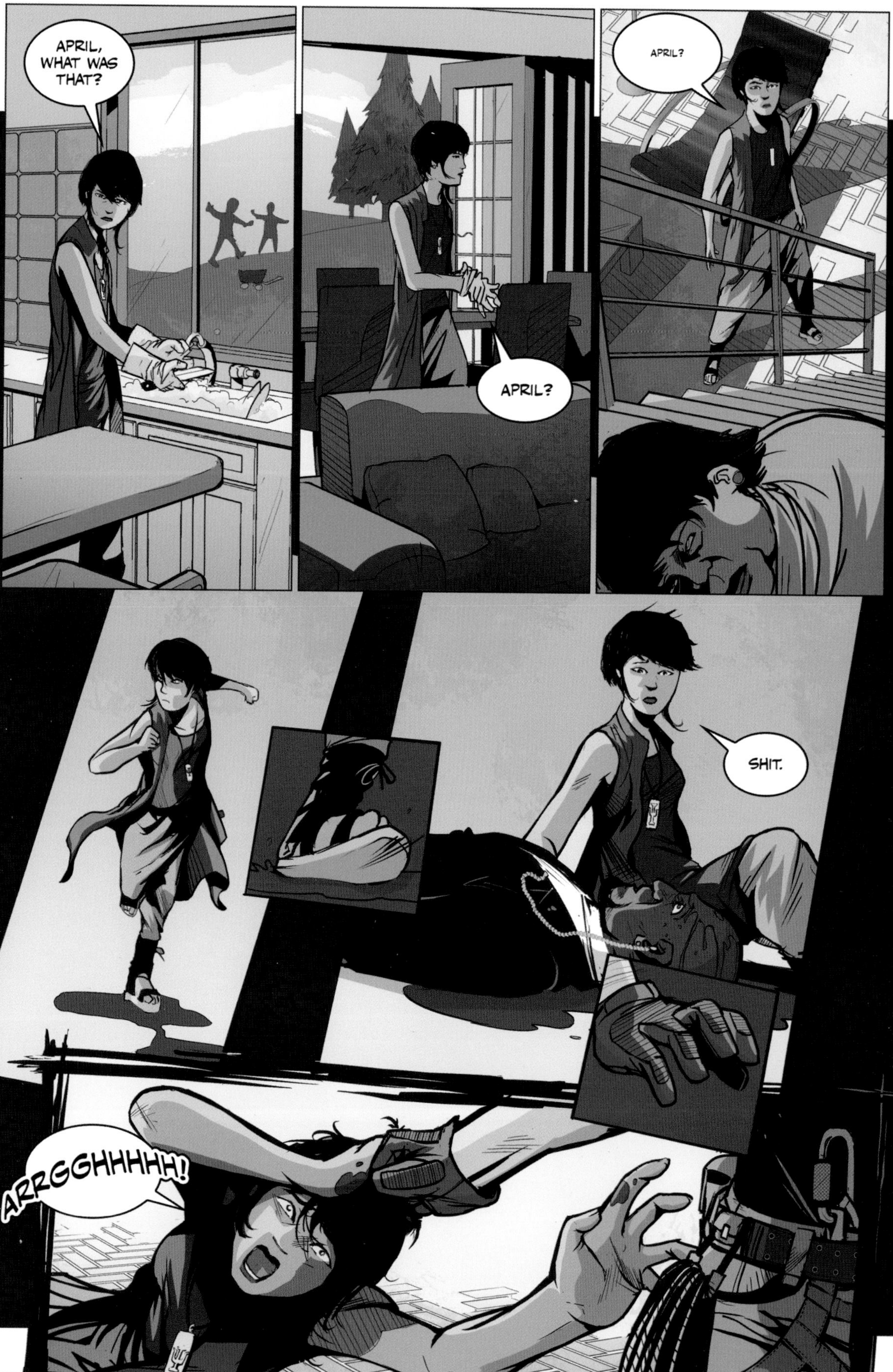
APRIL, WHAT WAS THAT?
APRIL?
APRIL?
SHIT.
ARRGGHHHHH!

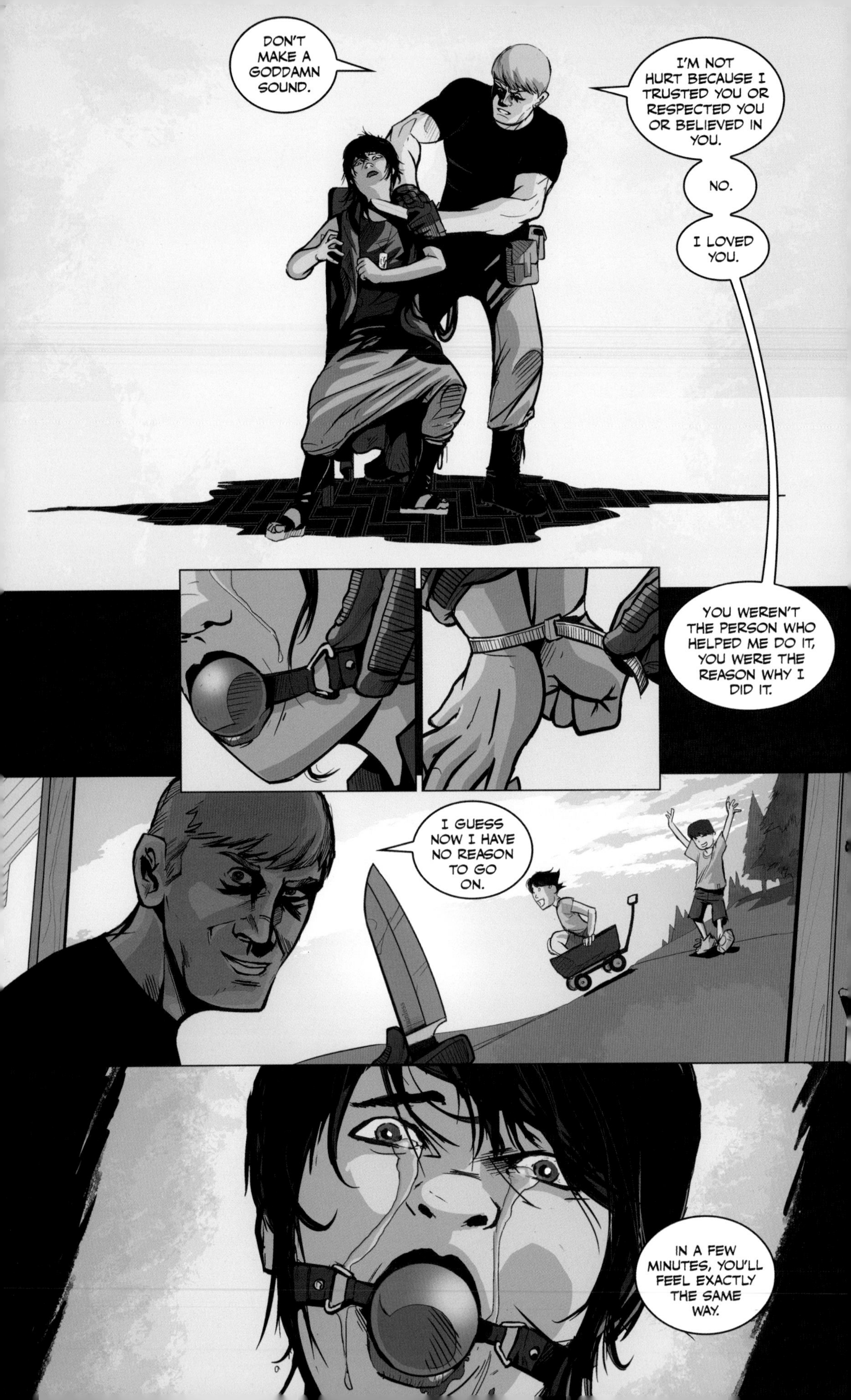
DON'T MAKE A GODDAMN SOUND.
I'M NOT HURT BECAUSE I TRUSTED YOU OR RESPECTED YOU OR BELIEVED IN YOU.
NO.
I LOVED YOU.
YOU WEREN'T THE PERSON WHO HELPED ME DO IT, YOU WERE THE REASON WHY I DID IT.
I GUESS NOW I HAVE NO REASON TO GO ON.
IN A FEW MINUTES, YOU'LL FEEL EXACTLY THE SAME WAY.

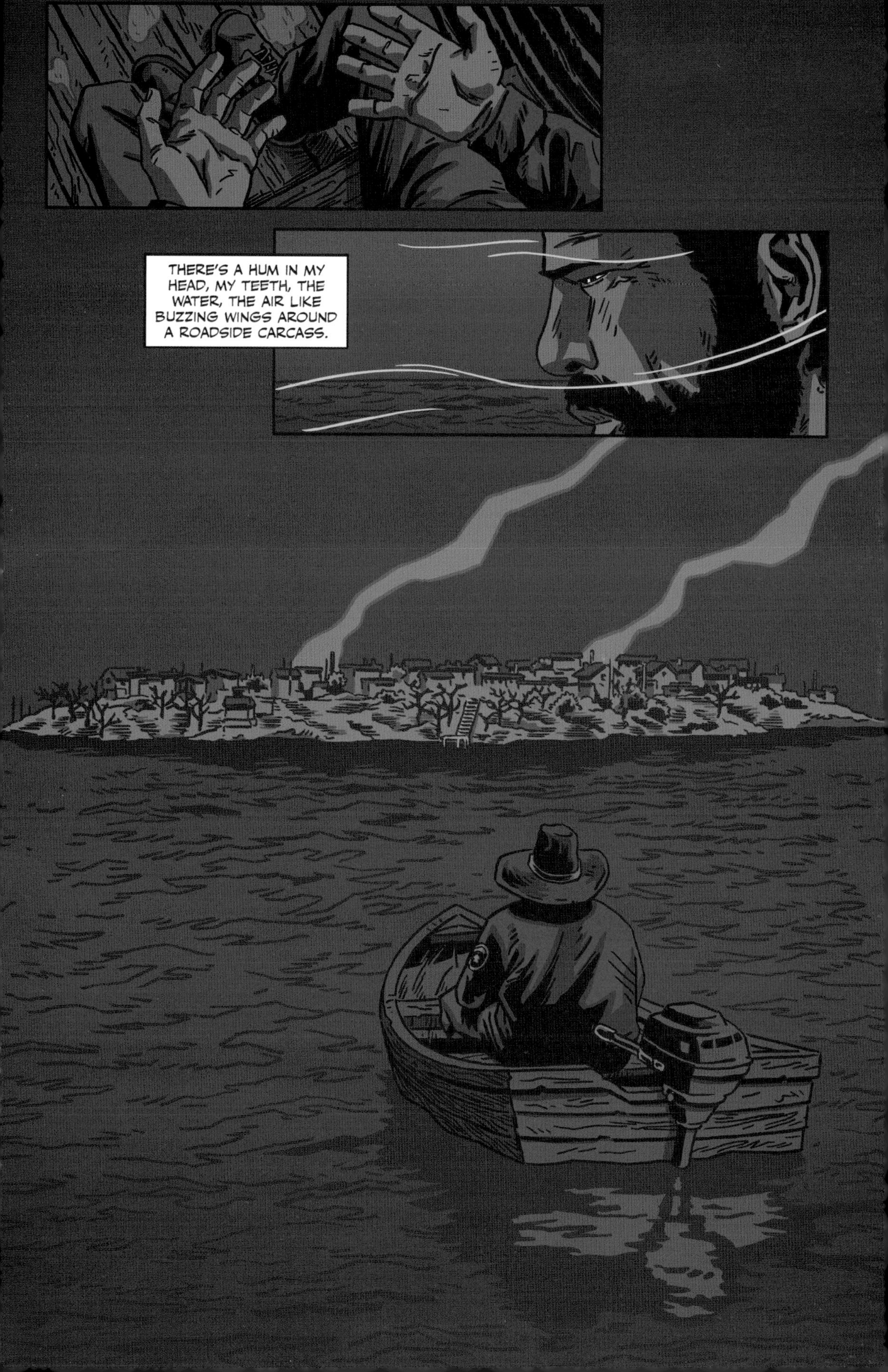
THERE'S A HUM IN MY HEAD, MY TEETH, THE WATER, THE AIR LIKE BUZZING WINGS AROUND A ROADSIDE CARCASS.

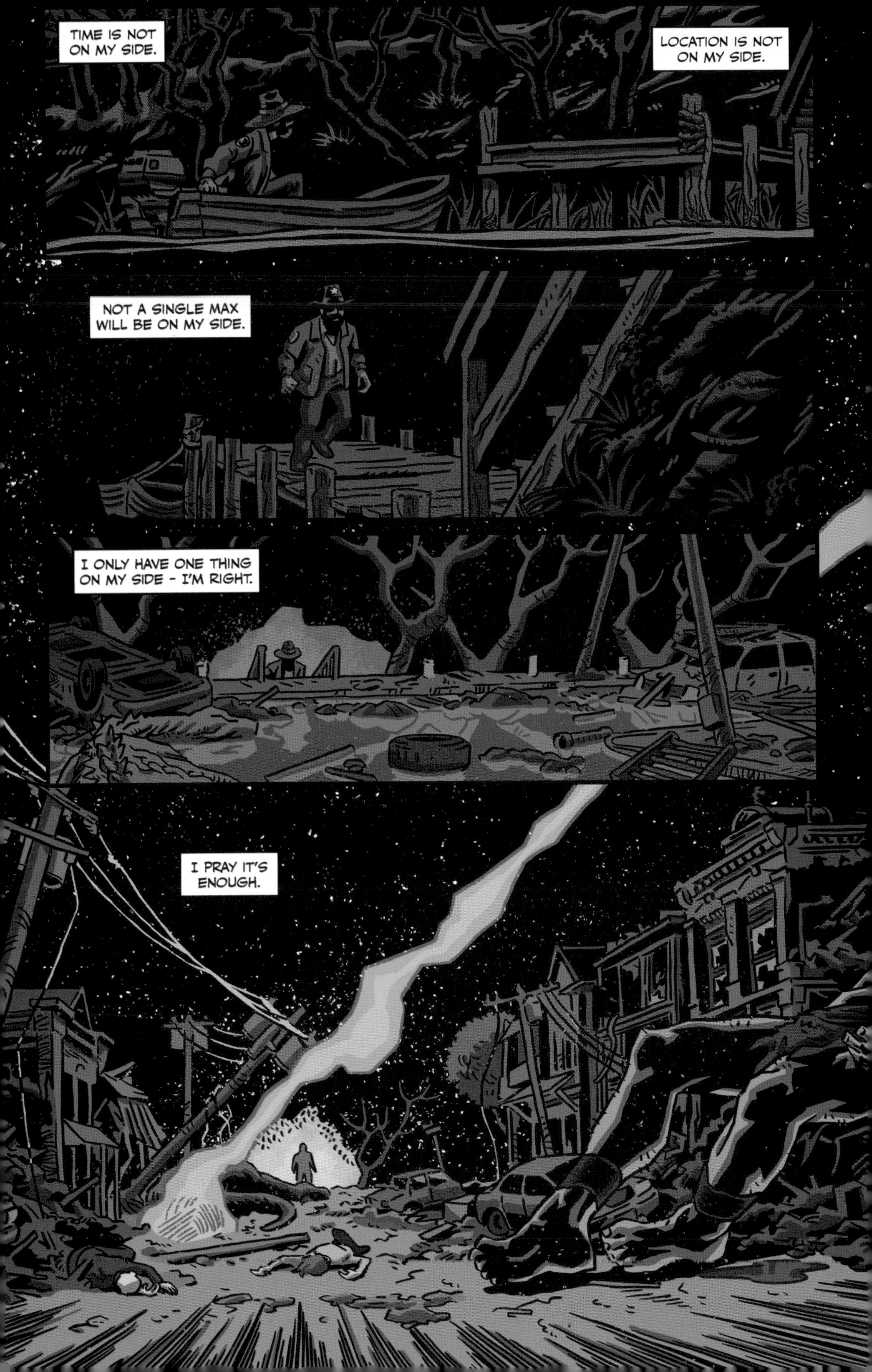
TIME IS NOT ON MY SIDE.
LOCATION IS NOT ON MY SIDE.
NOT A SINGLE MAX WILL BE ON MY SIDE.
I ONLY HAVE ONE THING ON MY SIDE - I'M RIGHT.
I PRAY IT'S ENOUGH.

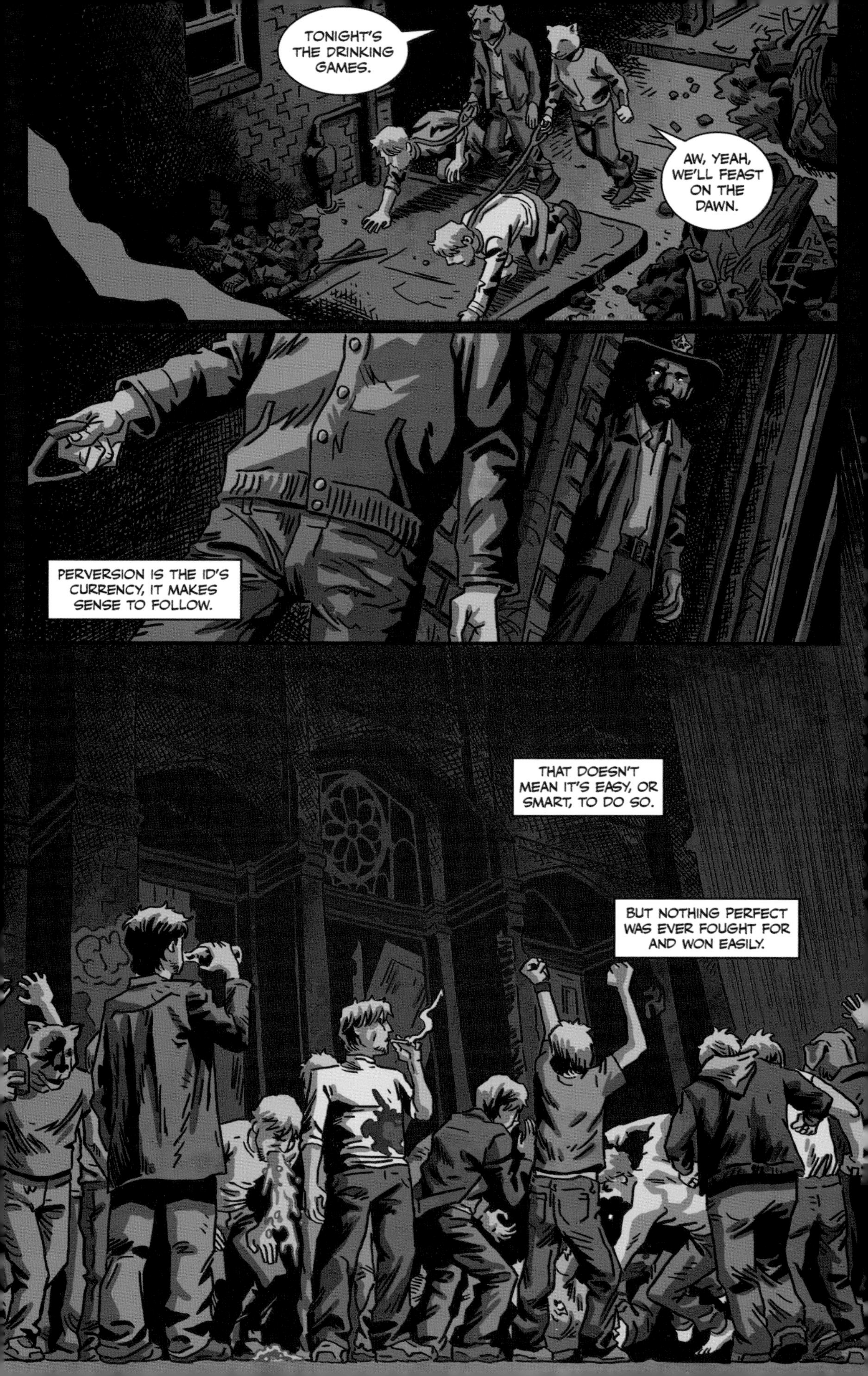
TONIGHT'S THE DRINKING GAMES.
AW, YEAH, WE'LL FEAST ON THE DAWN.
PERVERSION IS THE ID'S CURRENCY, IT MAKES SENSE TO FOLLOW.
THAT DOESN'T MEAN IT'S EASY, OR SMART, TO DO SO.
BUT NOTHING PERFECT WAS EVER FOUGHT FOR AND WON EASILY.

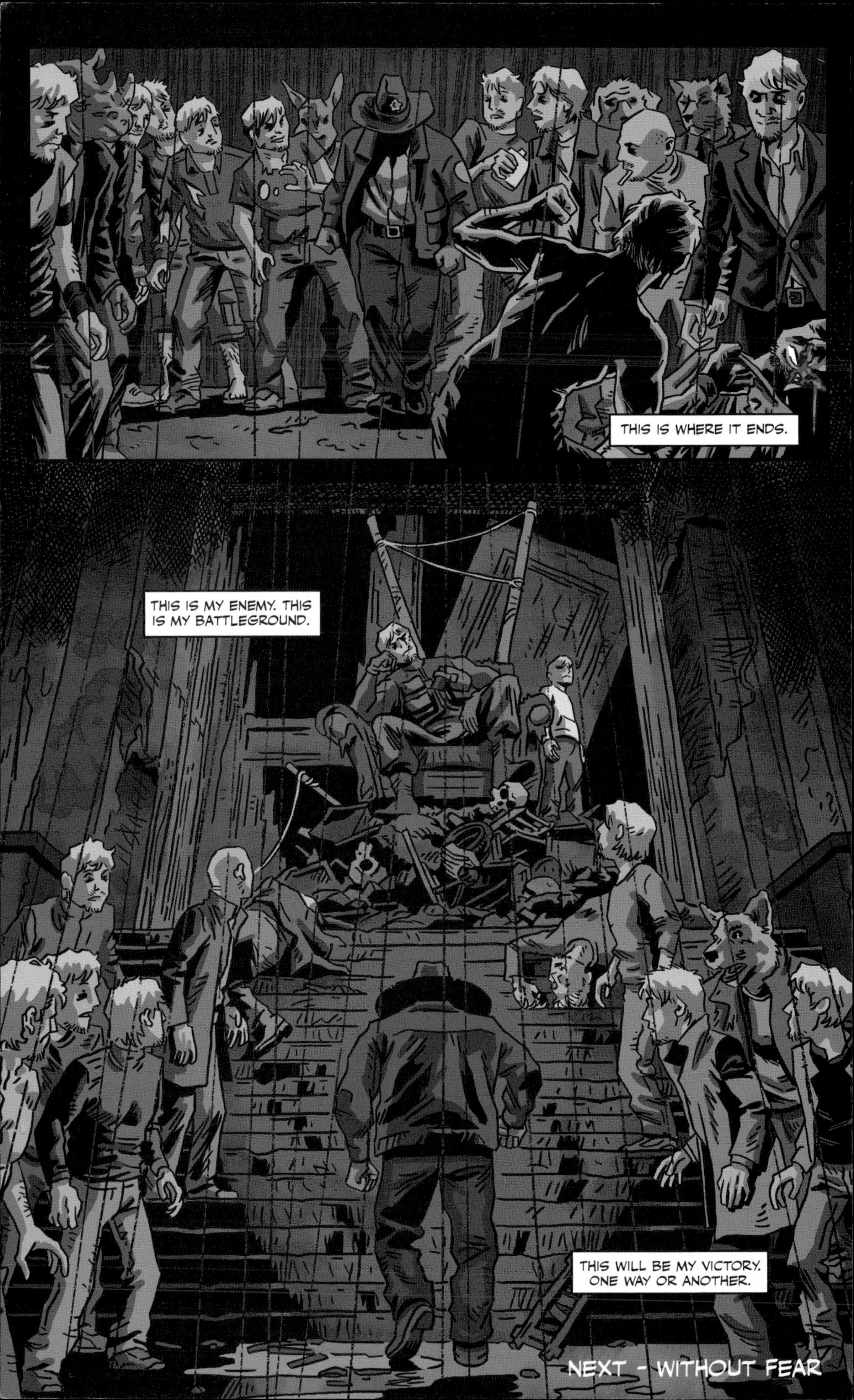
THIS IS WHERE IT ENDS.
THIS IS MY ENEMY. THIS IS MY BATTLEGROUND.
THIS WILL BE MY VICTORY. ONE WAY OR ANOTHER.
NEXT - WITHOUT FEAR

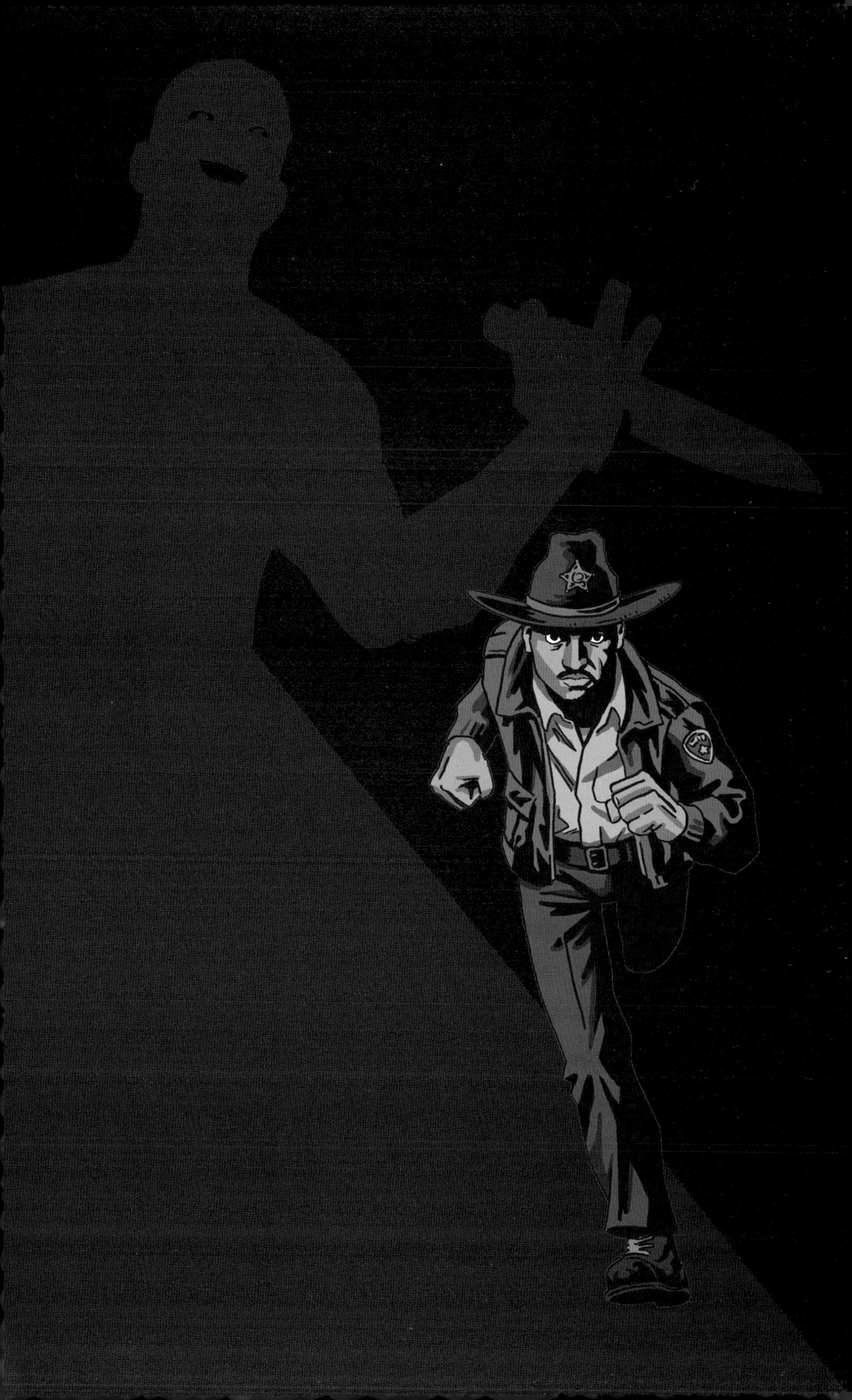

CHAPTER 8

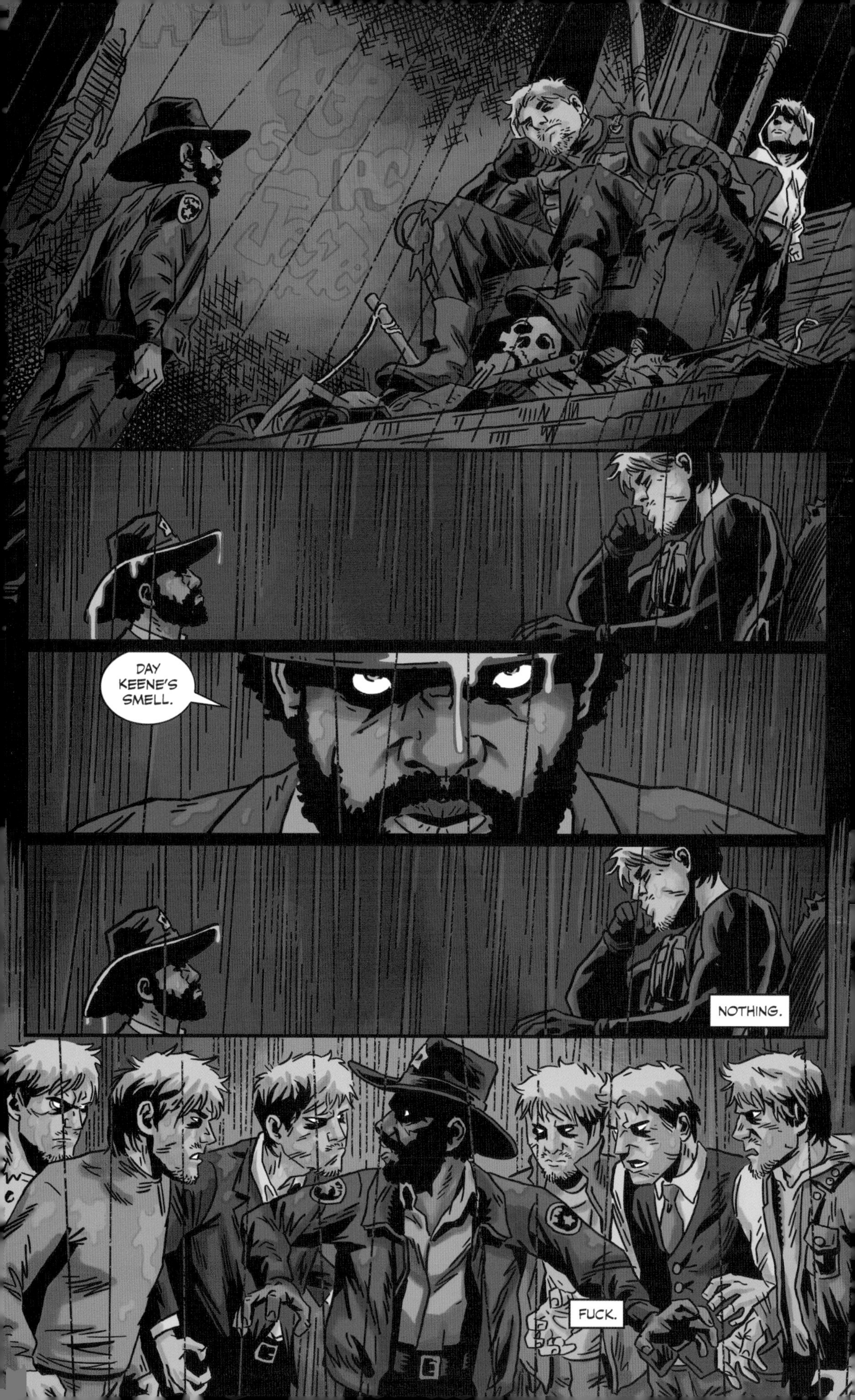
DAY KEENE'S SMELL.
NOTHING.
FUCK.

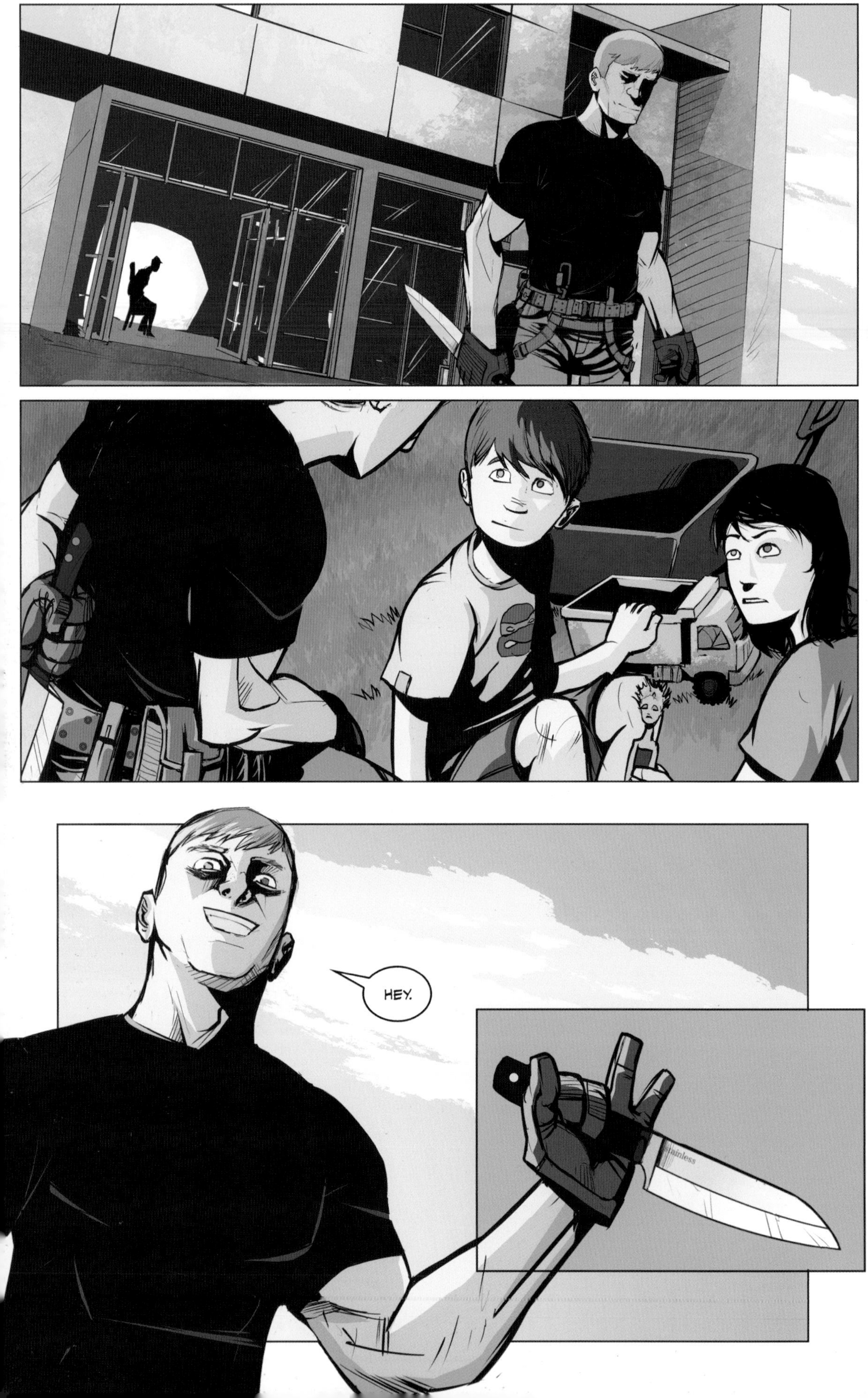
HEY.
Stainless

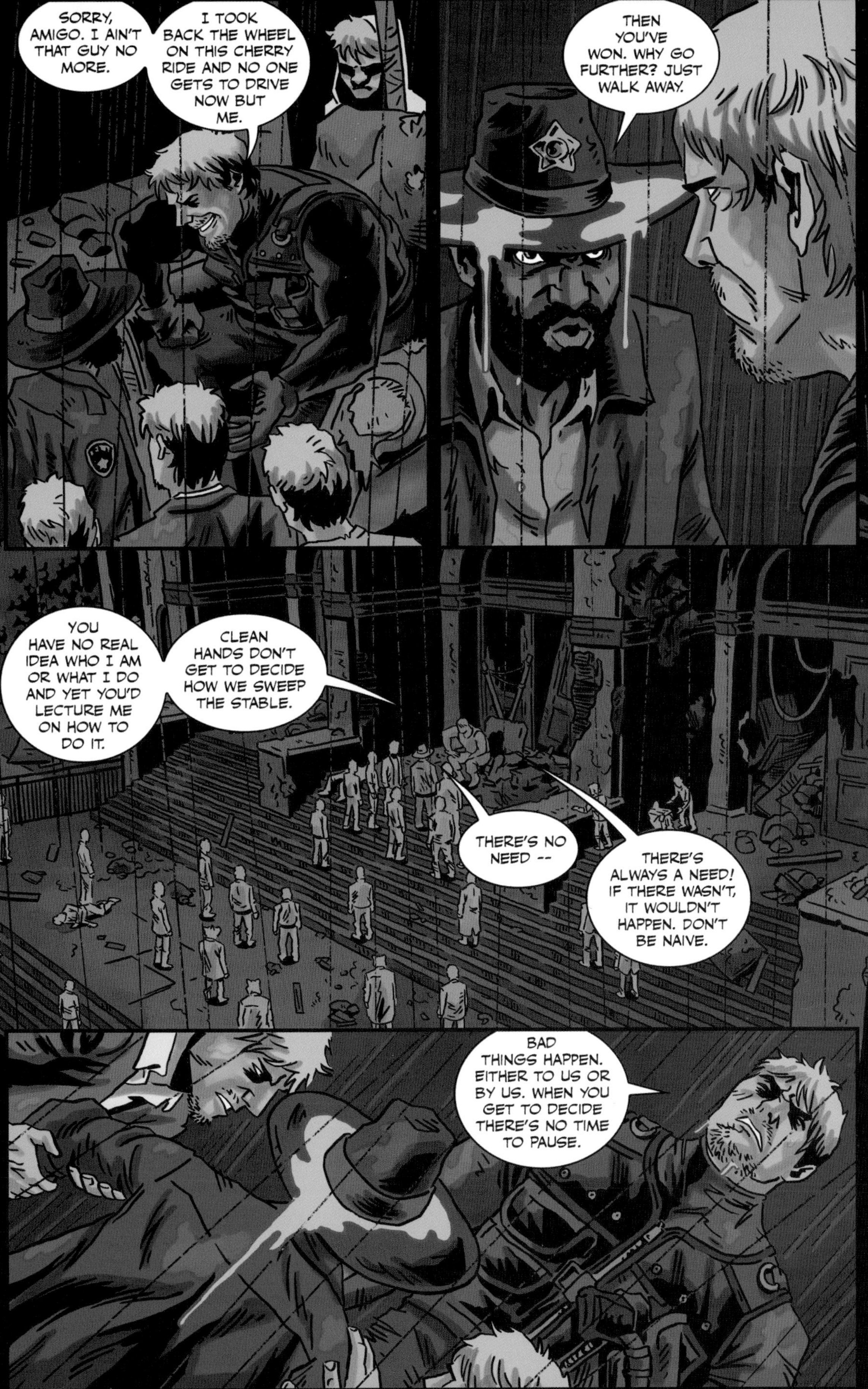
SORRY, AMIGO. I AIN'T THAT GUY NO MORE.
I TOOK BACK THE WHEEL ON THIS CHERRY RIDE AND NO ONE GETS TO DRIVE NOW BUT ME.
THEN YOU'VE WON. WHY GO FURTHER? JUST WALK AWAY.
YOU HAVE NO REAL IDEA WHO I AM OR WHAT I DO AND YET YOU'D LECTURE ME ON HOW TO DO IT.
CLEAN HANDS DON'T GET TO DECIDE HOW WE SWEEP THE STABLE.
THERE'S NO NEED --
THERE'S ALWAYS A NEED! IF THERE WASN'T, IT WOULDN'T HAPPEN. DON'T BE NAIVE.
BAD THINGS HAPPEN. EITHER TO US OR BY US. WHEN YOU GET TO DECIDE THERE'S NO TIME TO PAUSE.

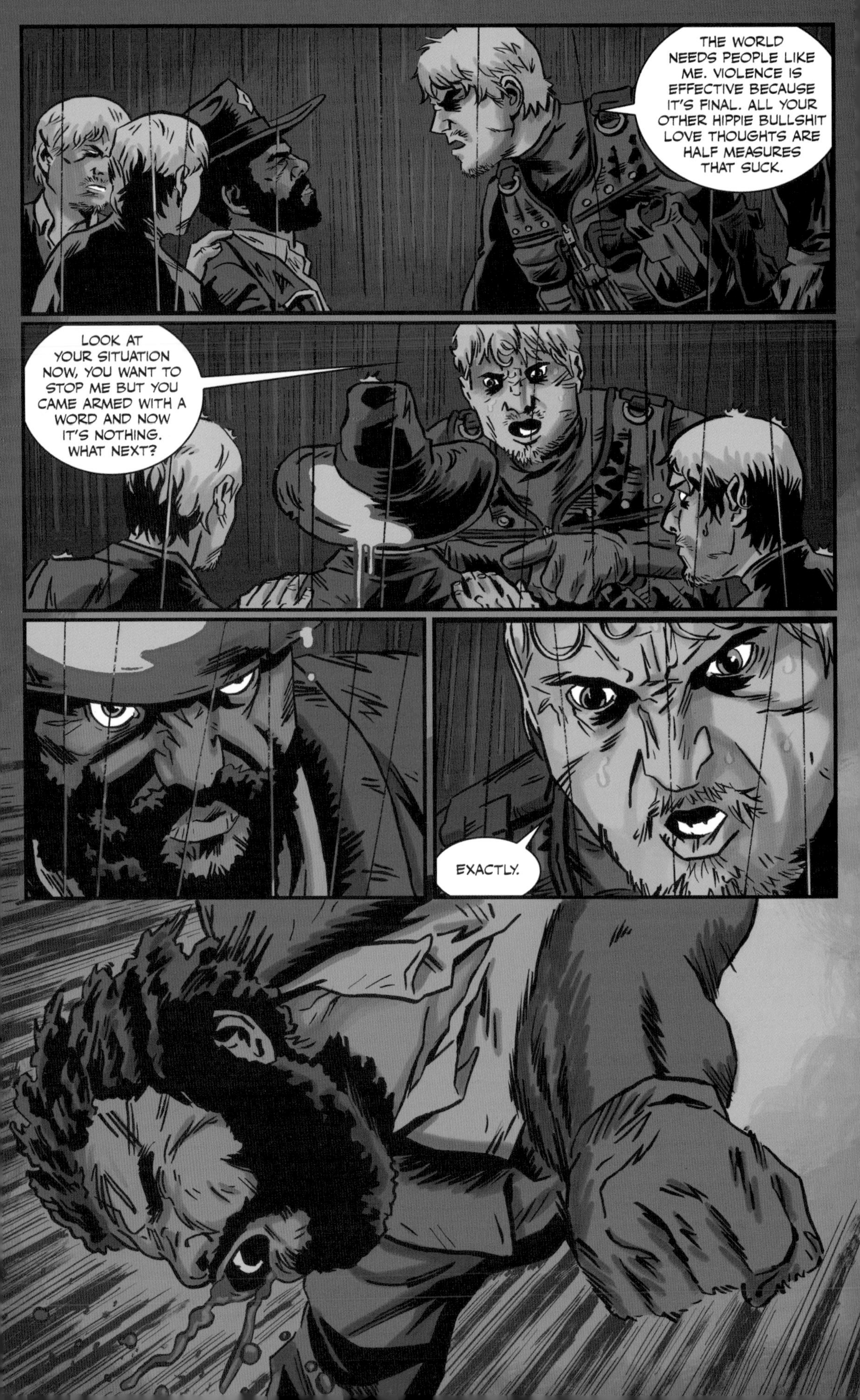
THE WORLD NEEDS PEOPLE LIKE ME. VIOLENCE IS EFFECTIVE BECAUSE IT'S FINAL. ALL YOUR OTHER HIPPIE BULLSHIT LOVE THOUGHTS ARE HALF MEASURES THAT SUCK.
LOOK AT YOUR SITUATION NOW, YOU WANT TO STOP ME BUT YOU CAME ARMED WITH A WORD AND NOW IT'S NOTHING. WHAT NEXT?
EXACTLY.

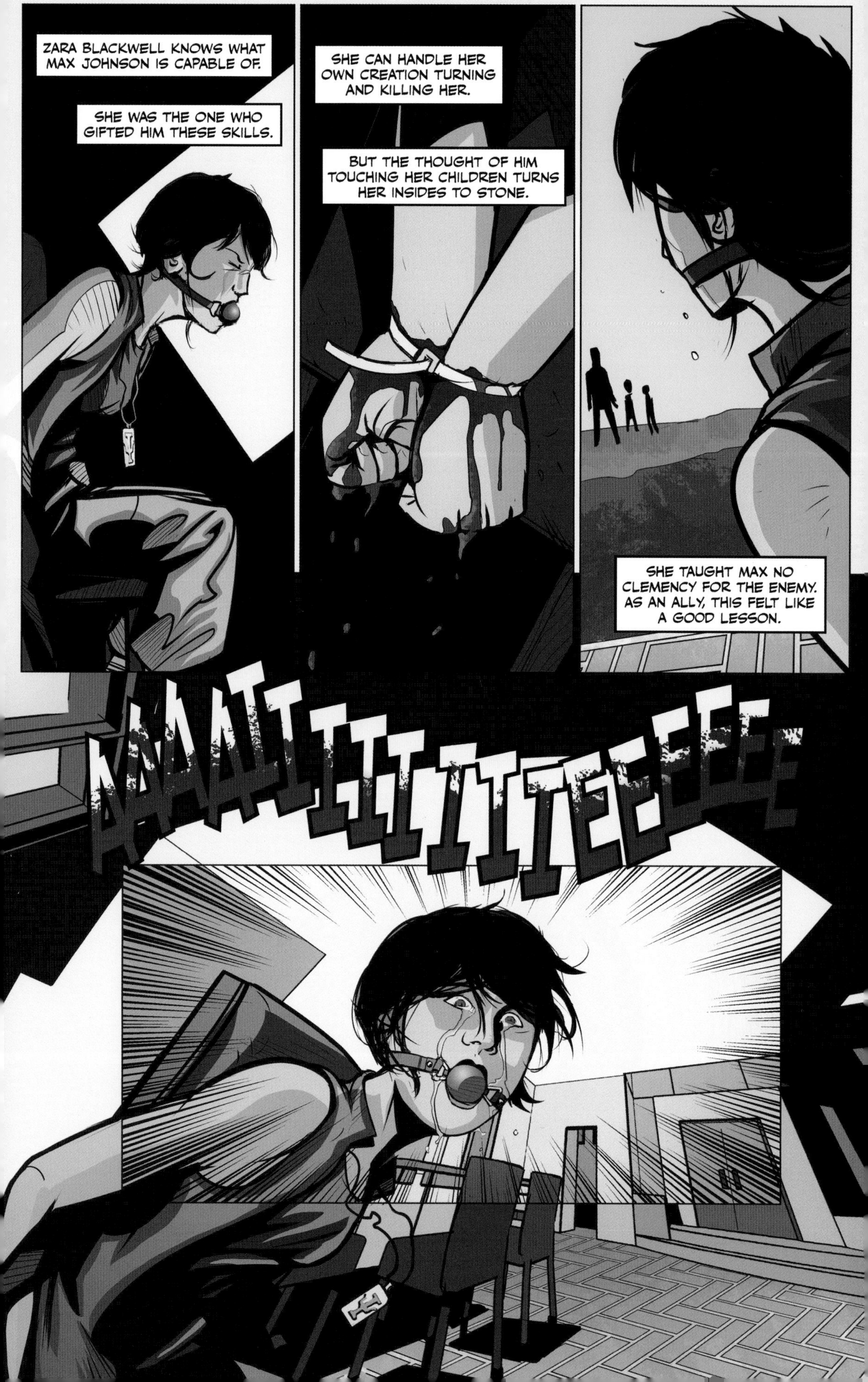
ZARA BLACKWELL KNOWS WHAT MAX JOHNSON IS CAPABLE OF.
SHE WAS THE ONE WHO GIFTED HIM THESE SKILLS.
SHE CAN HANDLE HER OWN CREATION TURNING AND KILLING HER.
BUT THE THOUGHT OF HIM TOUCHING HER CHILDREN TURNS HER INSIDES TO STONE.
SHE TAUGHT MAX NO CLEMENCY FOR THE ENEMY. AS AN ALLY, THIS FELT LIKE A GOOD LESSON.
AAAIIIIIEEEE

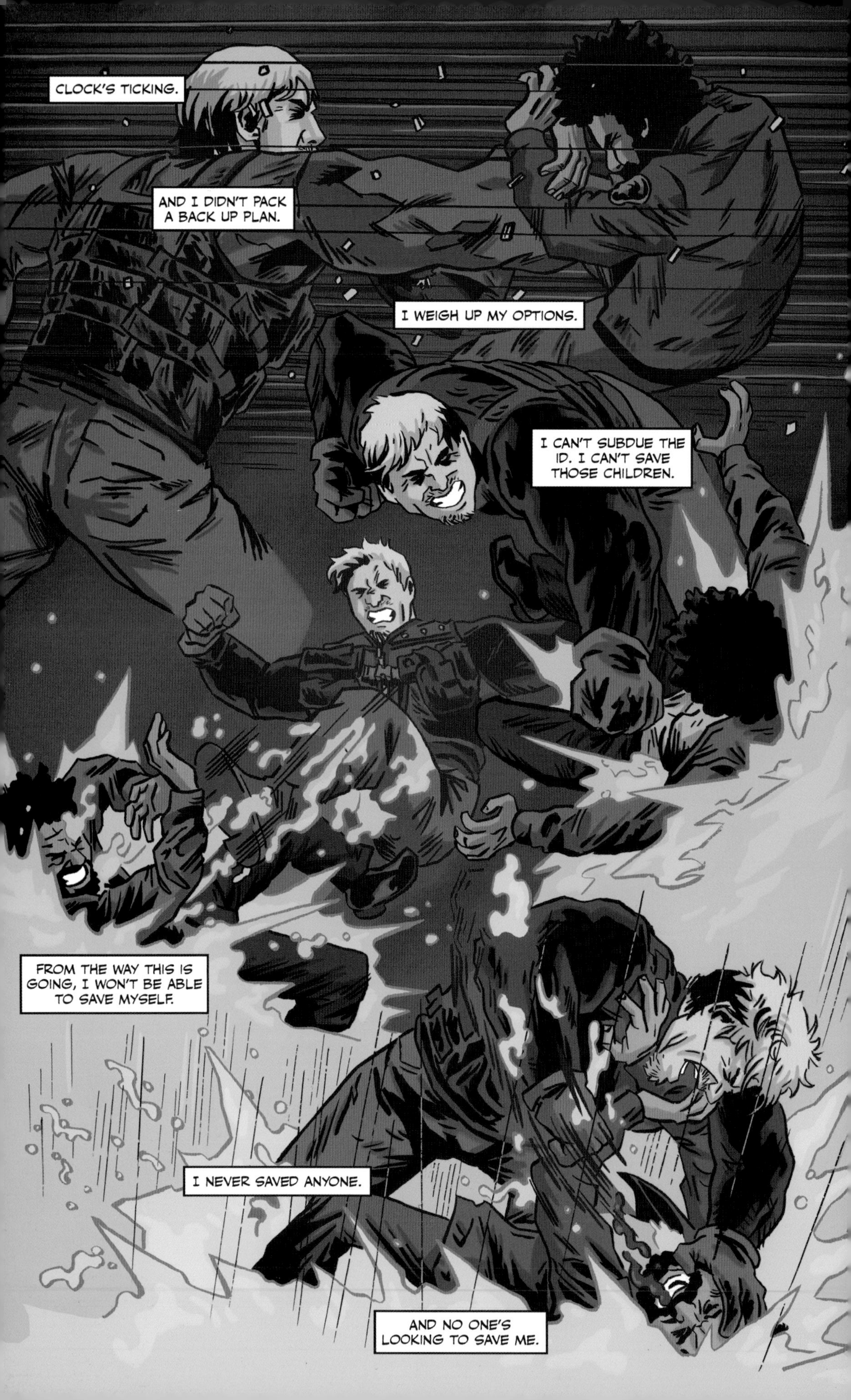
CLOCK'S TICKING.
AND I DIDN'T PACK A BACK UP PLAN.
I WEIGH UP MY OPTIONS.
I CAN'T SUBDUE THE ID. I CAN'T SAVE THOSE CHILDREN.
FROM THE WAY THIS IS GOING, I WON'T BE ABLE TO SAVE MYSELF.
I NEVER SAVED ANYONE.
AND NO ONE'S LOOKING TO SAVE ME.

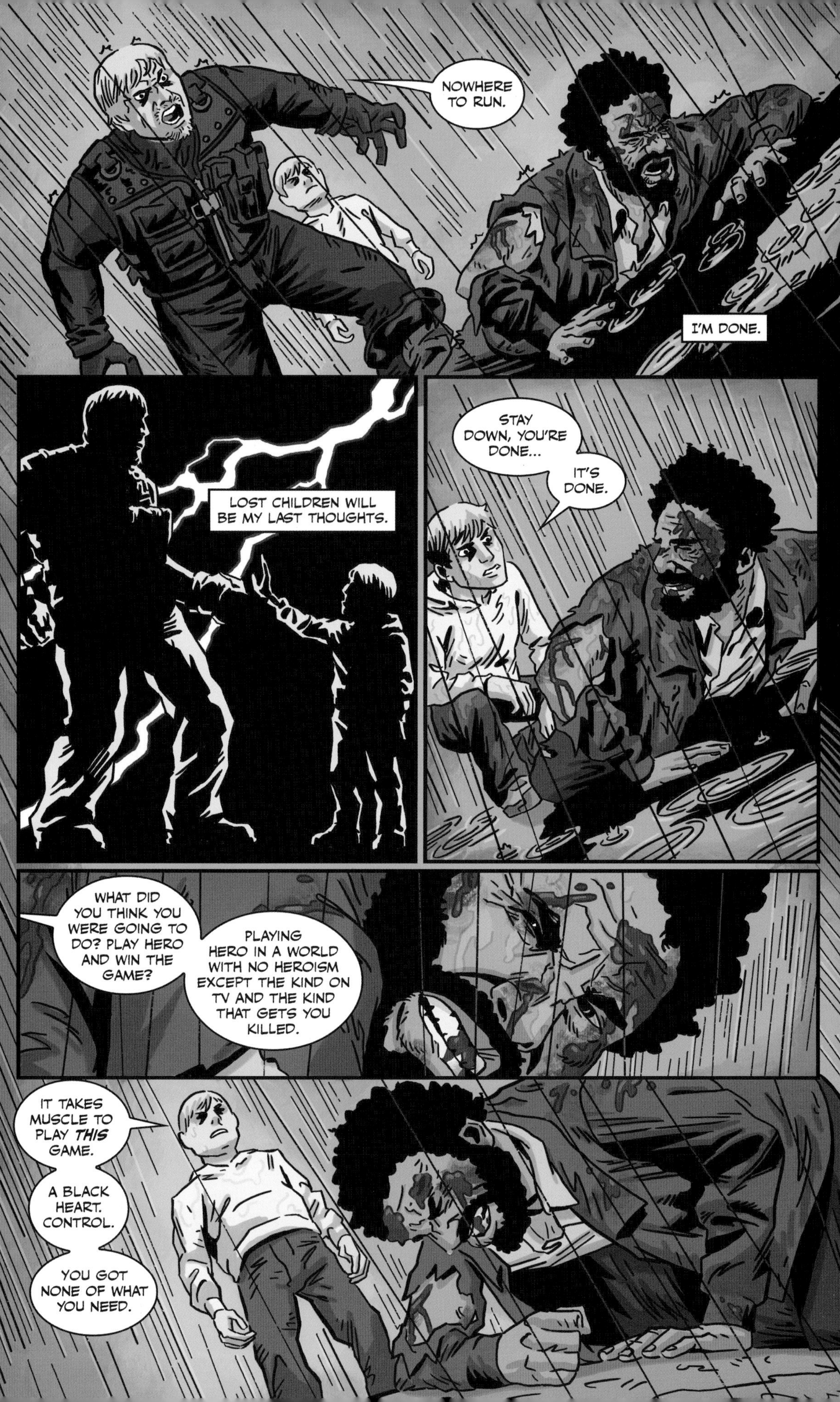
NOWHERE TO RUN.
I'M DONE.
LOST CHILDREN WILL BE MY LAST THOUGHTS.
STAY DOWN, YOU'RE DONE...
IT'S DONE.
WHAT DID YOU THINK YOU WERE GOING TO DO? PLAY HERO AND WIN THE GAME?
PLAYING HERO IN A WORLD WITH NO HEROISM EXCEPT THE KIND ON TV AND THE KIND THAT GETS YOU KILLED.
IT TAKES MUSCLE TO PLAY *THIS* GAME.
A BLACK HEART. CONTROL.
YOU GOT NONE OF WHAT YOU NEED.

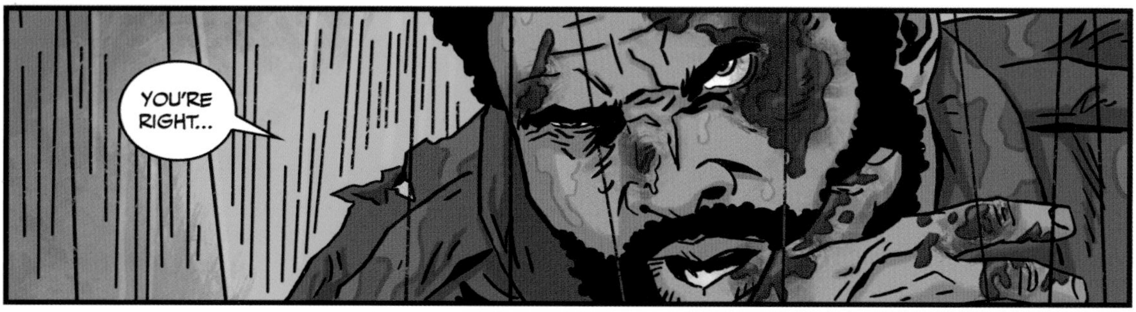
YOU'RE RIGHT...

I SEE IT NOW. THE ID IS THE MUSCLE BUT THE KID'S THE ONE WITH THE CONTROL.

OUR WORST DOESN'T COME FROM IMPULSES. TRUE EVIL IS CALCULATED, MEDITATED, BELIEVED.

THE VERY BEST IN US SHOULD COME FROM THE SAME PLACE.

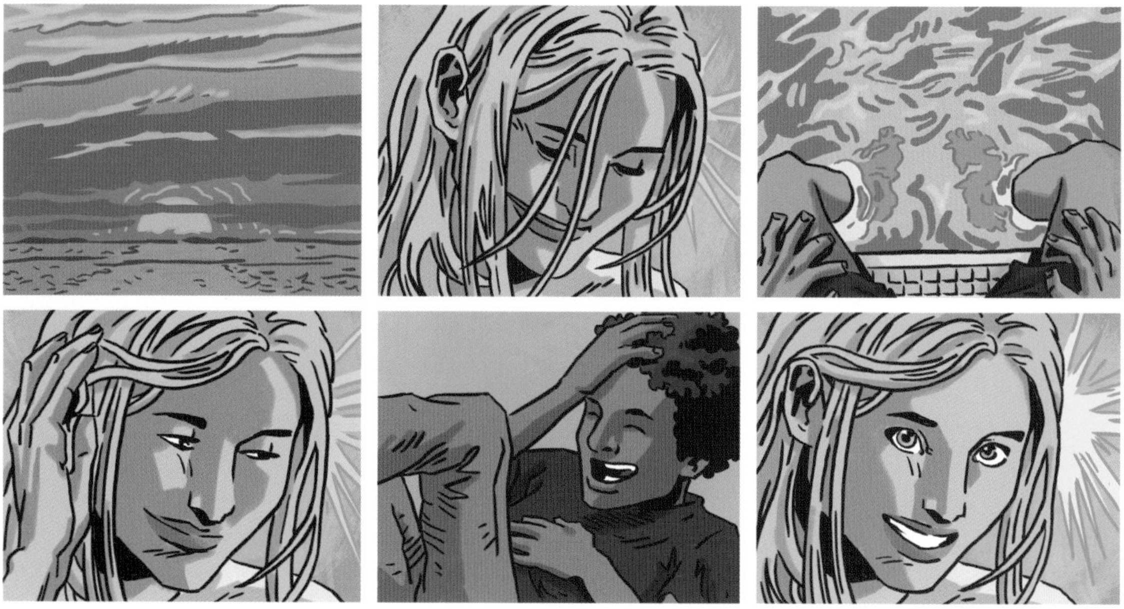

THE KID IS WHERE MAX TRULY BEGAN. HE'S THE CORE, THE ROOT, THE ORIGIN...

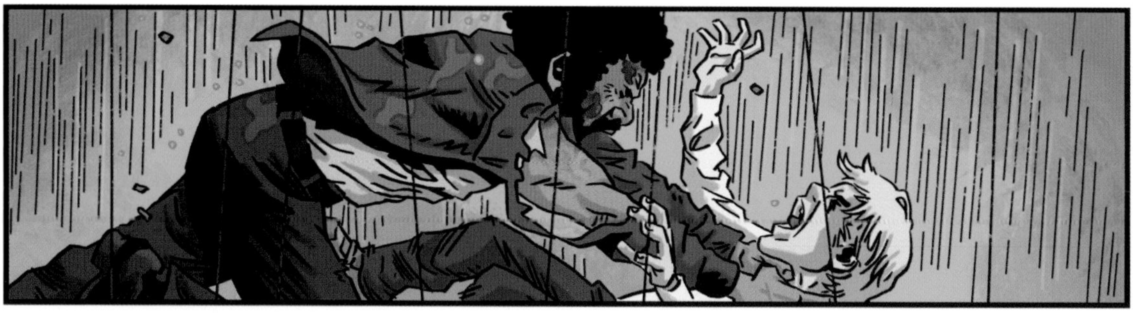

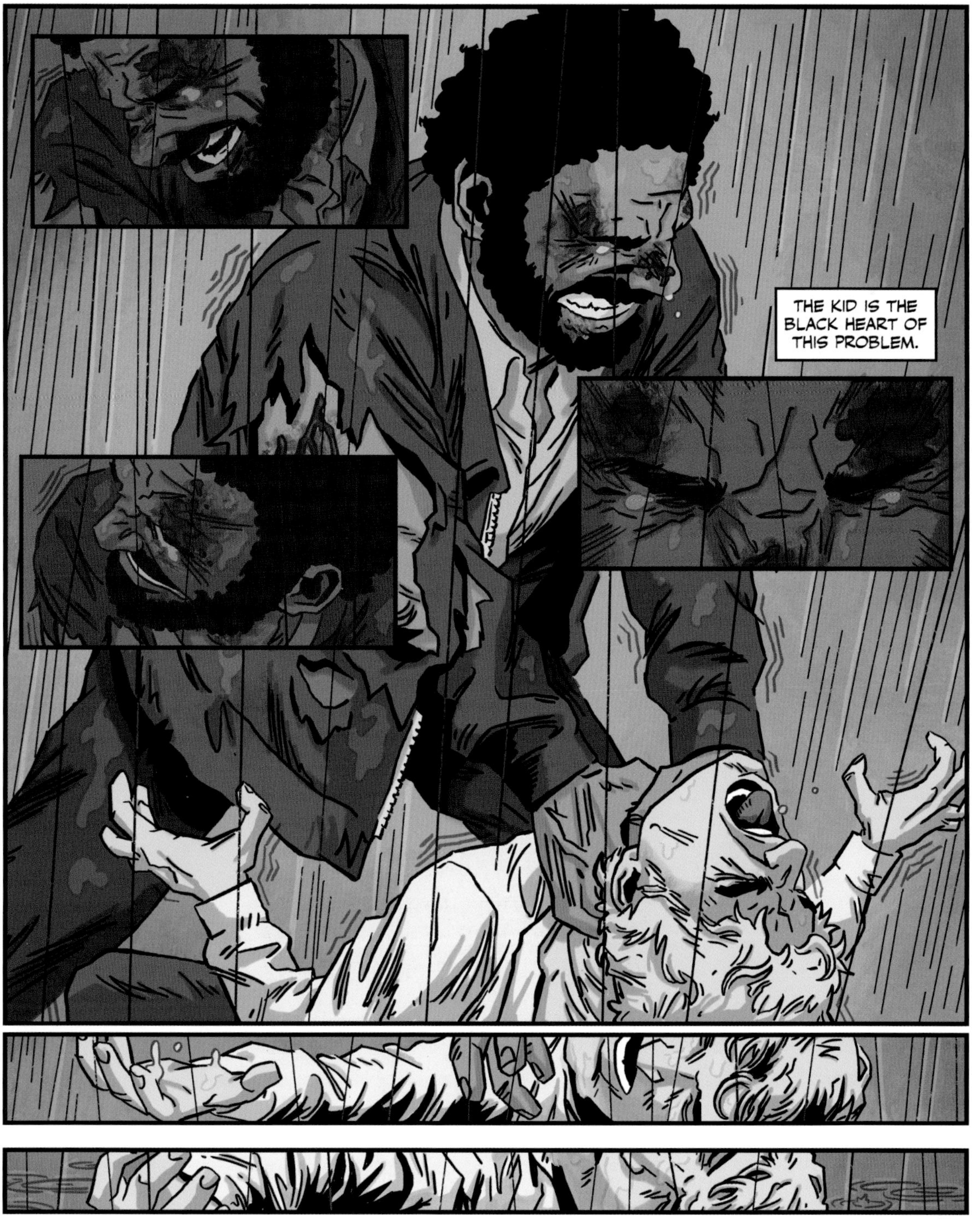
THE KID IS THE BLACK HEART OF THIS PROBLEM.

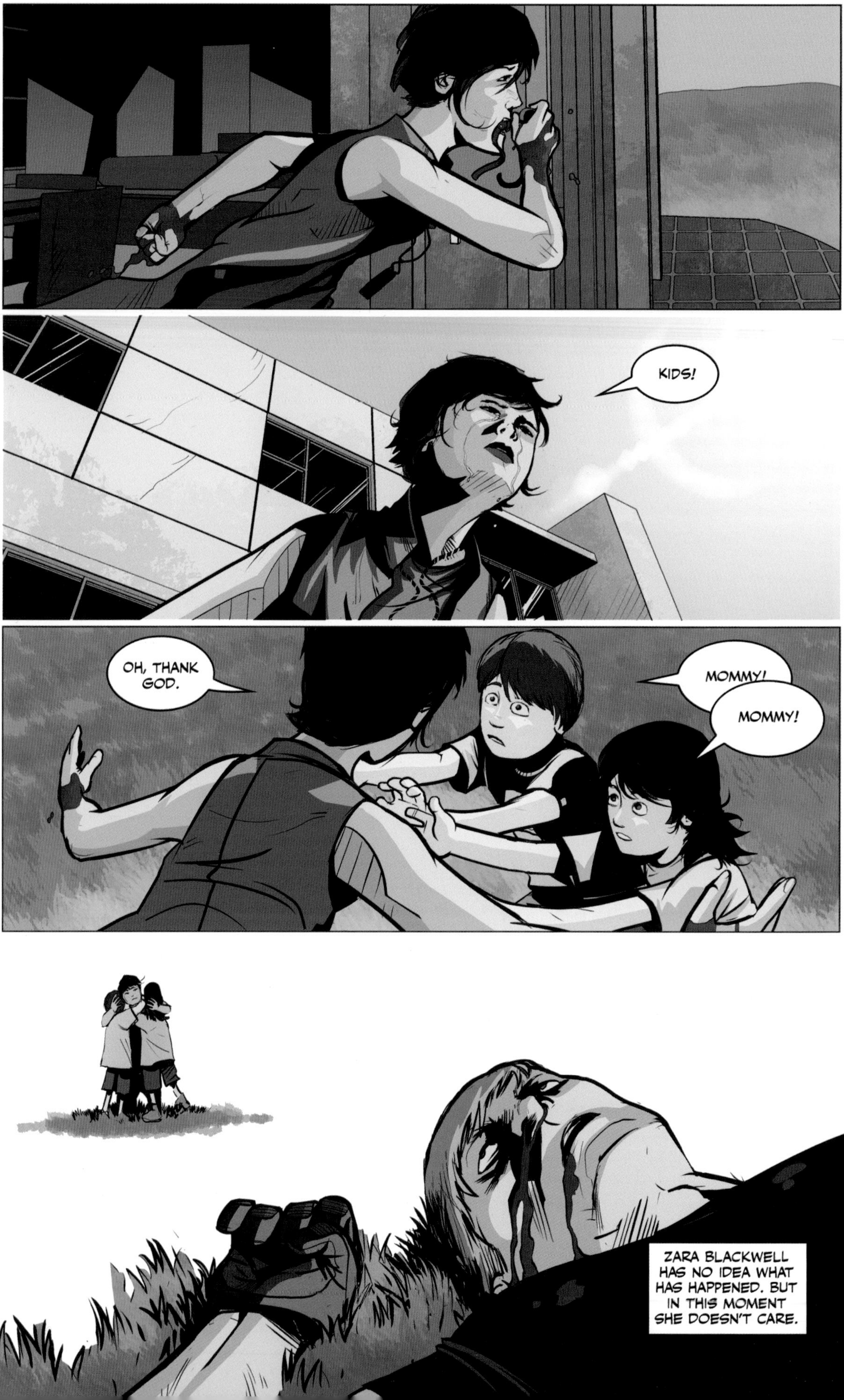
KIDS!
OH, THANK GOD.
MOMMY!
MOMMY!
ZARA BLACKWELL HAS NO IDEA WHAT HAS HAPPENED. BUT IN THIS MOMENT SHE DOESN'T CARE.

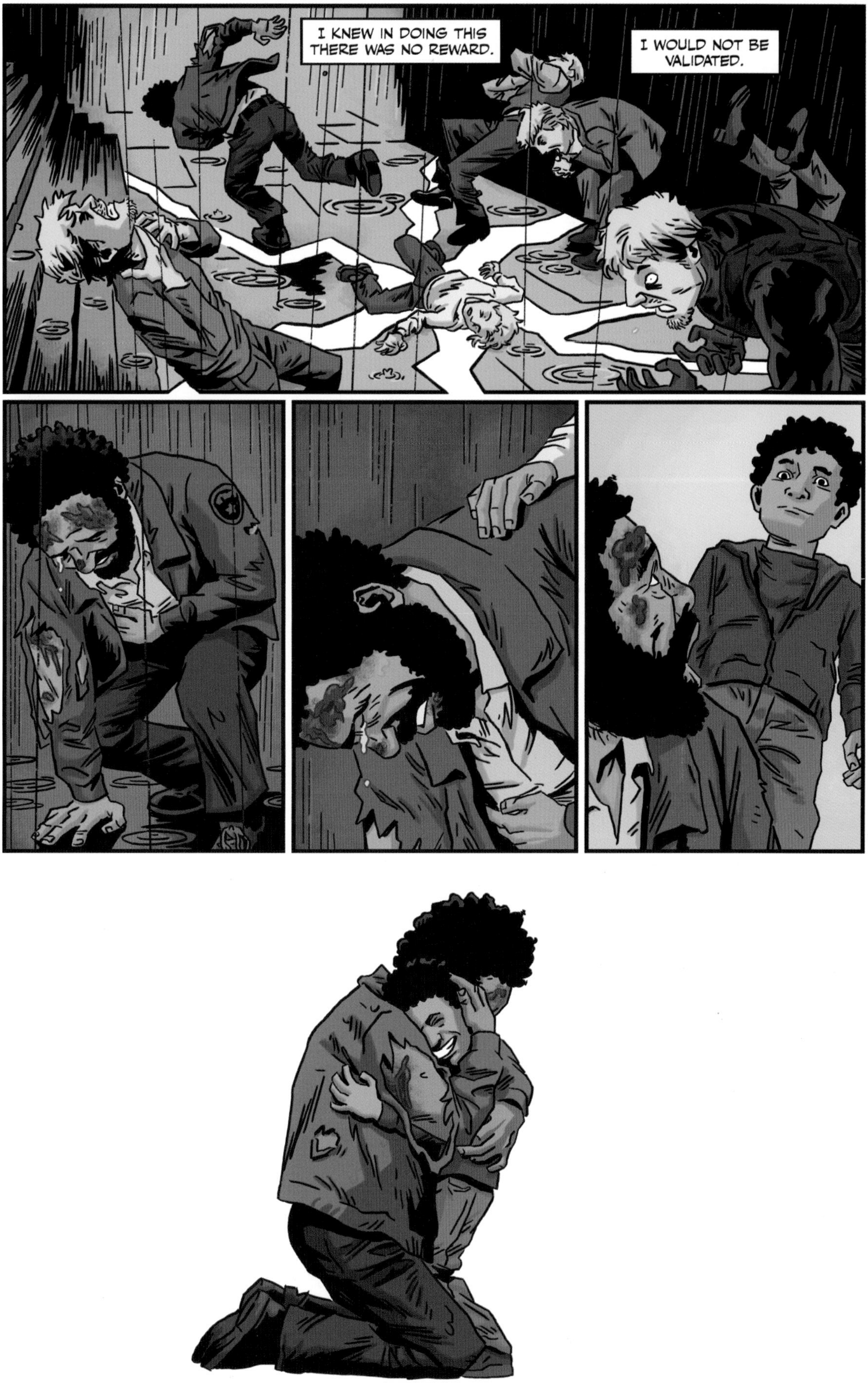
I KNEW IN DOING THIS THERE WAS NO REWARD.
I WOULD NOT BE VALIDATED.

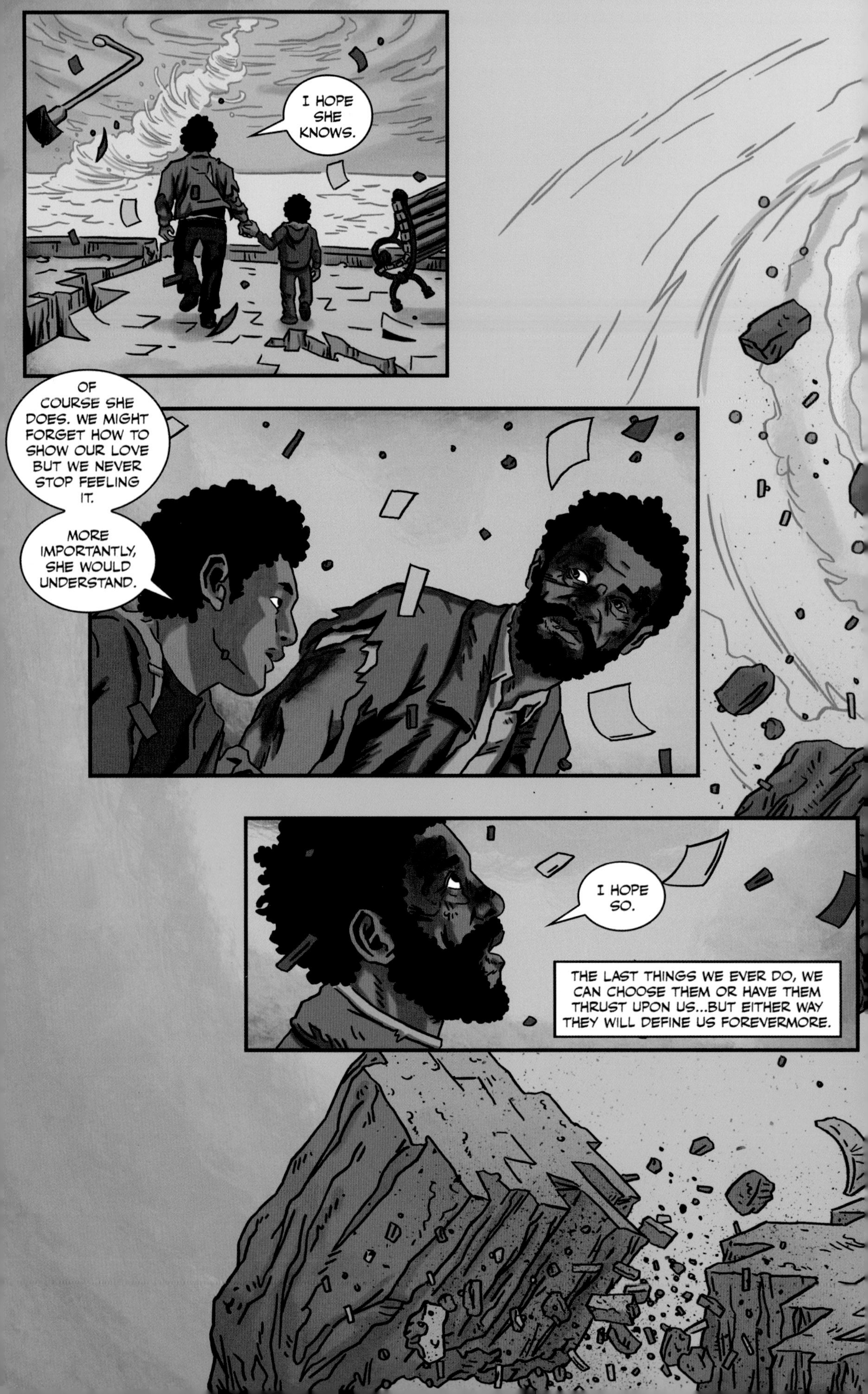
I HOPE SHE KNOWS.
OF COURSE SHE DOES. WE MIGHT FORGET HOW TO SHOW OUR LOVE BUT WE NEVER STOP FEELING IT.
MORE IMPORTANTLY, SHE WOULD UNDERSTAND.
I HOPE SO.
THE LAST THINGS WE EVER DO, WE CAN CHOOSE THEM OR HAVE THEM THRUST UPON US...BUT EITHER WAY THEY WILL DEFINE US FOREVERMORE.

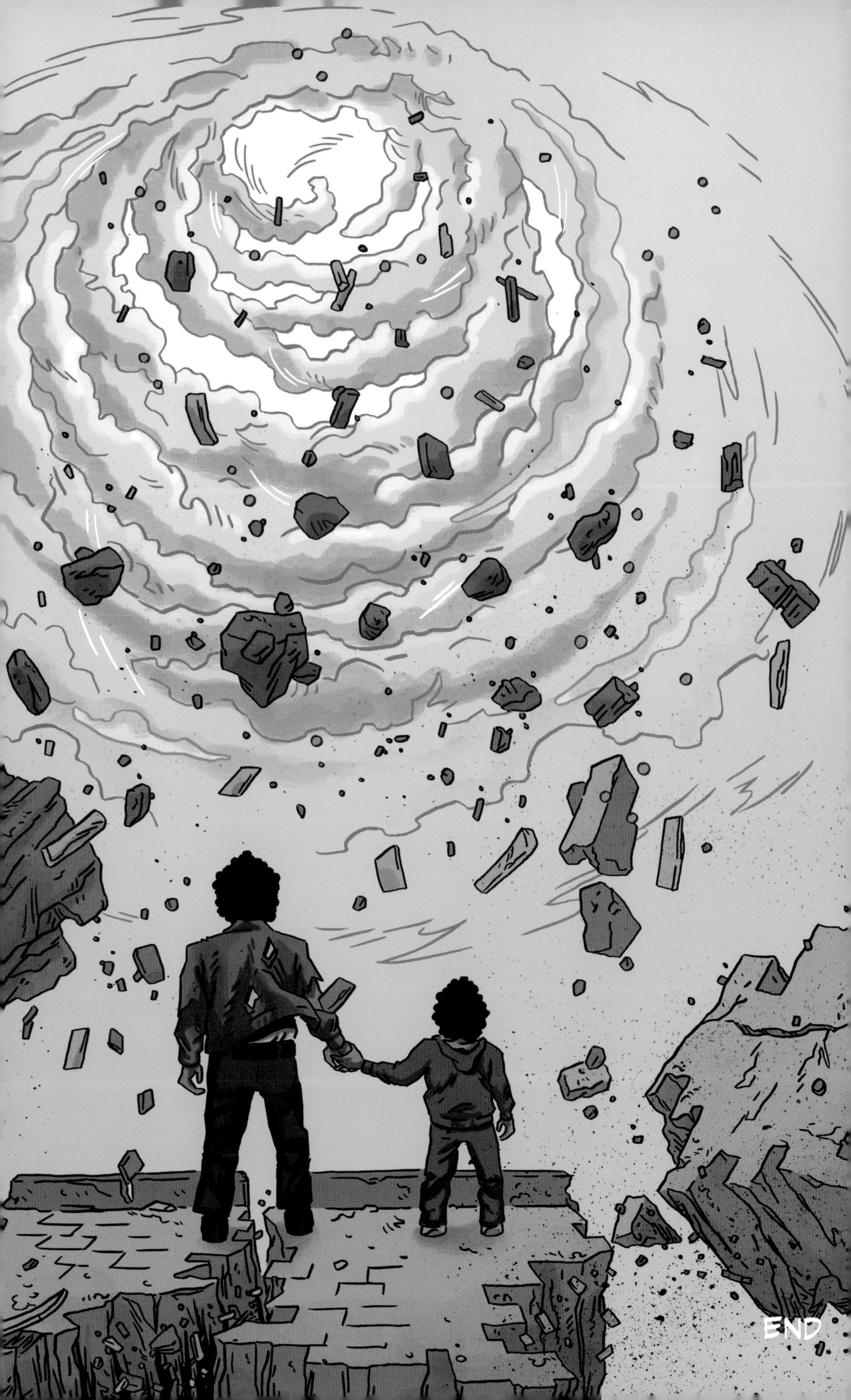
END

Afterword

I never worried if Schrodinger's cat was dead, I just always wondered if it was supposed to be, and what the ramifications of its subsequent death/life might be. This is because I overthink things, because I know every action has an equal and opposite reaction. And this knowledge constantly terrifies me.

When you consider the next 300 beats of the butterfly's wings, it's hard to gauge if your action caused more good in the world or not. Sometimes, you have to lunge for the closer or the greater good, and be damned what comes down the track. As someone who has absorbed enough time travel fiction in my life, I know life can tumble away from you. There is only the moment and what you feel in your gut, any more and he who hesitates is lost.

In *HEADSPACE* I wanted to consider the idea of good versus evil. And we look at this dichotomy through a lens where there is no actual evil, and where everyone is a little good and a lotta wrong. This book is about the fact life is grey. And sometimes our definition of what's the best choice might not align with another person. Every action is informed by our values, our personal situations, and our myopic view of the world.

Is Shane right in his final choice? I'd rather the question be raised than the answer delivered. We can only hope you agree. Or disagree, ha.

The only truth and light and right I know in this world is that working on this book has been one of the grandest experiences of my life. From cooking this up with Eric Zawadzki way back in the primordial swamp of 2012, to bringing aboard Sebastian Piriz and Marissa Louise and Dee Cunniffe, and Dan Hill and Chris Kosek. A man couldn't ask for a better platoon to join him on the downward spiral. Thank you, team, you humble me and dragged me across the finish line.

Flat out, this book doesn't even exist without Allison Baker and Chris Roberson at Monkeybrain Comics (with an assist from Christopher Sebela, the drunk chain-rattling ghost of Barcon's past). There's a chapter in the future of comics and it's written about these two amazing people. Their support and tireless efforts truly meant the world to me.

In the end, you're about to close the book on something I hold dear to my heart. A book full of amazing collaboration (hunt out the digital versions and my back matter there for some real insights), a book I am intensely proud of, and a book that stands for actual things in the world. I hope you have enjoyed it.

Ryan K. Lindsay
February 2015

Pin Up Gallery

The Carpenter Cove Beautiful Towns
Committee wishes to thank:
Brian Level
Sandy Jarrell
Matt Horak, w/Marissa Louise colours
Justin Greenwood, w/Marissa Louise colours
Sami Kivela
Vic Malhotra
Marissa Louise
Owen Gieni

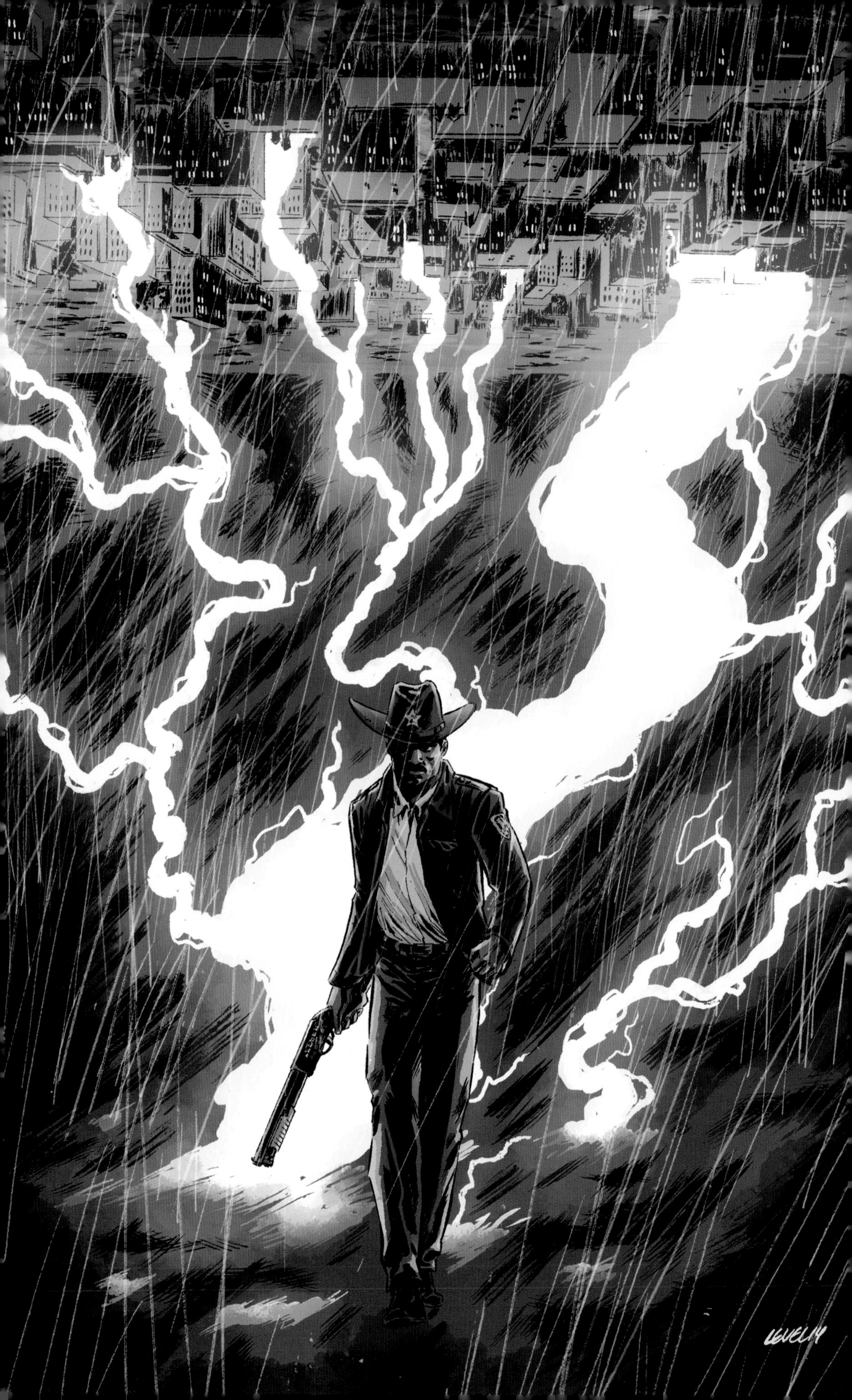

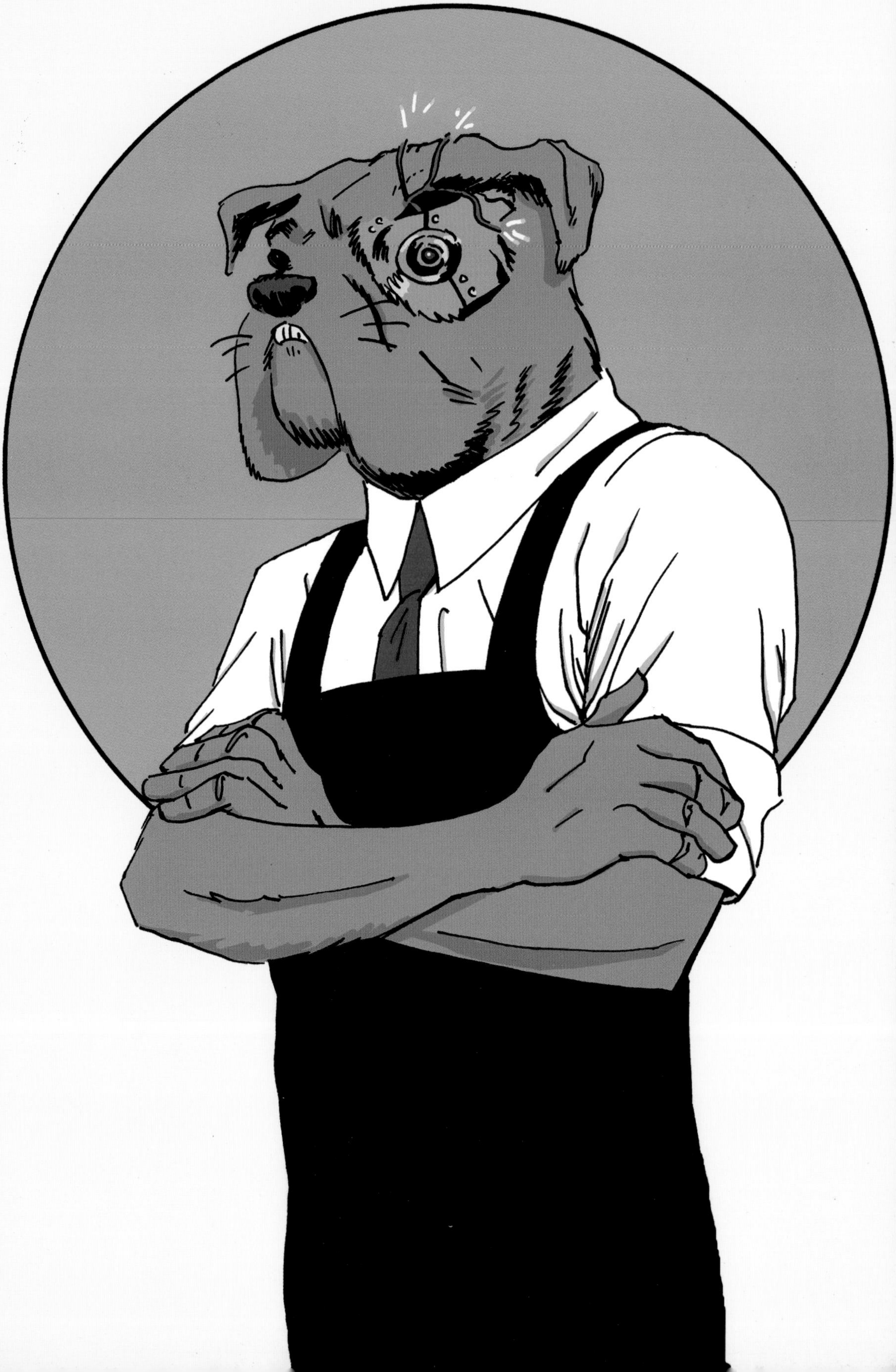

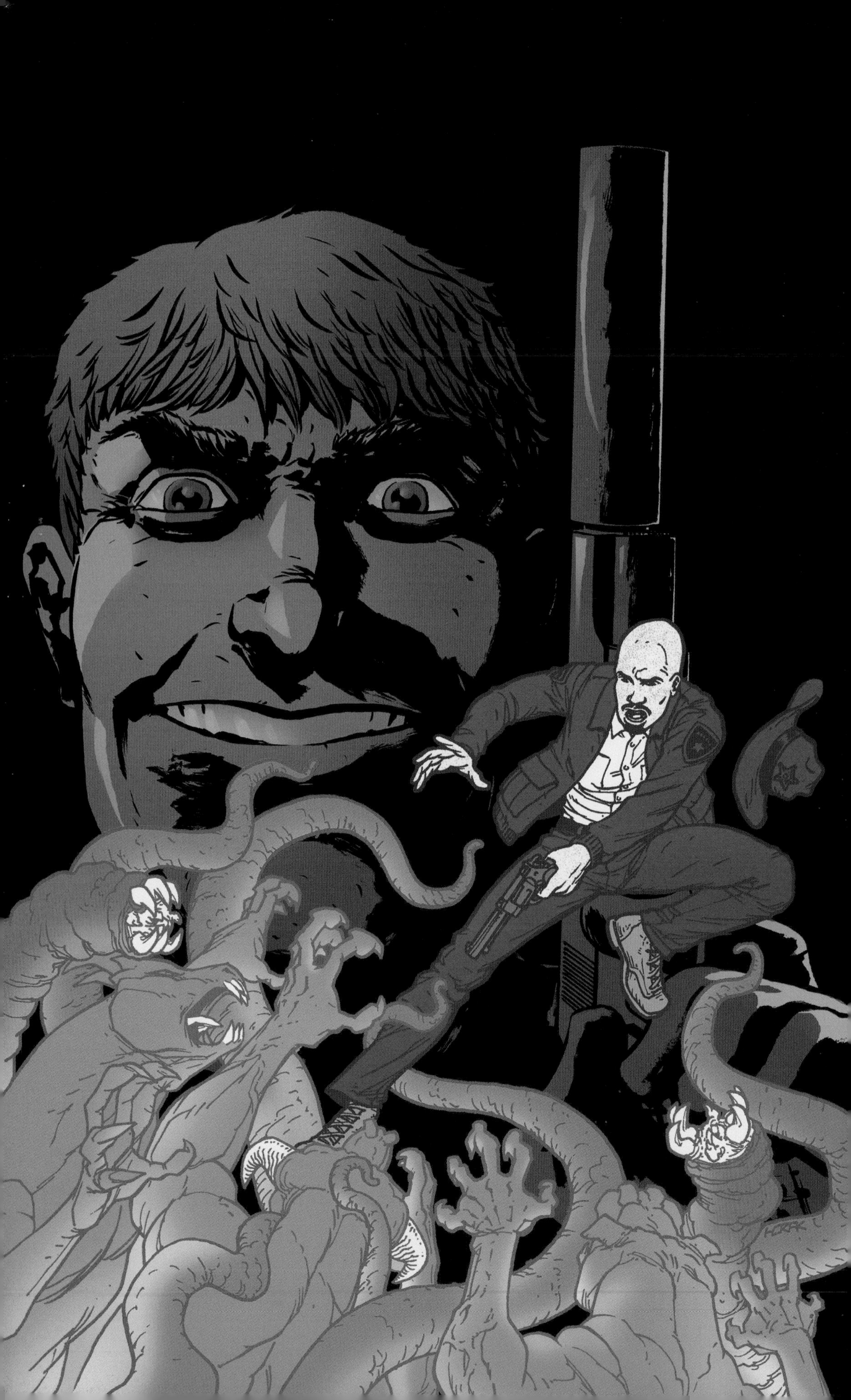

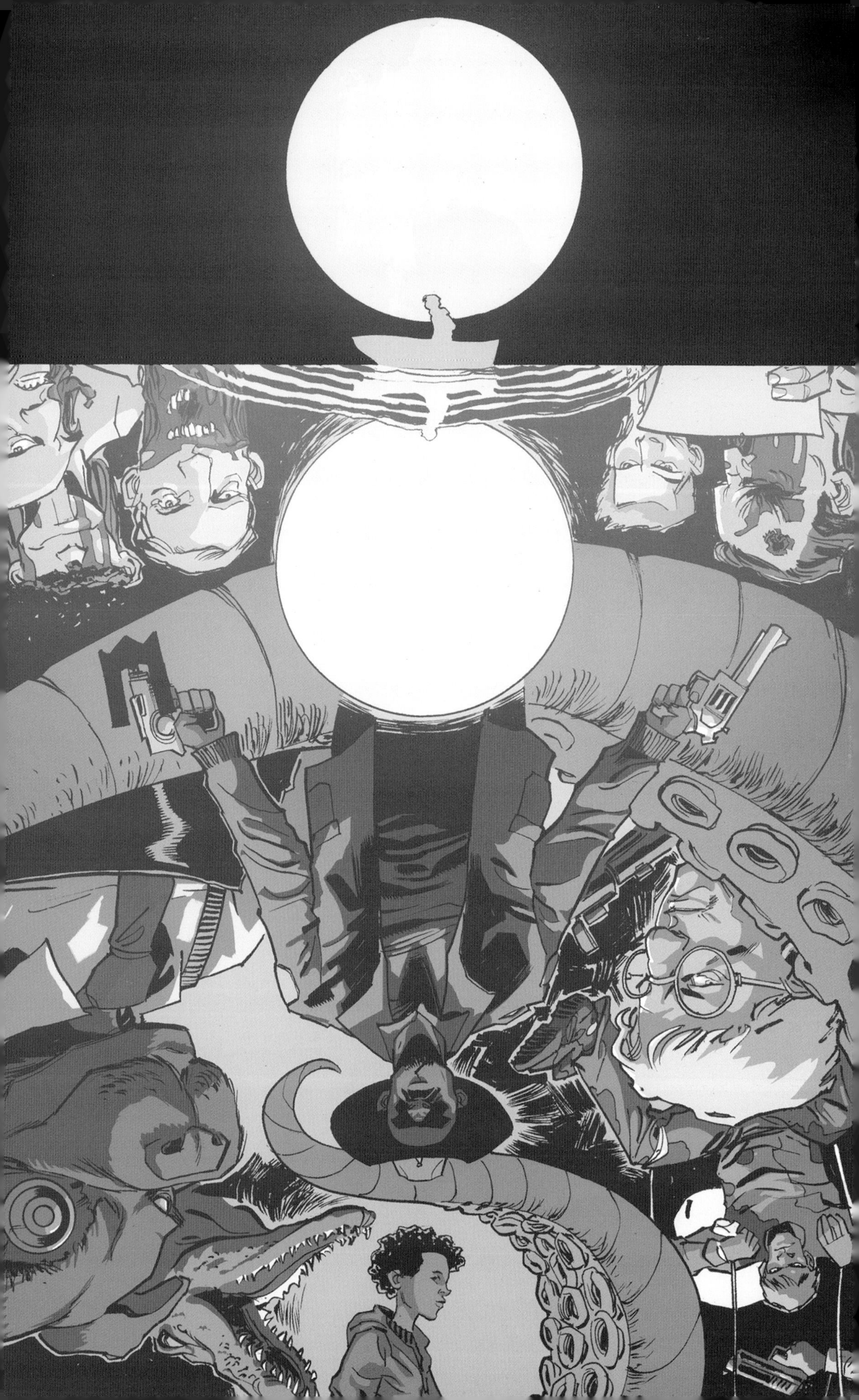

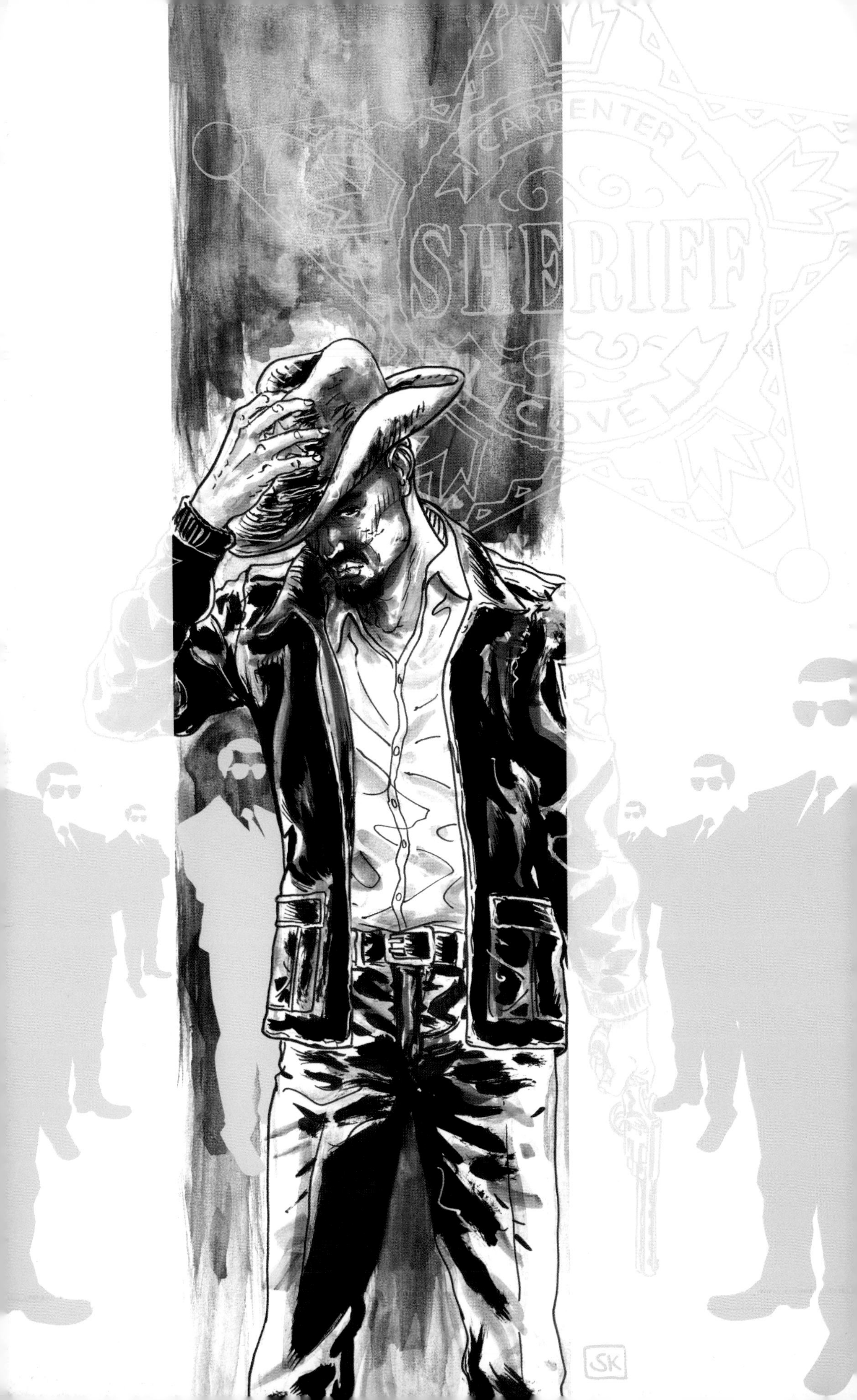
CARPENTER
SHERIFF
COVE
SK

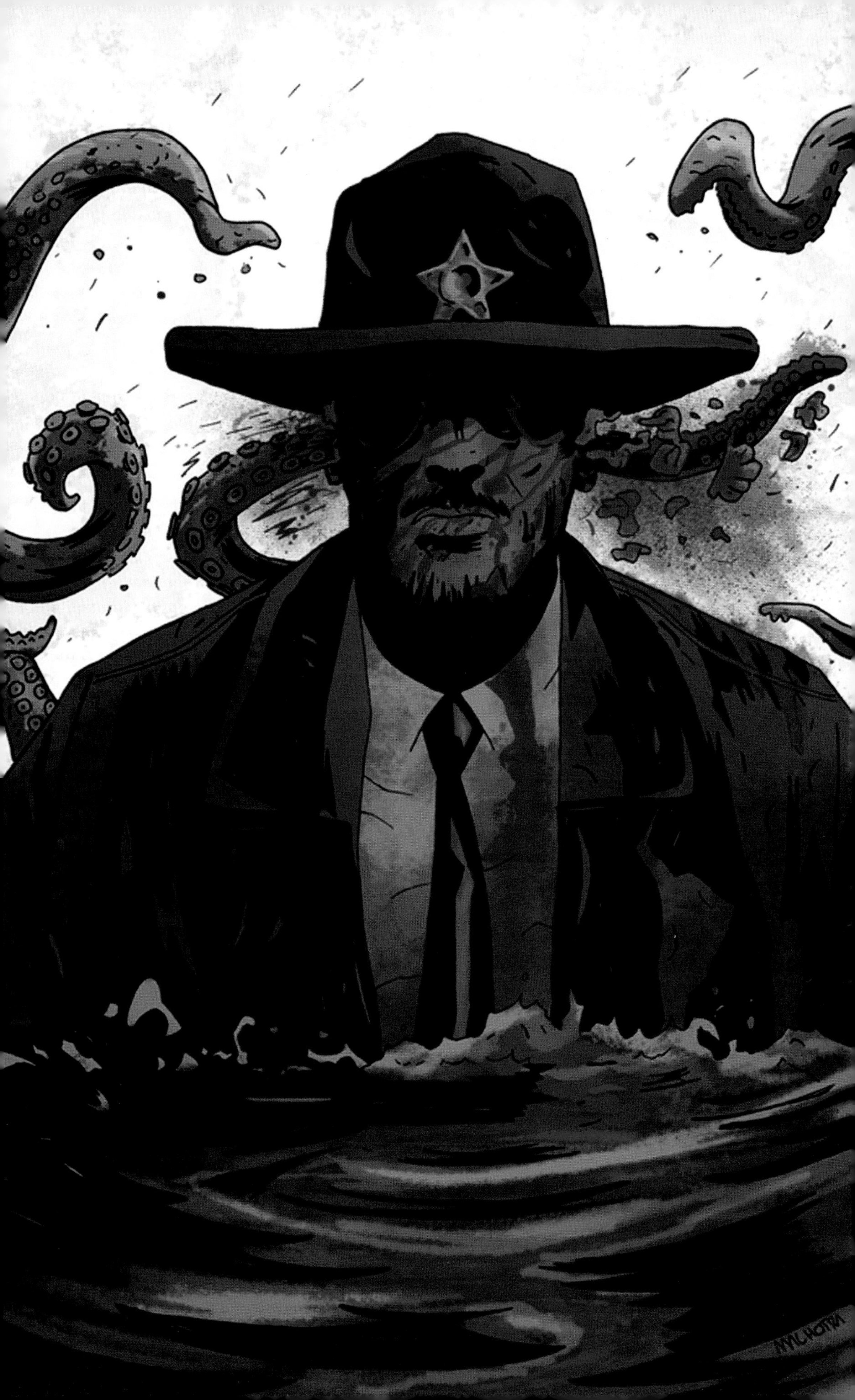

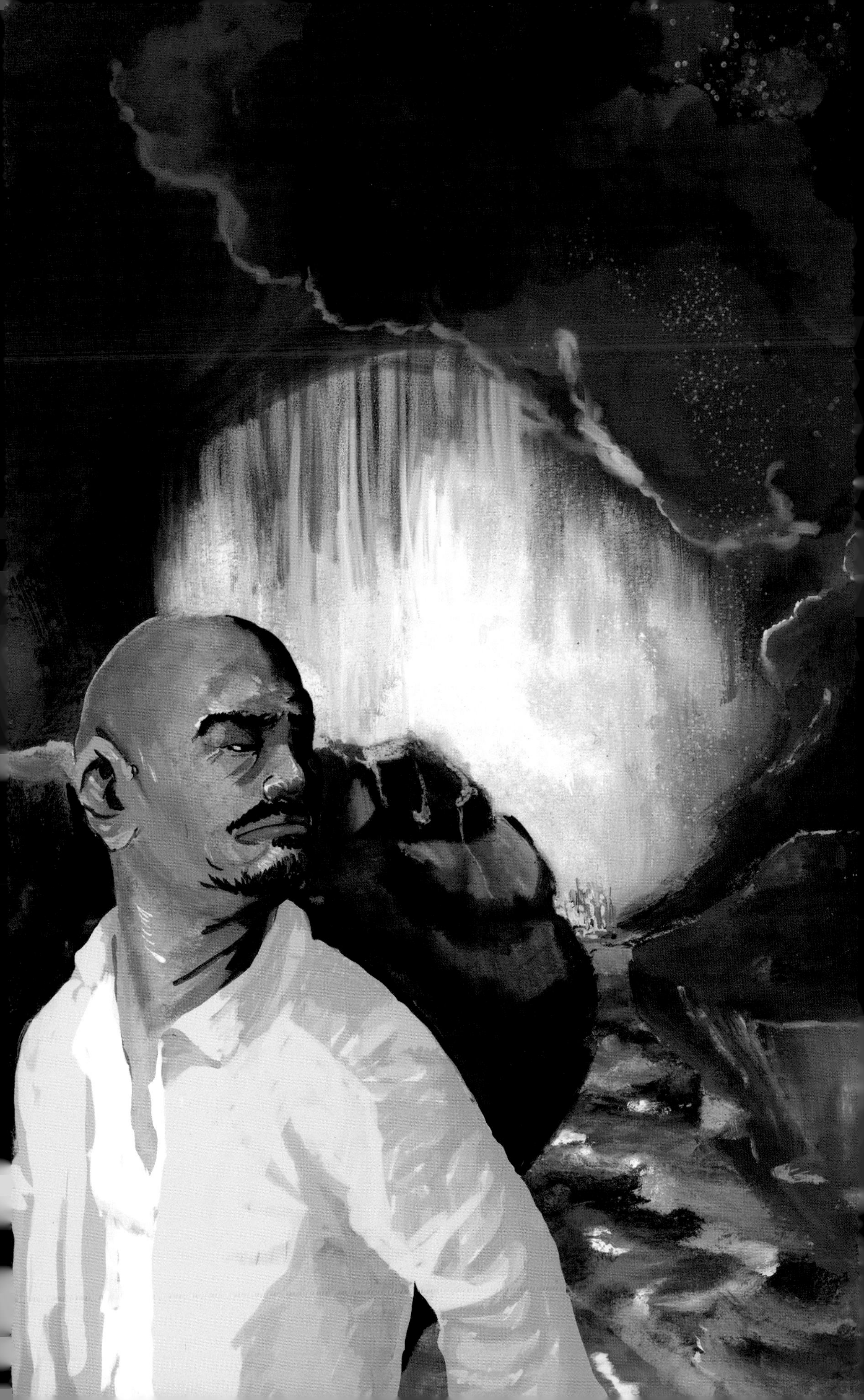

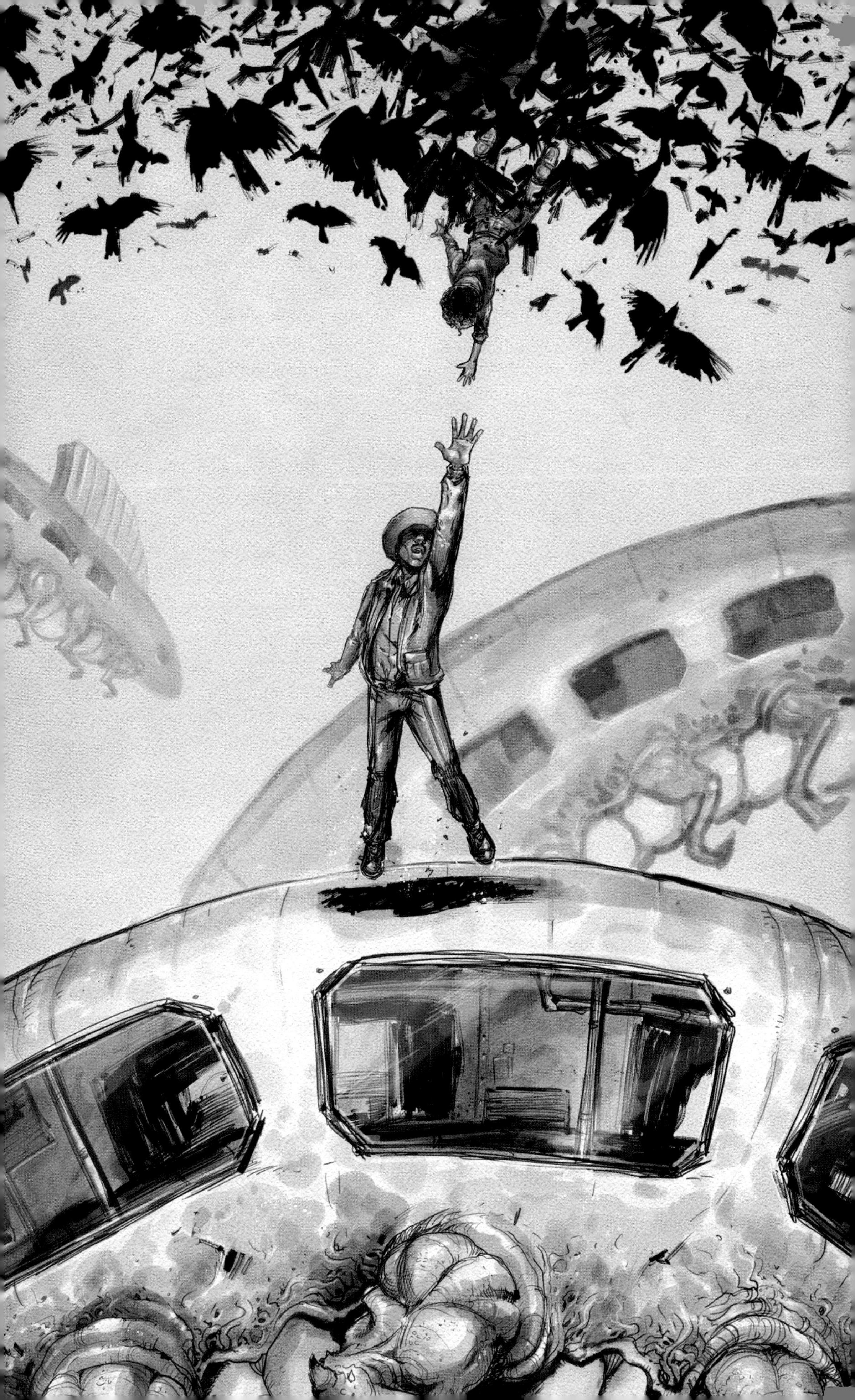

Headspace Creator Bios

Eric Zawadzki

Eric Zawadzki is a Vancouver based comic book artist. In addition to his work on *HEADSPACE*, he has contributed to a number of anthologies which include the *OCCUPY COMICS ANTHOLOGY* and Showtime's *CONTINUUM: WAR FILES*. He has also co-created and illustrated *THE GHOST ENGINE, LAST BORN,* and *PANIC KIDS*. Follow him on Twitter @ericxyz.

Sebastián Piriz

Sebastián Piriz has been working on comics for a few years now, doing things for Arcana, Boom, and Marvel Comics. He's currently working on www.demonarchives.com. You can find him on Twitter @sebastianpiriz.

Marissa Louise

Marissa Louise has a terrifying tongue twister for a last name, you'll never see it. Fortunately, her work is much nicer and you'll see a lot of that. She is an illustrator turned colorist whose work has appeared in *ESCAPE FROM NEW YORK, ROBOCOP,* and various galleries in New York, NY and Portland, OR. Follow her on Twitter @marissadraws.

Dee Cunniffe

Dee is an award-winning designer who worked for over a decade in publishing and advertising. He gave it all up to pursue his love of comics. He currently colors, letters, and designs comics every waking moment. He has worked on nearly every comic for every publisher as a flatter/color assistant to some of the world's top colorists.

Recent credits include Image Comics' *THE WICKED AND THE DIVINE,* and *ODY-C*. He also colored *GRAINUAILE: QUEEN OF STORMS* for O'Brien press and lettered *THE HOUND,* both released in 2015. Follow him on Twitter @deezoid.

Ryan K Lindsay

Ryan K Lindsay writes comics, about comics, and other prose. His credits include *DEER EDITOR* at Four Colour Ray Gun, the *FATHERHOOD* one-shot at Challenger Comics, a *MY LITTLE PONY* one-shot at IDW about Rainbow Dash, *GHOST TOWN* at Action Lab, and other shorts published by Vertigo, Image/Shadowline, ComixTribe, and in the *HBVB* anthology. He's had essays published in *CRIMINAL, GODZILLA, SHELTERED, STRANGE NATION,* and has a book of them in Sequart's *THE DEVIL IS IN THE DETAILS: EXAMINING MATT MURDOCK AND DAREDEVIL.* He is Australian. You can follow him on Twitter @ryanklindsay.